Practicing Disability
Studies in Education

Disability Studies in Education

Susan L. Gabel and Scot Danforth
General Editors

Vol. 17

The Disability Studies in Education series is part of
the Peter Lang Education list.
Every volume is peer reviewed and meets
the highest quality standards for content and production.

PETER LANG
New York • Bern • Frankfurt • Berlin
Brussels • Vienna • Oxford • Warsaw

Practicing Disability Studies in Education

ACTING TOWARD SOCIAL CHANGE

EDITED BY DAVID J. CONNOR,
JAN W. VALLE, & CHRIS HALE

PETER LANG
New York • Bern • Frankfurt • Berlin
Brussels • Vienna • Oxford • Warsaw

Library of Congress Cataloging-in-Publication Data
Connor, David J.
Practicing disability studies in education: acting toward social change /
edited by David J. Connor, Jan W. Valle, Chris Hale.
pages cm. — (Disability studies in education; v. 17)
Includes bibliographical references.
1. Students with disabilities—Education. 2. Special education.
3. Inclusive education. 4. Disability studies. 5. Sociology of disability.
I. Valle, Jan W. II. Hale, Chris III. Title.
LC4065.C66   371.9—dc23   2014033108
ISBN 978-1-4331-2552-2 (hardcover)
ISBN 978-1-4331-2551-5 (paperback)
ISBN 978-1-4539-1446-5 (e-book)
ISSN 1548-7210

Bibliographic information published by **Die Deutsche Nationalbibliothek**.
Die Deutsche Nationalbibliothek lists this publication in the "Deutsche
Nationalbibliografie"; detailed bibliographic data are available
on the Internet at http://dnb.d-nb.de/.

Cover art by David J. Connor

The paper in this book meets the guidelines for permanence and durability
of the Committee on Production Guidelines for Book Longevity
of the Council of Library Resources.

© 2015 Peter Lang Publishing, Inc., New York
29 Broadway, 18th floor, New York, NY 10006
www.peterlang.com

Printed in the United States of America

To my nieces and nephew:

Emily, Joseph, Lucy, and Abbey

—David

To my sisters:

Pam Carter and Marcia James

—Jan

To my wife and daughter:

Angela and Serena

—Chris

Table of Contents

A Note on the Cover Art

As with many academic projects, the concept of this book changed from its inception toward its completion. At the onset, we chose *Practicing Disability Studies in Education: Acting Toward Social Change* as our working title. It was strong, solid, and simply stated. Those of us who work within a disability studies in education (DSE) framework, grounded in ideals of social justice, seek to change how we "do business" in education. The impetus for this book emerged from a desire to share examples of DSE "at work" for teachers, teacher educators, professors, researchers, and policymakers. Our intent was not to provide a "how-to manual," but rather to showcase examples that foreground ways in which DSE scholars have moved forward in rethinking education and disability and how a DSE framework (re)shapes practice.

Toward the end of the project, we sought to change the book's title to *Syncopation, Improvisation, and Collaboration: Disability Studies in Education Within Theory, Research, Practice, and Policy.* Alas! We were too late, as production had already began. That said, the sentiment of the not-to-be title reflected our experience as book editors–reading and analyzing chapters, providing feedback to our contributors—that, in turn, shaped all contributions to varying degrees. What struck a chord for us, so to speak, is the role that "co-creation" played not only in the writing of this book, but also in the myriad ways DSE scholars have collaborated to rethink, reframe, and reshape the current educational response to disability. Largely confined to the limitations of traditional educational discourse, this collective (and growing) group has—and continues to—push limits, break molds, assert the need for plurality, explore possibilities, move into the unknown, take chances, strategize to destabilize, and co-create new visions for what can be, instead of settling for what is. Jazz seemed to us an apt analogy for the synergistic work of DSE scholars.

Much like jazz musicians who rely upon one another on stage to create music collectively, DSE scholars have been—and continue to—"riff" with one another in creating the growing body of DSE literature. In the way that syncopation, improvisation, and collaboration disrupt traditional musical frames, we contend these jazz elements likewise describe the work of DSE scholars that contravenes tightly bound rules, regulations, categorization, operations, and technical approaches within special education. *Syncopation* is the practice of emphasizing the "weak beats," foregrounding what is usually backgrounded. *Improvisation* is the act of creation "in the moment," an open-mindedness in the form of understanding within a specific context and time. *Collaboration* is participation within a group of individuals working together toward a common goal, yet creating a synergy that produces something greater than the sum of its parts. Consider jazz elements—weaving, tripping, riffing, bouncing, and stretching through DSE, sometimes smooth, and at other times dissonant, played within and circulated by a quartet of theory, research, practice, and policy.

We invite you to listen.

Foreword

Disability Studies in Education and the Sociological Imagination

SCOT DANFORTH

This volume of outstanding essays continues a critical scholarly tradition in the growing field of disability studies in education (DSE) of examining, exploring, and interrogating cultural and professional portrayals of disability and issues of human difference in the schools. To the reader familiar with disability studies (DS) scholarship, these essays will chime familiar tones while searching the terrains of childhood and schooling for insight and possibility. For readers more accustomed to reading research in American special education, this book may bring new and unusual notions to the frontal lobe while flipping standard assumptions and discourses upside down.

Understanding how DSE and the American field of special education overlap and diverge, coalesce, and conflict is not a simple matter. Undoubtedly, both deal with the education of young persons with disabilities in the public schools. Further, some special education researchers and the vast majority of DSE scholars have an investment in the development of successful programs of inclusive education. But beyond those bare simplicities, how are the two related ... or not?

I will begin this volume of DSE essays by pointing to two historical moments in the early twentieth century, two events that display many of the political and conceptual emphases of special education and DSE, allowing us to envision each in contrast to the other. I will offer a historical scene from the biography of noted American special educator Samuel A. Kirk as illustrative of the primary theoretical features of the field of special education. Then I will supply a story of disabled persons protesting federal government hiring practices as a portrait offering insight into the theoretical emphases of the field of DSE. The result is a contrast in political priorities, professional purposes, and discursive styles.

Early Intervention

The first historical moment is a scene involving a young Samuel A. Kirk, the man who by the end of his storied career would be called the "father of special education" (Mather, 1998, p. 35; Minskoff, 1998, p. 20). He developed many of the essential elements of contemporary special education thought and practice, including "the basic format of the IEP" (Minskoff, 1998, p. 16), the standard scheme of psychoeducational assessment (Minskoff, 1998), the federal definition of learning disabilities (Danforth, 2009; Bos & Vaughn, 1998), and the common framework and content of the university special-education textbook (Brantlinger, 2006; Kirk, 1962). Additionally, Kirk was a prominent political advisor and advocate in the development and passage of the Education of Handicapped Children Act of 1975 (Danforth, 2009; Gallagher, 1998).

In 1929, when he was a graduate student in psychology at the University of Chicago, Kirk was working evenings caring for delinquent children in an Oak Forest, Illinois, institution. There he discovered a ten-year-old boy was unable to read. This was hardly surprising news to the hospital staff. It was widely understood that "mental defectives" did not have the intellectual capacity for reading. But Kirk began secretly tutoring the boy anyway, teaching him in the doorway of a bathroom after the other children had fallen asleep. The ambitious, perhaps unreasonable graduate student and the institutionalized boy sat beneath a small corridor light, whispering in soft tones so as not to be caught by the ward nurses.

Knowing that he needed help in dealing with this unusual teaching challenge, Kirk consulted with reading assessment and remediation specialist Marion Monroe. Monroe (1928, 1932) was working at the same time on her own research project, teaching children with "reading defects." She validated and encouraged Kirk's thinking about the ability of some "feebleminded" children to learn to read. Her approach relied on a complex set of assessments of intelligence and reading ability. She ignited Kirk's lifelong interest in the use of systems of psychological measurement as a way of understanding the cognitive strengths and weaknesses of children with learning difficulties.

In this brief historical scene, the basic features of the purpose and the practices of the American field of special education are illustrated. First, Kirk believed that some children who were viewed by others as uneducable and lacking the physiological and psychological capacities necessary to benefit from instruction, could indeed learn. Hidden, untapped learning talent resided among the population of disabled students. With proper measurement instruments and great pedagogical skill, this talent could be located, drawn forth, and cultivated. Second, those children could only learn if provided with highly specialized instruction by persons prepared to understand their unique learning needs. This was a form of teaching unlike any other. It required a specific professional foundation of knowledge and skill. By the 1960s, this belief would become Kirk's clarion call for the national birth of the new field of special education (Danforth, Slocum, & Dunkle, 2010).

Third, when confronted with a need to understand more about his student, Kirk turned to psychometric measurements, early instruments in the historical development of the American field of psychological and educational measurement. Undoubtedly, this specialized instruction required a professional knowledge base. The best knowledge, in Kirk's view, involved ranking his student in comparison to the abstract cognition and reading abilities of other children. Systems of mental measurement resulting in the hierarchical classification of young minds were the epistemic backbone of the new profession.

The Audacity of Cripples

The historical scene offering insight into the conceptual orientation of DSE is set in New York City, in May 1935. A group of six persons with physical disabilities—Florence Haskell, Sylvia Flexer, Hyman Abramowitz, and three other young adults—sat down on the floor of the office of Oswald W. Knauth, director of the Emergency Relief Bureau (ERB), a federal New Deal program agency. They refused to move, acting in protest of the agency's policy of not hiring disabled persons. This scene may have been the first disability-rights protest in American history.

When the Roosevelt administration built a series of federal employment programs to offset the high unemployment during the Great Depression, some disabled adults hoped that the New Deal work programs would be less discriminatory than employers in the private sector. The work relief programs provided by progressive federal agencies such as the Public Works Administration, the Works Progress Administration (WPA), and the Civilian Conservation Corps were specifically designed to supply government jobs to unemployed workers. But the New Deal programs routinely snubbed disabled job applicants as "unemployable," worthy only of low levels of charitable relief (Longmore & Goldberger, 2000, p. 898). In compliance with official WPA policy, the ERB of New York City refused to hire persons with disabilities

(Longmore, 1998; Longmore & Goldberger, 2000). Within 24 hours, hundreds of supporters had gathered outside in support of the sit-in. The local and national news media, including the *Daily News, New York Post, New York Herald Tribune,* and the *Washington Post,* carried the story (Fleischer & Zames, 2011; Pelka, 1997; Longmore, 1998).

After five days, Director Knauth agreed to meet with the protest group leaders. They demanded that Knauth hire 50 disabled workers immediately and then add ten more each week. They demanded reasonable wages working side by side with nondisabled workers in integrated work settings.

"This is not an organization to give work to those who are permanently unemployable," responded Director Knauth (Longmore, 1998, para. 10). He rejected the demands. On the ninth day of the protest, Knauth called in the police. They broke up the demonstration and arrested 11 people.

This small group of 1930s, disability-rights activists called themselves the League for the Physically Handicapped. Although they eventually took their protest to Washington, DC to confront top New Deal policymakers head on, they did not succeed in changing the prejudicial hiring policy. Their great achievement was a new kind of political association that defined disability in a new way, creating "a precursor of disability pride" (Pelka, 1997, p. 191).

Disability historian Paul Longmore commented:

> Their audacity is surprising given that era's attitudes toward cripples. To resist society's prejudice, they had to engage in public acts of defiance at a time when the president of the United States found it necessary to keep his disability largely hidden. (Longmore & Goldberger, 2000, p. 904)

They were willing to think the unthinkable and imagine a society far more pluralistic, inclusive, and respectful than even the most progressive politicians of their time.

The actions of these early activists are emblematic of the thinking and strategies of the field of DSE in a number of ways. First, the League members viewed themselves as a group unified not by the incapable nature of their bodies but by the political circumstances that excluded and marginalized them. The problem was not their deficient physiology. The problem was the social conventions that casually and cruelly tossed them aside. Today, we often refer to this justice concept as the social model of disability, the broad theoretical basis of the fields of DS and DSE.

Second, the League members came together as coalition of persons with disabilities with a distinctly educational goal. They worked to shift the thinking of citizens and leaders away from disability as an individual failing and toward disability as the lived consequence of unjust policies and social practices.

They "fought job discrimination and contested the ideology of disability that dominated early-twentieth-century public policies, professional practices, and societal arrangements" (Longmore & Goldberger, 2000, p. 888).

Third, they cast the proper role of disabled persons as not merely the recipients of the assistance offered by non-disabled persons. They pushed the government leaders to jettison their conventional image of persons with disabilities as objects of charity, as persons who receive financial support because they are incapacitated. In its place, the League disseminated a new, progressive concept of disabled persons. They portrayed themselves as workers, as talented employees capable of making a substantial contribution. They also represented themselves as citizens, as highly engaged participants taking part in the democratic political process.

Finally, the knowledge base that supported and drove their actions was their own subjective knowledge, their own understandings and insights based on their experiences in the world. They did not turn to an objective science developed by non-disabled persons about disabled persons. They did not, per se, reject the validity or utility of scientific disciplines. What they did assert that lasts today in DS and DSE scholarship was the centrality of disabled persons' experiential knowledge to any activity seeking the social and political improvement of their lives.

Engaging Our Sociological Imagination

Eminent scholar C. Wright Mills (1959) coined the term "sociological imagination" to describe how we might employ scholarship to help us view individual lives in relationship to the broader workings of society. What may appear to us to be taking place within an individual's life narrative is, upon further investigation, also a function of the complex social and political dynamics of the larger culture. DSE scholars, while respecting Kirk's deep desire to teach the supposedly unteachable, also seek broader opportunities for participation and equality.

This volume of essays engages our sociological imagination with a democratic vengeance, playing repeatedly on the dialectic of individual and society while asking us serious political and ethical questions about human differences, relationships, and community. The authors wield keyboards with a jagged edge. They echo the audacity of the League of the Physically Handicapped, pushing forward with the (un)realistic hope that schools and societies may become more hospitable, respectful, and participatory for all children and families. They each ask that we spend nine days sprawled uncomfortably on the floor of ERB director Oswald W. Knauth's office, wondering what the future may bring, hoping for a more supportive and valuing democracy for all.

References

Bos, C. S., & Vaughn, S. (1998). Samuel Kirk's legacy to teaching reading: The past speaks to the present. *Learning Disabilities Research and Practice, 13*, 22–28.

Brantlinger, E. A. (2006). The big glossies: How textbooks structure (special) education. In E. A. Brantlinger (Ed.), *Who benefits from special education? Remediating (fixing) other people's children* (pp. 45–76). Mahwah, NJ: L. Erlbaum.

Danforth, S. (2009). *The incomplete child: An intellectual history of learning disabilities.* New York: Peter Lang.

Danforth, S., Slocum, L., & Dunkle, J. (2010). Turning the educability narrative: Samuel A. Kirk at the intersection of learning disability and mental retardation. *Intellectual and Developmental Disabilities, 48*, 180–194.

Fleischer, D. Z., & Zames, F. (2011). *The disability rights movement: From charity to confrontation* (2nd ed.). Philadelphia: Temple University Press.

Gallagher, J. J. (1998). The public policy legacy of Samuel A. Kirk. *Learning Disabilities Research and Practice, 13*, 11–14.

Kirk, S. A. (1962). *Educating exceptional children.* Boston, MA: Houghton Mifflin.

Longmore, P. K. (1998). *Disability policy and politics, considering consumer influences.* Paper presented to 1999 Switzer Seminar. Retrieved from http://www.dimenet.com/dpolicy/archive.php?mode=A&id=11;&sort=D

Longmore, P. K., & Goldberger, D. (2000). The League of the Physically Handicapped and the Great Depression: A case study and the new disability history. *Journal of American History,* 888–922.

Mather, N. (1998). Dr. Samuel A. Kirk: The complete professor. *Learning Disabilities Research and Practice, 13*, 35–42.

Mills, C. W. (1959). *The sociological imagination.* Oxford: Oxford University Press.

Minskoff, E. H. (1998). Sam Kirk: The man who made special education special. *Learning Disabilities Research and Practice, 13*, 15–21.

Monroe, M. (1928). Methods for diagnosis and treatment of cases of reading disability. *Genetic Psychological Monographs,* 335–456.

Monroe, M. (1932). *Children who cannot read: The analysis of reading disabilities and the use of diagnostic tests in the instruction of retarded readers.* Chicago: University of Chicago Press.

Pelka, F. (1997). *The ABC-CLIO companion to the disability rights movement.* Santa Barbara, CA: ABC-CLIO.

Introduction

A Brief Account of How Disability Studies in Education Evolved

DAVID J. CONNOR, JAN W. VALLE, AND CHRIS HALE

It is not without irony that the interdisciplinary field of disability studies (DS) was allegedly a little slow to warm up to the field of disability studies in education (DSE). After all, many disabled scholars within DS report having experienced firsthand, more often than not, schooling practices that institutionalized and segregated, stigmatized and pathologized their sensory, physical, cognitive, and/or emotional differences. Moreover, the terms *disability* and *education* have long been monopolized by the field of special education whose foundational knowledge base is predicated upon scientific, medical, and psychological understandings of human difference. Thus, special education came to conceptualize disability as a deficit, something absent, suggesting an incomplete human who needs to be fixed, cured, remediated, and shaped into the mold of normalcy at all costs. As DS scholar Mike Oliver (1996) noted, there was a marked mistrust of research methodologies and related knowledge claims as they were deemed by people with disabilities to be "at best irrelevant, and at worst, oppressive" (p. 129).

In contrast, DS, an academic discipline that grew out of grassroots, rights-based politics in the 1970s, focused upon the ways historical, social, cultural, political, and economic framings of disability simultaneously came into play with other discourses of disability (including those previously mentioned that undergird special education)—impacting the degree of access that people with disabilities have to all aspects of society. In sum, a basic feature that distinguished DS from other fields that engaged in the study of disability was its critical stance against what is usually perceived as the "master narrative" of disability perpetuated in science, medicine, and psychology. This critical stance, with its radical departure from "traditional" understandings of disability, can be seen in two relatively fluid threads of thought: (1) the minority model of disability that arose in the U.S., and (2) the social model of disability that emerged in the U.K. (for a more detailed description and discussion of these, see Gabel, 2005). In reality, over the past few decades, these models have grown, morphed, overlapped, extended, and been redefined by scholars who seek to use them in different ways. What has not changed, however, is the drive of DS to understand disability in varied, lived, eclectic ways that encompass exponential understandings—rather than the reductive, prescriptive renderings constructed by the "master narrative," symbolized, for example, by checklists of "symptoms" in the *Diagnostic and Statistical Manual of Mental Disorders* (American Psychiatric Association, 2013).

All that said, DS has served as the seeding ground in which ideas contrary to those held within the field of special education have taken root and flourished. Within the U.S., the formalization of DS was encapsulated in 1988 through the formation of the Society for Disability Studies (SDS), an interdisciplinary scholarly organization devoted to the study of disability. During the 1990s it remained the hub of DS in the U.S. with its annual conferences and a journal, *Disability Studies Quarterly* (*DSQ*) (parallel to the growth of DS in the U.K. including the journal *Disability & Society*). Educators by profession, Phil Ferguson, Susan Gabel, and Susan Peters were active in disability studies during this time and their presence kept educational research visible within the U.S. disability studies community. All three scholars discovered that SDS provided a place where they could experiment with the intersections of disability studies and educational research. By the late 1990s, several other DSE-identified scholars became involved in the SDS annual conferences, including Beth Ferri and Linda Ware, further establishing educational research in the annual program, indicating the deepening links between critical special education and disability studies.

Also during the 1990s, disability research using a post-positivist lens by critical special educators had been evolving not only in the U.S., but also in parts of Europe, Australia, and New Zealand. Importantly, they offered a critical response to special education's tenacious, singular embrace of positivism, a way of doing social science that attempts to imitate the ideology and practices of the natural sciences (i.e., belief in a detached objectivity to conduct quantitative measurement that leads toward "finding the truth"). Many of these scholars were members of an organization called the International Council in Inclusive Education (ICIE). In June 1999, Linda Ware, with the support of a Spencer Grant, organized an international conference in Rochester, New York, bringing together many of these scholars for the first time. The forum allowed the continuation of nascent re-workings toward DSE as it was emerging across various parts of the world. The keynote speaker was Ellen Brantlinger, admired for her willingness to openly critique the powerful body of researchers that dominated the field of special education (Brantlinger, 1997). Other attendees included Julie Allan, Keith Ballard, Len Barton, Tony Booth, Lous Heshusius, Roger Slee, Tom Skrtic, and Sally Tomlinson, along with a large sampling of graduate students. This conference played a pivotal role in encouraging continued international engagement with disability studies among educators, evidenced in the publication of *Ideology and the Politics of (In)Exclusion* (Ware, 2004), a collection of essays by educational researchers who attended the event.

The Critical Beginnings of DSE

In 1999, Scot Danforth, Ellen Brantlinger, Phil Ferguson, Lous Heshusius, and Chris Kliewer submitted a proposal to the national conference of the Association for Severely Handicapped (TASH) under the name of Coalition for Open Inquiry in Special Education (COISE). In this session, *Ways of Constructing Lives and Disabilities: The Case for Open Inquiry*, the panel asked questions such as: Why should a person with a disability or a teacher or a parent care what the academics say in their research and writings? Why should you care about the seemingly distant and esoteric writings in research journals and university textbooks? What is happening in these words that makes a difference? All participants discussed the social and political value of current trends and developments in disability research. In brief, they made a case for "open inquiry," an expansion and diversification of what was considered legitimate and valuable writing within special education publications.

In 2000, a DSE Special Interest Group was formed at the American Educational Research Association (AERA) conference in New Orleans, with Susan Gabel presenting a paper at the first business meeting on what constituted disability studies. During the following year at AERA in Seattle, Gabel also presented a paper that elaborated upon her original work. Having a DSE Special Interest Group legitimized DS as a field of study *within* educational research and reinforced the sub-field of DSE within DS. Both chairpersons and program chairs played a vital role in initiating and maintaining a high quality of presentations in research related to DSE.

DSE Annual Inter/National Conference

Parallel with the growth of DSE within AERA, the annual national conference of DSE (that has since grown into an international event) began. In

June 2001, a small, inaugural national meeting hosted by National-Louis University in Chicago titled *The Second City Disability Studies and Education Conference: Critical Reflections on the Themes of Policy, Practice, and Theory*, was held in Chicago, with Ellen Brantlinger, Scot Danforth, Susan Gabel, Deborah Gallagher, Bill Rhodes, and Linda Ware as featured speakers. Coordinators Valerie Owen, Paula Neville, and Terry Jo Smith provided a safe space for scholars and graduate students to present papers, listen to speakers, and discuss areas of common interest to explore disability studies and education. The success of the initial conference led to its establishment as an annual event that attracted scholars, researchers, professors, doctoral students, teachers, and other individuals who actively sought changes in theory and practice within both education and rehabilitation services for people with disabilities. Subsequent conferences have been held in other parts of the U.S., Belgium, New Zealand, and Australia. The conference has maintained a number of traditions, including annually recognizing a senior and junior scholar in the field of DSE. These meetings also inspired a listserv in which DSE researchers can share resources and ask questions within the community.

Growth in Publications

The annual conferences and DSE Special Interest Group have provided ongoing opportunities for networking, developing ideas, and providing mutual support in accomplishing research projects and scholarly writings. A major accomplishment has been Susan Gabel and Scot Danforth joining forces as co-editors of a DSE books series published by Peter Lang (of which this book is an example). To date there are 17 publications and the series is still growing. In addition, research from annual conferences is often documented through special editions of journals edited by DSE scholars. For example, in 2004 Scot Danforth and Susan Gabel were guest editors to an edition of *Disability Studies Quarterly (DSQ)* dedicated to educational issues. Likewise, Jan Valle, David Connor, and D. Kim Reid were guest editors for a special edition of *DSQ* featuring papers from the 5th Annual DSE Conference. In addition, a special edition of the *International Journal of Inclusive Education* was published in 2008, based on papers presented at the 7th Annual DSE Conference. Edited by David Connor, Susan Gabel, Deborah Gallagher, and Missy Morton, this special edition was the first publication to articulate what constituted a DSE framework and the tenets that upheld it. Continuing in this track, the conference committee of the 8th Annual DSE Conference edited a special edition of the *Teachers College Record* in 2012, based upon interdisciplinary presentations.

As we are critical special educators, we have simultaneously sought to engage the field of general and special education in conversation. For example, in 2008 Susan Baglieri, Jan Valle, David Connor, and Deborah Gallagher made a panel presentation at the national Annual Conference for the Council for Exceptional Children (CEC) in Boston entitled *Disability Studies in Education: The Need for a Plurality of Perspectives on Disability*. The presentation was well received and a subsequent article by the same name was published in *Remedial and Special Education* (Baglieri, Valle, Connor, & Gallagher, 2011). In an effort to appeal to a broader market and present DSE dispositions in the context of teacher education programs and good teaching, Jan Valle and David Connor wrote *Rethinking Disability: A Disability Studies Approach to Inclusive Practices*, which was published by McGraw-Hill (Valle & Connor, 2011). *Rethinking Disability* was recently translated into Portuguese, illustrating the growth of international interest in DSE. Likewise, in *Disability and Teaching* (2014), Susan Gabel and David Connor contributed to Erlbaum's Reflective Teaching series, edited by Daniel Liston and Ken Zeichner, that spans many general topics relevant to all teachers. This text was an unabashed attempt to take DSE into "the mainstream," and has been used by teacher education programs across the U.S. Other scholars in DSE have taken the lead in chronicling the foundations of DS along with contemplating contemporary contributions (Wappet & Arndt, 2013a, 2013b). DSE has also become present in some "mainstream" special education publications. For example, in the recent *Sage Handbook of Special Education* (Florian, 2014), six of the 44 chapters are by scholars who primarily define themselves within DSE (Connor, 2014; Slee, 2014; Biklen, Orsati, & Bacon, 2014: Ferguson, Hanreddy, & Ferguson, 2104; Gallagher, 2014; Harwood & McMahon, 2014), along with significant representation by progressive inclusionists (Ainscow, 2014; Dieker & Powell, 2014; Pugach & Blanton, 2014), and other critical special educators who are highly influenced by culture and context (de Valenzuela, 2014; Harry, 2014; Kozleski, Artiles & Waitoller, 2014; Thomas, 2014). All of these authors contribute to diversification within, and beyond, special education scholarship.

Opportunities to Share Ideas

Many scholars have used the DSE annual conference and/or the DSE Special Interest Group–sponsored events at AERA as a venue in which to present their latest work, whether work in progress or completed. Such scholars have included Julie Allan, Katrina Arndt, Christy Ashby, Jessica Bacon, Susan Baglieri, Len Barton, Lynne Bejoian, Liat Ben-Moshe, Gregg Beratan, Douglas Biklen, Ellen Brantlinger, Alicia Broderick, Cathy Cologon, Scot Danforth, Curt Dudley-Marling, Chris Hale, Nirmala Erevelles, Dianne Ferguson, Phil Ferguson, Beth Ferri, Susan Gabel, Deborah Gallagher, Annie

Guerin, Elizabeth Grace, Chris Hale, Lous Heshusius, Shelley Kinash, Paula Kluth, Bernadette McCartney, Erin McCloskey, Angus McFarlane, Margaret McLean, Emily Mintz, Missy Morton, Kagendo Mutua, Paula Neville, Srikala Naraian, Valerie Owen, Susan Peters, D. Kim Reid, Dan Rhodes, Nancy Rice, David Skidmore, Janet Sauer, Roger Slee, Phil Smith, Robin Smith, Terry Jo Smith, Susan Snellgrove, Santiago Solis, Edy Stoughton, Steve Taylor, Jan Valle, Julia White, Matthew Wappet, Linda Ware, Rod Wills, and Kathryn Young. We realize that this is a sample of participants, far from an exhaustive list, and in no way wish to neglect any of our colleagues in the field. However, in this sample, we wish to convey the scope of interests—from philosophical groundings to historical reinterpretations, from pedagogical innovations to reimagining commonplace practices. In addition, doctoral students, under-graduate students, and professionals in the field of rehabilitation have all tak-en the opportunity to present research, position papers, and creative works in a supportive atmosphere.

The first half of this chapter is admittedly a snapshot of how DS helped critical special educators who felt their disposition did not fit within the very real limits of the knowledge base and practices of their field of education to nurture an alternative field of study. In many ways, there is a long list of schol-ars throughout the decades who have pushed the proverbial envelope about what constitutes disability and how to best educate students so designated, and includes the likes of Alfredo Artiles, Bernadette Baker, Carol Christensen, Curt Dudley-Marling, Beth Harry, Alan Gartner, Janette Klingner, Elizabeth Kozleski, Dorothy Kerzner Lipsky, James Patton, and Tom Skrtic. We re-spectfully acknowledge that these scholars may or may not self-identify with DSE, but their professional work has undoubtedly critiqued aspects of special education in ways that are compatible with a DSE stance.

The Strength of Community

The evolution of DSE is the story of building community. At the turn of the last century, there were a few scholars who had a vision that encompassed dis-ability in different ways and the drive to see it actualized. As previously men-tioned, in the field of education "disability" meant "special education," and if a researcher or teacher held a different perspective, it was difficult to find a comfortable ideological place within the profession. It is not an exaggeration to say that our first conferences and meetings brought together many scholars who had been professionally attacked, dismissed, marginalized, or ignored, leaving them somewhat shocked, wounded, and professionally homeless. Since then, the DSE Special Interest Group, the annual conference, various publications, and professional listservs have served to build a community that, in turn, has empowered its members. Together we have created a common language, refined our purpose, identified practices consistent with theory, and explicitly articulated our beliefs about educational equity. We have been active in international discussions about civil rights and inclusion. We have invited leading scholars in other disciplines to join our conversation. We are present in compendiums dedicated to human diversity, multiculturalism, and social justice. We are community members who continue to push back against incessant demands of educational systems that pay lip service to diversity while aggressively demanding standardization and conformity.

However, while acknowledging the successful growth of an alternative discourse to the master narrative of disability reified within the institutions of special education, we also know that there is a long, long way to go in developing and circulating DSE as means to inspire, motivate, and inform actions within the field of education.

The Purpose of the Book

As co-editors and contributors, this book feels like a natural progression within the field of DSE. What do we mean by this? In some ways it is easy to explain, and in other ways, it is more complicated. The easy way pertains to our need to document what we do and what has been achieved through the significant influence of DSE within educational contexts. For those of us who have experienced the value of DSE, we know how useful it can be in a multitude of ways including: theorizing the very nature of what constitutes disability to whom, where, when, and why; researching all aspects of the phenomenon of disability in ways that render humans quite differently than traditional special education does; practicing inclusive pedagogies within the realm of universal design for learning; and impacting policies at international, national, regional, and local levels.

Conversely, the more complicated side of this natural progression involves imagining and negotiating ways in going forward that will benefit children, youth, and adults with disabilities both in educational settings and life in general. It is tempting to see DSE variously as the romanticized David to special education's Goliath, the underdog in a boxing ring who bobs and shifts in unexpected ways to challenge the established favorite of institutional knowledge, or even as a tick on the backside of the camel of special education—annoying, but equally a form of life with a right to exist. In many respects, DSE has definitely made its mark both within and outside of special education scholarship, including the cultivation of interdisciplinary exchanges. Some DSE scholars, including ourselves, have engaged the field of special education about its narrow focus that inhibits an expansion of the two related issues that we all care deeply about—disability and education (Baglieri et al., 2011; Connor, Gallagher, & Ferri, 2011; Danforth, 2006; Danforth & Rhodes, 1997; Reid & Valle, 2004). Unfortunately, instead of seeing this as an opportunity to grow knowledge, influential scholars in the field of special education seek to stifle or discredit DS. In a recent spate of articles that have the same message—disability studies is purely ideological and a corrupting influence on the integrity of special education—Anastasiou and Kauffman tellingly tie themselves into a Gordian knot of ineffective critiques (2010, 2011, 2013). One can only speculate that their vociferous, multi-pronged denouncement is in relation to their fear of an increased circulation of diverse ideas about disability that DS (and DSE) has introduced. And yet, as those who are being critiqued, we actually enjoy the debates and active intellectual exchange, urging that we move beyond the impasse—suggesting that the field of special education and DSE continue to engage with and inform one another (Gallagher, Connor, & Ferri, 2014). After all, despite this debate, which over the decades often seems acrimonious (Brantlinger, 1997; Kauffman, 1999; Kauffman & Sasso, 2006a, 2006b; Gallagher, 1998, 2006), DSE has developed and grown exponentially, indicating a substantive interest in our field.

Ultimately, this book is consciously proactive. We have been developing ideas within DSE for a decade and a half, and "before it had a name" (Taylor, 2006), this alternative ideology was being forged by individual scholars (see, for example: Biklen, 1990; Heshusius, 1984; Iano, 1990; Rhodes, 1995; Skrtic, 1991). We know the ideas that have emerged within DSE have entered educators' practices, allowing them to think and act in ways that have a positive impact on the lives of others. This text, therefore, is meant to showcase ways in which DSE is currently used by many educators in tangible ways.

The Format of the Book

The book is divided into four parts that foreground the interrelated domains of education—theory, research, practice, and policy. We believe that the domains deserve their own sections as this allows for clear examples of DSE "at work" with each one. Of course, these examples are illustrative rather than prescriptive, instances of how scholars working within DSE have utilized its grounding tenets to do, as Gallagher (this volume) would argue, what they believe is morally justifiable or, more simply put, "the right thing to do." At the same time, although we have allowed the domains of theory, research, practice, and policy to have their own sections that provide opportunities to hone in on specific instances of DSE in action, we all know that each domain does not exist in isolation. It is more accurate, we believe, to consider the domain in constant interplay with, and always informing, the others.

It can be said, therefore, that our choice of format is intended to encourage the reader to have the best of both worlds. Namely, you can read across three chapters consisting of distinct and sometimes contrasting "takes" of DSE within the four domains of theory, research, practice, and policy. Simultaneously, the reader also has the opportunity to consider—as you read through the four domains—ways in which each relates to the others. We encourage this multi-dimensional reading that will serve to deepen the reader's understanding of, and appreciation for, ways in which DSE has been enacted within everyday situations across a variety of settings. In the remainder of this introduction, we briefly describe each chapter.

Section I focuses on theory and opens with Deborah Gallagher's chapter titled "Exploring Some Moral Dimensions of the Social Model of Disability," in which she asserts the need to acknowledge disability as a moral category. As she notes, regardless of whether disability is "real" or "socially constructed," and whether a medical or a social model is the correct stance toward human difference, it is rather each individual's core set of values that ground and inform our personal and cultural responses to disability. To help us better understand how we consider disability as a moral category, Gallagher invokes utilitarianism, libertarianism, and communitarianism schools of thought within moral philosophy to help clarify how moral principles shape our larger social/cultural responses to disability. Ultimately, she reveals ways in which a communitarianism framework is compatible with a DSE grounding in education that emphasizes inclusive education and the pedagogical practices that support it.

In Chapter 2, "'As a cripple, I swagger': The Situated Body and Disability Studies in Education," Beth Ferri utilizes feminist disability studies and reveals interdisciplinary ways in which we come to know "the body." Ferri notes how DS scholars locate disabilities within structures of society as opposed to the biology or essence of individuals. These critical understandings of disability as a social and political construct, Ferri believes, implicitly build upon Simone de Beauvoir's critique of biological determinism encapsulated in her famous phrase "Woman is made, not born." Thus, the dis/abled body functions as a cultural text created ("made") through social relations of power, discursively inscribed with meaning. However, Ferri claims that social models of disability oftentimes inadvertently reify an artificial binary between the social and the personal/individual, between disability as socially produced and impairment as biological and inherent. By focusing on the writing of disabled author Nancy Mairs, and making connections to Simone de Beauvoir's concept of situated embodiment, Ferri illustrates how both women understand the body as both *situation* and *point of view*, thereby offering a more complex model of disability. Mairs' work, for example, can be viewed as fertile ground for thinking through how to reconsider disability as much more than a sum of oppressive and exclusionary forces, and instead as an equally valid way of knowing and being in the world.

Chapter 3 (coming at you crazy right now) is Phil Smith's poetic "BEyon|ce|D inclusion: Wud mite[ymouse] be NEXTERATED X". This piece, like much of Smith's work, defies simple categorization in terms of form or content. He does, however, center his thoughts around the radical question: "What if a goal of inclusion—across oppressions and identities—is not a useful trajectory for this thing we call education?" Better yet, Smith proceeds to answer the question posed by presenting the case about corruption and immorality circulating within historical and contemporary forces within education. Whether you find this chapter to be nihilistic, refreshing, "telling it like it is," destabilizing, depressing, liberating, visionary, dystopian, or a kaleidoscopic moving mosaic incorporating all of the above—if you like it, then you better put a ring on it.

Section II focuses on research and begins with Chapter 4, Jan Valle's "Enacting Research: Disability Studies and Performative Inquiry." In this work, Valle makes the case for integrating arts-based research, specifically theater arts, and DSE as a means to provide access to DSE research and practice for an audience beyond the academy and to the general public. Valle describes three examples within her own practice of how she integrates DSE and theater arts by: (1) a cross-program collaboration between herself and a colleague that allows Valle to integrate theater into teaching artists who seek teacher certification; (2) developing a partnership between herself, a playwright, and a musician to co-create and produce an ethnodrama based on research narratives by mothers of children with disabilities; and (3) a case example of graduate students applying DSE to arts-based research. This body of work demonstrates the transformative potential of integrating DSE and theater arts—allowing theater artists to apply new understandings of disability and inclusion to theater contexts in public schools and within the greater community.

In Chapter 5, Subini Annamma's "'It was just like a piece of gum': Using an Intersectional Approach to Understand Criminalizing Young Women of Color With Disabilities in the School-to-Prison Pipeline," embraces a topic that is largely neglected within traditional special education. Despite an increased knowledge of the School-to-Prison Pipeline, there is still very little known about the actual experiences of students within it. Annamma's research focuses on how five queer young women of color with disabilities experienced the process of criminalization via the mechanisms of labeling, surveillance, and punishment that, in turn, made them more vulnerable to juvenile incarceration. The intersectional identities of the young women are portrayed and viewed through a theoretical framework consisting of Critical Race Theory (CRT), DisCrit, and Queer Crit, affording a better understanding of how females of color labeled with an emotional disability experience criminalization in the School-to-Prison Pipeline.

Chapter 6, titled "An 'In-Betweener' Ethnographer: From Anxiety to Fieldwork Methods in a Cross-Cultural Study of Bilingual Deaf Kindergartners," is Joseph Valente's autoethnographic account of how his anxieties, fears, and insecurities (along with many other factors) constantly inform and shape all aspects of his research as a deaf person. Such vulnerability, Valente asserts, permits him to constantly reflect upon what is important, to whom, and why, and how that can shift unpredictably with the passage of time and exposure to increased experiences and different forms of knowledge. He notes that being a researcher involves understanding one's position as an outsider who values the genre of ethnography. As such, researchers sometimes see patterns and ascribe significance that insiders do not recognize, and equally, vice versa. Valente's chapter is not only about growing pains as a novice researcher, and a deeper awareness of his limitations, it is also a meditation about how DSE helps broker the ongoing questions and dilemmas we have about our role as researchers.

Section III focuses on practice and opens with David Connor's "Practicing What We Teach: The Benefits of Using Disability Studies in an Inclusion Course." As a teacher educator, Connor describes how a course that he has taught on inclusive education for 15 years has changed and evolved, largely through his interaction with—and adoption of—DS and DSE to inform readings, practices, assignments, and assessments. In describing the architecture of the course, he highlights how a framing of disability using DS/DSE theory within what is largely a traditional special-education program at his educational institution can actively serve to challenge and inform students' rethinking of familiar topics including: challenging stereotypes; working with parents; instructional planning, delivery, and assessment of diverse learners; managing classrooms; selecting responsible curricula; and engaging with universal design for learning (UDL). This chapter features personal observations, anecdotes of students, and a selection of artifacts within inclusive pedagogy used—all of which coalesce to purposely destabilize the current educational worldview of students, while simultaneously preparing them to work within diverse classrooms.

In Chapter 8, Geert Van Hove and Elisabeth De Schauwer's "Why We Do What We (Think We) Do: Creating a Campus Coalition From the Perspective of Disability Studies in Education," the authors highlight progressive practices involving the University of Ghent in Belgium. Van Hove and De Schauwer explain how, since 1999, they have been part of a group that has been building a university environment in which DSE is more than just a theoretical framework, a way of thinking, or a topic of class discussion. Within their community/university network, these DSE scholars have strong connections to people identified as having intellectual disabilities and their families, who participate in, and help shape the group's agenda. In addition, Van Hove and De Schauwer relate how they constantly look at ways to collaborate within their network in research, education, and service to the community.

In Chapter 9, "Madness and (Higher Education) Administration: Ethical Implications of Pedagogy Using Disability Studies Scholarship," Nirmala Erevelles explores how universities respond "reasonably" to the topic of madness. Beginning with a general discussion of the socio-political climate in which madness/mental illness and violence are constructed synonymously, Erevelles moves to the implications such rhetoric has on administrative policies within the context of higher education. To challenge such a limited, institutional response, Erevelles uses Margaret Price's book, *Mad at School* (2011), as an example of DSE scholarship as a critical tool to analyze normative notions of the mind/body split and the implications for students and professors with madness/mental illnesses. Sharing how she engages students in ethical theories informed by critical disability-studies scholarship, Erevelles describes ways to help students construct an oppositional/transformative analysis of commonsensical understandings of mental illness, and discusses the implications that such disruptions can have for the critical engagement of difference.

Section IV focuses on policy and begins with Chapter 10, Julie Allan's "Critiquing Policy: Limitations and Possibilities." This work examines the limited success of formal critiques of educational policy and considers the specific contexts of Sweden, the U.K., and the U.S., each with different educational traditions and trajectories but with some convergences in patterns of critique. Allan strongly advocates for the potential of analytical resources derived from within DSE and through its orientation to the humanities to deliver acceptable and appropriate critique and to mobilize political action within education. Most importantly, Allan points out the consequences of moving forward *without* critiques of educational policy, and the need for respectful engagement around actions and practices that impact students, teachers, and administrators on a daily basis.

In Chapter 11, Missy Morton's "Using Disability Studies in Education to Recognize, Resist, and Reshape Policy and Practices in Aotearoa New Zealand" describes the country's policy of striving toward a world-class inclusive education system. Morton's chapter illustrates ways in which DSE can be utilized to work within a less-than-ideal environment influenced by neoliberal ideologies of standardization. She addresses ways in which committed educators can and do push back against policies and within education structures to maintain a humanist rather than a technicist disposition toward teaching. Morton believes that an integral part of teacher education must be designed to recognize and resist deficit discourses of human differences and shows how this can be incorporated into national policy—including the student-centered context of individualized education programs.

In Chapter 12, titled "A Disability Studies in Education Analysis of Corporate-Based Educational Reform: Lessons From New Orleans," Kathleen Collins tells a powerful tale of educational reform in the wake of Hurricane Katrina that has created a class of "leftover" children who are systematically denied access to public schooling. Collins notes that despite media reports upholding New Orleans as an example of the success of privatized school reform, insufficient attention has been paid to understanding the constellation of effects that corporate school-reform policies have had on students with complex support needs. In this chapter, Collins draws from DSE to analyze *P. B. et al. v. Paul Pastorek* (2010), a pending class-action lawsuit, and ably critiques policies and practices that actively exclude children with disabilities from public schooling.

In the concluding chapter, "Using Disability Studies in Education to (Re)Envision the Applied Field of (Special) Education," we co-editors analyze and reflect upon how all 12 chapters hold great potential for interacting with, and influencing, DS in general and other disciplinary areas of study. By analyzing each chapter individually as well as all chapters together as a body of work, we aim to further our collective thinking about ways in which DSE visibly and tangibly demonstrates the impact it has upon people's lives within the interconnected domains of theory, research, practice, and policy. As members of an established and growing community, it is our intention to continue documenting the work that arises from DSE that translates into actions. Finally, we acknowledge that the examples of "DSE at work" in this volume are only a glimpse into what is occurring in everyday lives of teachers, scholars, researchers, and activists around the world who are interested in disability and education. We hope you enjoy reading them as much as we did.

References

Ainscow, M. (2014). From special education to effective schools for all: Widening the agenda. In L. Florian (Ed.), *The Sage handbook of special education* (pp. 171–186). Sage: London.

American Psychiatric Association. (2013). *Diagnostic and statistical manual of mental disorders* (5th ed.). Arlington, VA: APA.

Anastasiou, D., & Kauffman, J. M. (2010). Disability as cultural difference: Implications for special education. *Remedial and Special Education*, *33*(3), 139–149. DOI: 10. 1177/0741932510383163. Retrieved from http://rse.sagepub.com/content/early/2010/09/21/0741932510383163

Anastasiou, D., & Kauffman, J. M. (2011). A social constructionist approach to disability: Implications for special education. *Exceptional Children*, *77*(3), 367–384.

Anastasiou, D., & Kauffman, J. M. (2013). The social model of disability: Dichotomy between impairment and disability. *Journal of Medicine & Philosophy*, *38*(4), 441–459.

Baglieri, S., Valle, J., Connor, D. J., & Gallagher, D. (2011). Disability studies and special education: The need for plurality of perspectives on disability. *Remedial and Special Education*, *32*(4), 267–278.

Biklen, D. (1990). Communication unbound: Autism and praxis. *Harvard Education Review*, *60*(3), 291–315.

Biklen, D., Orsati, F., & Bacon, J. (2014). A disability studies frame for research approaches in special education. In L. Florian (Ed.), *The Sage handbook of special education* (pp. 351–368). London: Sage.

Brantlinger, E. (1997). Using ideology: Cases of non-recognition in the politics of research and practice in special education. *Review of Educational Research*, *67*(4), 14–22.

Connor, D. J. (2014). Social justice in education for students with disabilities. In L. Florian (Ed.), *The Sage handbook of special education* (pp. 111–128). London: Sage.

Connor, D. J., Gallagher, D., & Ferri, B. (2011). Broadening our horizons: Toward a plurality of methodologies in learning disability research. *Learning Disability Quarterly*, *32*(2), 107–121.

Danforth, S. (2006). From epistemology to democracy: Pragmatism and the reorientation of disability research. *Remedial and Special Education*, *27*(6), 337–345.

Danforth, S., & Rhodes, W. C. (1997). Deconstructing disability: A philosophy for inclusion. *Remedial and Special Education*, *18*(6), 357–366.

de Valenzuela, S. J. (2014). Sociocultural views of learning. In L. Florian (Ed.), *The Sage handbook of special education* (pp. 299–314). London: Sage.

Dieker, L. A., & Powell, S. (2014). Secondary special education and inclusive practices: Pitfalls and potential for the success for all. In L. Florian (Ed.), *The Sage handbook of special education* (pp. 659–674). London: Sage.

Ferguson, D. L., Hanreddy, A. N., & Ferguson, P. M. (2014). Finding a voice: Families' roles in schools. In L. Florian (Ed.), *The Sage handbook of special education* (pp. 763–784). London: Sage.

Florian, L. (2014). Reimagining special education: Why new approaches are needed. In L. Florian (Ed.), *The Sage handbook of special education* (pp. 9–22). London: Sage.

Gabel, S. L. (Ed.) (2005). *Disability studies in education: Readings in theory and method.* New York: Peter Lang.

Gabel, S. L., & Connor, D. J. (2014). *Teaching and disability.* Mahwah, NJ: Erlbaum.

Gallagher, D. J. (1998). The scientific knowledge base of special education: Do we know what we think we know? *Exceptional Children, 64*(4), 493–502.

Gallagher, D. J. (2006). If not absolute objectivity, then what? A reply to Kauffmann and Sasso. *Exceptionality, 14*(2), 91–107.

Gallagher, D. J. (2014). Challenging orthodoxy in special education: On longstanding debates and philosophical divides revisited. In L. Florian (Ed.), *The Sage handbook of special education* (pp. 763–784). London: Sage.

Gallagher, D. J., Connor, D. J., & Ferri, B. A. (2014). Beyond the far too incessant schism: Special education and the social model of disability. *International Journal of Inclusive Education.* DOI: 10.1080/13603116.2013.875599. Retrieved from http://www.tandfonline.com/loi/tied20

Harry, B. (2014). The disproportionate placement of ethnic minorities in special education. In L. Florian (Ed.), *The Sage handbook of special education* (pp. 73–96). London: Sage.

Harwood, V., & McMahon, S. (2014). Medicalization in schools. In L. Florian (Ed.), *The Sage handbook of special education* (pp. 915–930). London: Sage.

Heshusius, L. (1984). Why would they and I want to do it? A phenomenological theoretical view of special education. *Learning Disabilities Quarterly, 7,* 363–367.

Iano, R. P. (1990). Special education teachers: Technicians or educators? *Journal of Learning Disabilities, 23*(8), 462–465.

Kauffman, J. M. (1999). Commentary: Today's special education and its messages for tomorrow. *Journal of Special Education, 32*(4), 244–254.

Kauffman, J. M., & Sasso, G. M. (2006a). Toward ending cultural and cognitive relativism in special education. *Exceptionality, 14*(2), 65–90.

Kauffman, J. M., & Sasso, G. M. (2006b). Certainty, doubt, and the reduction of uncertainty: A rejoinder. *Exceptionality, 14*(2), 109–120.

Kozleski, E., Artiles, A., & Waitoller, F. (2014). Equity in inclusive education: A cultural historical comparative perspective. In L. Florian (Ed.), *The Sage handbook of special education* (pp. 231–250). London: Sage.

Oliver, M. (1996). Understanding the hegemony of disability. In M. Oliver (Ed.), *Understanding disability: From theory to practice* (pp. 126–144). New York: St. Martin's Press.

P. B. et al. v. Paul Pastorek et al. (2010). E.D. La. 2:10-cv-04049.

Price, M. (2011). *Mad at school: Rhetoric's of mental disability and academic life.* Ann Arbor: University of Michigan Press.

Pugach, M., & Blanton, L. P. (2014). Inquiry and community: Uncommon opportunities to enrich professional development for inclusion. In L. Florian (Ed.), *The Sage handbook of special education* (pp. 873–888). London: Sage.

Reid, D. K., & Valle, J. W. (2004). The discursive practice of learning disability: Implications for instruction and parent-school relations. *Journal of Learning Disabilities, 37*(6), 466–481.

Rhodes, W. C. (1995). Liberatory pedagogy and special education. *Journal of Learning Disabilities, 28*(8), 458–467.

Skrtic, T. M. (1995). The special education paradox: Equity as a way to excellence. *Harvard Educational Review, 61*(2), 148–206.

Slee, R. (2014). Inclusive school as an apprenticeship in democracy? In L. Florian (Ed.), *The Sage handbook of special education* (pp. 217–230). London: Sage.

Taylor, S. J. (2006). Before it had a name: Exploring the historical roots of disability studies in education. In S. Danforth & S. Gabel (Eds.), *Vital questions facing disability studies in education* (pp. xiii–xxiii). New York: Peter Lang.

Thomas, G. (2014). Epistemology and special education. In L. Florian (Ed.), *The Sage handbook of special education* (pp. 267–280). London: Sage.

Valle, J., & Connor, D. J. (2011). *Rethinking disability: A disability studies guide to inclusive practices.* New York: McGraw-Hill.

Wappet, M., & Arndt, K. (Eds.) (2013a). *Foundations of disability studies.* New York: Palgrave Macmillan.

Wappet, M., & Arndt, K. (Eds.) (2013b). *Emerging perspectives on disability studies.* New York: Palgrave Macmillan.

Ware, L. (Ed.) (2004). *Ideology and the politics of (in)exclusion.* New York: Peter Lang.

Section I
Theory

1. Exploring Some Moral Dimensions of the Social Model of Disability

Deborah Gallagher

Years of debate about the epistemological and ontological status of disability have ensued since the face-off between the long dominant medical versus the insurgent social models of disability (See for example: Anastasiou & Kauffman, 2010, 2011). In the midst of these disputes, disability studies scholars have further probed the sufficiency with which the social model of disability captures or represents the experience of disability (See for example: Crow, 1996; Davis, 2002; French, 1993; Shakespeare, 2006, 2014). These discussions, too, have revolved largely around questions of epistemology and ontology that have perhaps done as much to exhaust and divide as to illuminate and unite.

The purpose of this chapter is threefold. First, I put forth what I hope is a convincing case that the longstanding disputes over the epistemological and ontological status of disability are, at this point, unavailing, and that we would be far better served simply to regard disability explicitly as a moral category. This approach, I suspect, has the potential to expand the emancipatory impact of the social model. Second, I offer an exploration of three areas of moral philosophy in an effort to provide some initial context or scaffolding useful for engaging disability as a moral category. Finally, I discuss the three schools of moral philosophy in terms of their compatibility with the social model of disability and their implications for disability studies in education.

Moral philosophy, or ethics as it is most often referred to, is a branch of philosophy encompassing an extensive array of theories and schools of thought, none of which can be covered extensively in the context of one paper. For this reason, I have selected *utilitarianism*, the moral bases for the political philosophy known as *libertarianism*, and *communitarianism* as the three lenses through which to explore the moral nature of disability. My goal is to draw upon major philosophers to examine three schools of moral/political thought of interest to the disability community, specifically the promotion of inclusion/equity and implications for the social model of disability.

The Social Model and Disability as a Moral Category

When 1970s activists and scholars refuted the medicalist account of disability, they succeeded not only in exerting the social model as a politically powerful counter-narrative, but also in creating new spaces for probing the intricate dimensions of disability as a lived experience. Given the hegemony of the then ascendant medical framework, the social model constituted an audacious confrontation with the status quo by asserting that the origin of disability lay not in the bodies or minds of those pathologized, but rather in the cultural interpretations, social conventions, and professional practices to which they were subjected. Disability as asserted by the social model is a constructed phenomenon, not an objective one. The piercing indictment embedded within this conceptual shift was not lost on those who heard it—the problem lies not in a given person's physical or mental differences but in your personal (and our collective) responses to those differences.

In accomplishing this shift, though, the social model retained impairments (differences) as distinct from disabilities, the former as epistemological and ontological facts and the latter as cultural creations, thus creating a disjuncture of no small consequence. And while some objected to this disconnection on the grounds of philosophical incoherence (Tremain, 1998, 2002), others protested that the force of the constructivist assertion served to deny the very real lived experiences of pain, illness, and emotional anguish (Crow, 1996; French, 1993). In an attempt at reconciling the two concerns, Thomas (2004) offered a social relational understanding of disability that accounts for "impairment effects" but also expressed misgivings that this approach might blunt the social model's forceful repudiation of the presumption of defective citizenship. In the final analysis, she concluded that:

> The social advances achieved by oppressed groups are always of much greater significance than any loss in clarity of ideas along the way. The social model remains, and should remain, in place as a powerful organizing principle, a rallying cry, and a practical tool (Oliver, 2004) for the disabled people's movement. (p. 581)

The social model's greatest strength, in other words, lies in its potential to eradicate disabling barriers, and this goal trumps concerns about philosophical coherence.

Thomas's social relational understanding of disability is consonant with Shakespeare and Watson's (2002) attempt to reconcile the social model's disability/impairment dichotomy. From their perspective, "impairment and disability are not dichotomous." Instead, together they are best understood as "dialectic of biological, cultural, [and] socio-political factors" (p. 24). Extending this kind of inquiry further, Shakespeare (2006) pointed out that a "plurality of approaches" or conceptual frameworks can be useful for understanding disability, and toward that end he has drawn upon post-structuralism, postmodernism, social constructionism, feminist theory, and critical realism among others.

If the conceptual tools one might use are not the point, then the question becomes how the tools are used and more specifically toward what ends. Tools, whether they are physical or intellectual, are always selected with a goal in mind. One's goals subsume intention, and intention is essentially moral. My reading of and engagement with the philosophical literature over the past many years, whether the topic has involved the impassioned quarrels over research methodology, the intricate deliberations about the social model, or the interminable conflict between inclusive schooling advocates versus the preservationists of segregation, has led me to conclude that, regardless of the quality, depth, clarity, or coherence of any given analysis, arguments are largely lost on those for whom these issues interfere with or undermine their moral positioning on that topic. In plain terms, conceptual frameworks both contain and serve moral intentions, which is why any discussions about them are most often so very impassioned.

That being the case, then, we might ask why we debate the merits, coherence, or veracity of various frameworks as they pertain to important issues rather than simply getting to the moral substance of the issue itself. Are these debates mostly if not entirely proxy disputes and border skirmishes? This is not to say that these discussions are pointless but that they confine us to the more comfortable margins of academic debate rather than plunging us into the much more demanding work of moral deliberation. Now, clearly the epistemological framework of the social model makes for a useful conduit for articulating this indictment because it deftly exposes the conceits of the medical model's much acclaimed detachment. But as I specified above, the real power of the social model is its assertion that no one is disabled alone, that disablement in fact requires either the active and passive complicity of the rest of us. It is an indictment of self-centeredness and the cultural abandonment of consideration for what we owe each other. At its core, it affirms the personhood and accordant worth of us all. Because it speaks to the issue of disability, an issue that is fundamentally a moral one, the social model is a moral assertion more than an epistemological one (see: Gallagher, Connor, & Ferri, 2014).

If indeed that is the case, if analyzing and engaging disability is essentially a moral endeavor, then it seems rather self-evident that valuable perspectives might be sought through an exploration of moral philosophy. And there are endless paths one might take in such an exploration. As mentioned earlier, I have chosen libertarianism, utilitarianism, and communitarianism as three schools of moral philosophy that I think are worthwhile, most particularly because they have figured prominently into contemporary and very public discussions about disability. Consequently, these schools of thought no doubt are in a position to exert substantial influences in shaping public discourse, attitudes, and perspectives about disability in general. In what follows, I first provide an overview of each of these schools of thought. Here I want to state pointedly that my intention is to aim for a useful clarity rather than offer exhaustive expositions of the intricacies involved in the many strains and strands of these moral theories. From there I'll draw on their tenets to discuss how prominent contemporary moral philosophers who have publically weighed in on matters important to the disability community applied their chosen frameworks to assert their respective positions and conclusions.

Three Schools of Moral Philosophy: An Overview

Utilitarianism

As a theory within the branch of moral philosophy known as normative ethics, utilitarianism advances the position that the most defensible, hence correct, course of action is one that maximizes utility, meaning that it expands happiness or well-being and minimizes suffering to the greatest extent or for the greatest number of people. As a form of consequentialism, the moral worth of any act is judged by its overall consequences. Utilitarianism, as it was most prominently articulated by Bentham and Mill, represented a reformist bent toward the establishment of a rational and enlightened system of morality quite apart from the reigning religious dogma of the late-eighteenth century. Emerging in the historical context of the enlightenment, early utilitarians sought to establish an ethical system concordant with science—a single law of morality with virtually limitless explanatory capacity. Utilitarians were also, quite pointedly, social and political reformers who supported such advances as the extension of suffrage to women and the poor, the abolition of slavery, rehabilitation of rather than retribution against lawbreakers, and, intriguingly, the elimination of cruelty to animals.

A particular strain of egalitarianism is a defining feature of utilitarian ethics, most particularly in the bedrock principle that each person's happiness is of equal value to all others. But because the interests of one or more people are often in conflict with the interests of others, commonsense rules that one would generally follow (obey laws and don't lie, cheat, or steal) can and even should be broken if and when the consequences of breaking them extends greater happiness or decreases overall suffering. For example, lying to save someone's life is consistent with utilitarian ethics, as is the time-honored practices of lying to spare someone's feelings. Few would find these practices problematic, but what about killing or causing someone's death in the event that many other lives will be saved as a result? Committed utilitarians could, according to the logic of their framework, find this choice not just acceptable but morally requisite. For them, choosing not to act is not a way out of a moral dilemma. Errors of omission are just as indefensible as wrongs of commission. Where some contemporary utilitarian philosophers and bio-ethicists begin to part company with a great many other people, though, is in their defense of euthanasia—a practice that, in this framework, justifies the killing of an innocent for the sake of ending pointless suffering.

Perhaps the most publicized contemporary utilitarian philosopher and animal rights advocate is Peter Singer, a bioethicist at Princeton University. As DSE scholars are well aware, since his appointment at Princeton University in 1999, Singer has relentlessly incited the ire of the disability rights community (Jung, 2009) with his very public advocacy for euthanizing disabled infants (Kuhse & Singer, 1985; Singer, 2011) and physician-assisted suicide (Singer, 2011). He has also continued to provoke outrage with, for example, his support for the parental decisions in the Ashley X case (Singer, 2012), and his frankly bizarre musings about whether healthcare for disabled people should be limited (see: Drake, 2009).

Although he was painstakingly careful to acknowledge and censure the oppression of disabled people, Singer based his defense of euthanizing some disabled infants on the premise that simply being biologically (genetically) human does not make them human in the sense that they possess personhood, or have "truly human qualities" (p. 73). Drawing on Locke's definition of personhood, he asserted that to be truly human in the sense of being a *person* requires that one possess self-awareness, a sense of the future, and so on.

Owing to its eloquent minimalism and subsequent ease of application, utilitarian ethics has enjoyed a wide appeal—even among those who know next to nothing about utilitarianism as a formal school of moral thought. Even so, there are some objections to which its academic adherents have had to respond. First, and most obviously, if the moral adequacy of one's action is predicated on its consequences (increasing happiness and minimizing suffering), it seems rather important that those consequences be known in advance. Yet, this kind of knowledge is not something we humans have at our disposal, and most of us are acutely aware that the consequences of any act are as complex as they are far-reaching. Utilitarian philosophers acknowledge as much while countering that we should act on the basis of what we have the most reason to believe given the possibilities available. Second, some counter, in a deontological sense, that some acts are simply immoral on their face, particularly when they involve exploitation, ruthlessness, or paternalism. Is it really morally defensible to harm a person to save multiple others? Utilitarianism would seem to suggest so. The utilitarian counter to this concern points out that such equations are seldom simple given the distinct possibility of spillover effects; that is, extreme acts that appear justifiable can serve to spread more harm by creating a sense of existential insecurity when others empathize with the person who is harmed.

Much depends, of course, on how strictly one adheres to utilitarian principles. As with other schools of moral philosophy, there are more who acknowledge and contend with its complexities than there are complete purists. That said, utilitarianism's powerful persuasiveness lies in the difficulty of arguing against something so basic to our existence as the desire for happiness and the dread of suffering. To advocate for a moral system squarely designed to increase the former and minimize the latter places the rhetorically skilled utilitarian on terrain that is difficult to contest.

Libertarianism

Although libertarianism is formally a political philosophy, its underlying core ethic holds personal liberty/autonomy as an organizing focus. As such, and given its ascendancy in virtually every sphere of contemporary politics, I am persuaded that this core ethic has decisive implications for the present discussion. Of particular interest is the degree to which libertarianism so fully embraces the tenet of freedom of association and the minimization of the role of government. As most readers will be quick to grasp, the major thrust of libertarianism's guiding ethic asserts self-sufficiency and independence. And, as Mary Johnson (2003) elaborated upon in some detail in her adroit analysis of the impact of the Americans with Disabilities Act (ADA), this strain of libertarianism has had considerable influence in blunting the impact of this landmark legislation. That said, libertarianism is a complex school of thought. Included among its adherents are, as one might expect, Friedrich Hayek, Milton Friedman, and Ayn Rand. But Noam Chomsky is also widely identified as a libertarian—of sorts.

At the core of libertarianism is the very fixed belief that individuals funda-mentally own themselves and are, as such, morally autonomous beings. This self-ownership confers liberty—the freedom from interference in one's per-sonal affairs so long as she is not interfering with others. In a vernacular sense, the animating credo of this school of moral thought is "live and let live." The meaning of justice (what we owe each other) emerging from self-ownership is one that says that we as individuals are under no obligation to help or aid others, although some libertarians, depending on their brand of libertarian-ism, would concede such an obligation in a situation where a fellow human being is in dire straits and the cost of coming to her aid would require little.

This does not mean that libertarians are full-stop against helping others, though. And they are loath to be framed as adhering to a soulless individ-ualism. For them, kindness, generosity, and service to others is not only distorted when it is required by the state (e.g., social welfare programs), but to their way of thinking such compulsion actually reduces the likelihood of such acts, creates resistances, and so on. Moreover, inducing people under threat of penalty to volunteer or contribute resources is a form of oppres-sion—forced servitude or outright thievery (see for example: Hayek, 1960). The only definitive circumstances under which one is indisputably obliged are those in which compensation is owed for having violated another's free-dom or personal autonomy. Under these circumstances, the individual for-feits her freedom.

The right to property ownership is an extension of the core right of self-ownership, so long as the property was legitimately appropriated. Con-servative libertarians believe that an individual has a right to and unencum-bered use of any natural resources to which they can legitimately make a first claim, so long as others are not left worse off than they were before the resources were acquired and used (see: Nozick, 1974). More centrist libertar-ians also accede to limitations based on the less acquisitive view that sufficient resources should be left for others. Leftist libertarians, on the other hand, as-sert that natural resources belong to us all and should only be used to benefit the common good. Along these lines, they see no need for state-sponsored and enforced social welfare programs because the assets of these resources should supply this kind of support in the first place.

Libertarians of all stripes fundamentally mistrust state power. Vallentyne (2012) summarized this anti-state position as follows:

> Libertarianism, then, is not only critical of the modern welfare state, but of states in general. Given that so much of modern life seems to require a state, libertar-ianism's anarchist stance is a powerful objection against it. In reply, libertarians argue that (1) many of the effects of states are quite negative, (2) many of the

positive effects can be obtained without the state through voluntary mechanisms, and (3) even if some positive effects cannot be so obtained, the ends do not justify the means in these cases. (n.p.)

With the exception of very few, however, libertarians tend to concede the necessity for publically funded and administered military, police, and fire departments in that these entities directly defend and protect property ownership.

Some reject or dismiss libertarianism owing to a visceral distaste for its intensely individualistic ethos. Beyond that, both its critics as well as its intellectual adherents have recognized other vulnerabilities in its philosophical edifice. In his précis of libertarian ethics, left-leaning libertarian scholar Peter Vallentyne (2012) discussed two rather momentous problems. The first has to do with the question of personal autonomy, an issue that goes to the heart of libertarianism's core principle of self-ownership. As with utilitarianism, libertarianism restricts personhood to beings who possess moral agency; that is, those who have moral duties, a biographical self (a theory of the self) as opposed to merely a biological existence, the capacity to originate interests or preferences, and so on.

This conception of personal autonomy thus makes a clear distinction between autonomous selves and non-autonomous sentient beings (animals, children, and those with significant intellectual impairments). But because non-autonomous sentient beings still have moral standing, this distinction raises the question of their status. One way out of this dilemma is to simply deny them moral standing; but most would find this unacceptable. Another is to grant them full self-ownership with others who (paternalistically) protect their interests rather than their choices. In the end, neither of these alternatives offers an adequate solution.

The second snag in the libertarian fabric significantly complicates the right to property ownership and can be summarized by asking the question: If libertarians justify ownership on the basis of the property in question being legitimately appropriated (not seized from others), how can they then account for historical wrongs such as imperialism or invasion? How far back in history can they go to establish the legitimacy of ownership, even if that were possible? There appears to be no definitive answer to this question other than to invoke an arbitrary statute of limitations as a fall-back solution (see: MacIntyre, 1984).

Despite these difficulties, the appeal of libertarianism appears to have grown in the recent decade (Silver, 2011), the reasons for which are open to speculation. Certainly this moral/political school of thought seems to offer something solid and clear to embattled young adults striving to find their way in an increasingly uncertain world. There is a certain moral appeal, a stability and sensibility, to its firm foundation of personal autonomy and responsibility. As well, its "live and let live" credo also resonates with this generation's more open and accepting attitudes toward various social issues that continue to animate its parents' political battles. Moreover, libertarianism cuts across the left-right divide of contemporary politics, making it attractive to those who wish to transcend this apparently intractable divide. And, like its consequentialist cousin, utilitarianism, it seems to possess a fairly uncomplicated intelligibility that many may find appealing in these complex times.

Communitarianism

At the center of communitarianism is the relationship between the individual and the community. In fact, communitarian philosophy is predicated on the recognition that individuality is a product of community relationships rather than individual traits. Put differently, philosophers associated with communitarianism question the very notions of the "individual" and "selfhood" in that each of us can only come to know ourselves through our relationships with others within the socially, culturally, and historically contingent contexts that give meaning to our choices, dispositions, proclivities, and so on. In his celebrated work, *Sources of the Self*, philosopher Charles Taylor (1989) prompted just such a fundamental reconstruction of our understanding of selfhood (see also: Taylor, 1991). Likewise, Alasdair MacIntyre (1984) had much to say about the notion of individuality in general as well as its relevance to the issue of disability in particular (1999). Still others, such as Michael Walzer (1983, 1987) and Michael Sandel (1998) offered incisive critiques of modern liberalism that are highly pertinent to the topic of disability. Interestingly, Sandel's (2009) book, *The Case Against Perfection*, spoke directly to the issue of modern genetic engineering, a matter of no small importance to the disability community.

In opposition to the libertarian and to some extent the utilitarian conception of the a priori self, communitarians contend that individuals do not exist in a vacuum. Rather, they emphasize that our individuality is ineluctably conceived and forged in and through communities. And as such, our individual well-being is bound to the various communities of which we are a part. So, while libertarians and utilitarians start from the assumption that there is such a thing as the fully autonomous self, communitarians would point out that their very notion of atomistic individualism is itself derived from a distinctive set of historical and cultural contingencies.

The emergence of communitarianism was kindled by increasing concerns about the precipitous tilt toward a self-centered, greed-driven culture that both disparages and seeks to penalize human dependency of any kind.

The organizing feature of communitarianism is solidarity—responsibility for each other and shared commitments forged through dialogue or what Taylor (1999) called "a genuine, unforced consensus." This emphasis on using dialogue to establish what Mary Ann Glendon (1991) characterized as a nuanced relationship between individual rights and responsibility for the common good is based on the understanding that:

> Moral voices achieve their effect mainly through education and persuasion, rather than through coercion. Originating in communities, and sometimes embodied in law, they exhort, admonish, and appeal to what Lincoln called the better angels of our nature. They speak to our capacity for reasoned judgment and virtuous action. (Etzioni, 1998, p. xxvi)

Very importantly, this call for consensus is not to be mistaken for a majoritarian position. Rather, communitarians emphasize the need for a strong, participatory democracy that is responsive to basic human needs, including the need for "individualism, autonomy, interpersonal caring, or social justice" (Etzioni, 1998, p. xxvii). No doubt this kind of disciplined consensus calls for a finely tuned and carefully fashioned balance; and, while communitarians recognize that striking such a balance is an arduous and ongoing task, they would invite viable alternatives from those skeptical of their position.

It is fairly self-evident that libertarians would be among the first to deride communitarian ethics for, among other transgressions, questioning the former's individual-rights fundamentalism and for encouraging what they view as an expansion of the "nanny state." But critiques of communitarianism (or more specifically the original movement communitarian positions) have surfaced from cultural feminists and those advocating a feminist ethic of care with whom they share substantial common ground. While they are united in their criticism of libertarian and utilitarian ethics, feminists have pointed out that communitarians have, at least in the past, paid insufficient attention to the inequality and oppression present in some communities.

Eva Kittay (2001) for example, observed that communitarians have only recently begun to account for the traditional role of women in caring for dependent others, including and perhaps most especially those with significant impairments. In calling attention to the fact that current economic and social structures also make dependent those (most often women) who provide care for others, she argued for, "a public ethic of care based on the idea that we are all embedded in nested dependencies" (p. 56). In other words, those who are dependent on the wider community due to their contribution to that community in return deserve care and reciprocity from that community.

Disability, the Social Model, and Theories of the Self

Clearly the three schools of moral thought diverge dramatically from one another; yet, quite apart from communitarianism, both utilitarianism and libertarianism share an essential theory of the individual self as existing prior to and holding a distinct status apart from its bonds from others. This assumption of the primacy of the self, what Sandel (1998) critically termed the "antecedently individuated" self (p. 64), is reflected in both the utilitarian and libertarian demarcation between those who count as *persons* and those who can be regarded only as sentient beings—between those possessing self-awareness, a sense of their past and future, and moral autonomy versus those deemed as lacking these attributes. That said, where they quickly part company is evident in the libertarian antipathy toward the utilitarian principle that the rights and freedoms of an individual can be legitimately sacrificed for the greater benefit of others. On this front, Nozick (1974) countered that:

> To use a person [for another's benefit] does not sufficiently respect and take account of the fact that he is a separate person, that his is the only life he has. *He* does not get some overbalancing good from his sacrifice. (Nozick, 1974, p. 33)

Thus their disagreement is not about the primacy of the self. Rather, it is about the libertarian dismay that utilitarians do not take individualism seriously enough.

This theory of the self likewise and rather conspicuously serves as foundational premise of the medical model of disability, reflecting, of course, the notion that disability resides within the individual, that one owns the disability, and so on. Accordingly, it should come as no surprise that adherents of these two schools of thought have been quite trenchant in their defense of the medical modelist position. Consider, for example, Singer's (2011) insistence that disabled people own (and should own up to) their inferior status:

> If disabled people who must use wheelchairs to get around were suddenly offered a miracle drug that would, with no side effects, give them the full use of their legs, how many of them would refuse to take it on the grounds that life with a disability is in no way inferior to life without a disability? In seeking to raise research funds to overcome and prevent disability, people with disabilities themselves show that the preference for a life without disability is no mere prejudice. Some disabled people might say that they make this choice only because society puts so many obstacles in the way of people with disabilities. They claim that it is social conditions that disable them, not their physical or intellectual condition. This assertion takes the simple truth that social conditions make the lives of the disabled much more difficult than they need be, and twists it into a sweeping falsehood. (p. 46)

One might note here that Singer's perfunctory nod to oppressive social conditions allowed him to import the social model only to trivialize it. And trivialize it he must because an individualist theory of the self is indispensable to his preference for utilitarianism. To concede too much to social conditions gets precipitously close to accepting a rival theory of the socially constitutive nature of the self.

Along the same vein, libertarians took aim at the social modelist underpinnings of the Americans with Disabilities Act's definition of disability, specifically scorning the law's affirmation that a person did not have to have an impairment to experience disability discrimination (see: Johnson, 2003). On a practical level, they protested that this part of the ADA's definition of disability was so vague that it would overestimate the number of people who could claim protection under the law. For example, writing for the Cato Institute, Hudgins (1995) complained that this definition was "confusing," and added that, "The category of mental disorders is open to the greatest abuse. Many kinds of aberrant behavior that might have cost an employee his job now merit ADA coverage. The nature of many suits bears this out" (p. 71). At a more conceptual level, the ADA's framing of disability as socially constructed strikes a very hard blow to the libertarian framework of justice, reliant as it is on the doctrinal theory of the self as a wholly discrete individual.

In contrast, the social model of disability accords with the communitarian theory of the self, which fundamentally effaces the self/other dichotomy. In the same way that the social model affirms that no one can be disabled by herself (apart from her relationships with others), communitarianism asserts that she cannot, in a wider sense, *be* herself apart from influences and ties with the community. It is on this pivotal point that the communitarian framework of justice places a central importance on the value of human solidarity. Consonant with this value is the need to place, as Sandel (1998) put it, the emphasis on the (common) good over (individual) rights; and, by extension, "do what we can to create social and political arrangements more hospitable to the gifts and limitations of imperfect human beings" (Sandel, 2009, p. 97). In that we all have gifts and limitations, the social and political arrangements he spoke of benefit us all alike whether directly or (seemingly) indirectly.

Because we are all differently situated, our involvement in these arrangements requires differing kinds and degrees of contribution—and at different times in our lives. What is required, quite emphatically, is a setting aside of the zero-sum ethos that considers someone else's gain my loss as a feature of the strict calculus of direct reciprocity. MacIntyre (1999) explicitly countered this ethos as follows:

> For to participate in this network of relationships of giving and receiving as the virtues require, I have to understand that what I am called upon to give may be quite disproportionate to what I have received and that those to whom I am called upon to give may well be those from whom I shall receive nothing. And I also have to understand that the care that I give to others has to be in an important way unconditional, since the measure of what is required of me is determined in key part, even if not only, by their needs. (p. 108)

To this point it can also be added that those who have contributed to our own needs and well-being are often forgotten—if they were ever known in the first place. Likewise, because we are all always the recipient of others' care, and because we are all always in need of this care whether we choose to recognize it or not, we owe a different kind of reciprocity—one that recognizes that what we have needed and received can never be measured or fully known. It is from this standpoint that the social model confirms the experience of disablement as belonging to us all.

Implications for Disability Studies in Education

Beyond its accordance with the social model of disability, the communitarian framework is, in my estimation, not only uniquely resonant with of inclusive education but also affirms many of the inclusive pedagogical practices widely recognized in the DSE literature. Decisively, this framework's emphasis on the dialectical role of community membership in the development of the self extends far beyond simply opposing exclusion or endorsing inclusion as a worthy goal. Specifically, it asserts that, "if a person is excluded by society, he or she is excluded from the opportunity not only of complete citizenship *but also of complete development as a person*" (Dickson, 2012, p. 1103, emphasis added). Further, and also in accordance with communitarian ethics, inclusive education benefits all students by affording them the opportunity to discover what they have in common and so to develop the bonds of kinship that form the basis of human solidarity. In turn, the experience of solidarity cultivates the "virtues of giving and receiving" (MacIntyre, 1999, p. 118) and a commitment to each other that makes possible the common good, and hence genuine participatory democracy.

On the level of inclusive practices, the communitarian framework's disavowal of the "antecedently individuated self" (Sandel, 1998) and Taylor's (1989) assertion that being a self is a communal project is echoed in DSE scholars' calls to end disability labeling in schools (see for example: Biklen, 1992; Connor, 2008; Harry & Klingner, 2005; Keefe, 1996; Kliewer & Biklen, 1996). Likewise, DSE's promotion of collaborative learning arrangements, universal design for learning (UDL), and, by extension, constructivist pedagogy (Baglieri, Valle, Connor, & Gallagher, 2011; Gallagher, 2004; Heshusius, 1984) is consonant with the communitarian emphasis on community. Finally, DSE scholars and practitioners have long embraced the concerted cultivation of schools and classrooms as inclusive communities animated by mutual respect, active valuing of diversity, and reciprocity (Baglieri & Knopf, 2004; Reid & Valle, 2004). In these schools and classrooms, "how the needs of the disabled are adequately voiced and met is not a special interest, the interest of one particular group rather than of others" MacIntyre, 1999, p. 130) precisely because these interests cannot be separated in the first place.

These parallels do not exhaust the possibilities for the influence of communitarianism as a guiding framework for disability studies in education. Given this framework's rather striking resonance with DSE's social modelist foundation, its stand on inclusive education, and advocacy for the practices cited above, further exploration may be well worth further consideration.

References

Anastasiou, D., & Kauffman, J. M. (2010). Disability as cultural difference: Implications for special education. *Remedial and Special Education*, 33(3), 139–149. DOI: 10. 1177/0741932510383163. Retrieved from http://rse.sagepub.com/content/early/2010/09/21/0741932510383163

Anastasiou, D., & Kauffman, J. K. (2011). A social constructionist approach to disability: Implications for special education. *Exceptional Children*, 77(3), 367–384.

Baglieri, S., & Knopf, J. H. (2004). Normalizing difference in inclusive teaching. *Journal of Learning Disabilities*, 37, 525–529.

Baglieri, S., Valle, J. W., Connor, D. J., & Gallagher, D. J. (2011). Disability studies in education: The need for a plurality of perspectives on disability. *Remedial and Special Education*, 32(4), 267–278.

Biklen, D. P. (1992). *Schooling without labels: Parents, educators, and inclusive education*. Philadelphia, PA: Temple University Press.

Connor, D. J. (2008). *Urban narratives. Portraits in progress: Life at the intersections of learning disability, race, and social class*. New York: Peter Lang.

Crow, L. (1996). Including all of our lives: Renewing the social model of disability. In J. Morris (Ed.), *Encounters with strangers: Feminism and disability*. London, UK: Women's Press.

Davis, L. J. (2002). *Bending over backwards: Disability, dismodernism and other difficult positions*. New York: New York University Press.

Dickson, E. (2012). A communitarian theory of the education rights of students with disabilities. *Educational Philosophy and Theory*, 44(10), 1093–1109.

Drake, S. (2009, July 17). Peter Singer in the New York Times: Disabled lives worth less, hypothetically. Not Dead Yet. Retrieved from http://www.notdeadyet.org/2009/07/peter-singer-in-ny-times-disabled-lives.html

Etzioni, A. (1998). The responsive communitarian platform: Rights and responsibilities. In A. Etzioni (Ed.), *The essential communitarian reader* (pp. xxv–xxxix). Lanham, MD: Rowman & Littlefield.

French, S. (1993). Disability, impairment or something in between. In J. Swain, S. French, C. Barnes, & C. Thomas (Eds.), *Disabling barriers, enabling environments*. London: Sage.

Gallagher, D. J. (2004). The importance of constructivism and constructivist pedagogy for disability studies in education. *Disability Studies Quarterly, 24*(2).

Gallagher, D. J., Connor, D. J., & Ferri, B. A. (2014). Beyond the far too incessant schism: Special education and the social model of disability. *International Journal of Inclusive Education*. DOI: 10.1080/13603116.2013.875599. Retrieved from http://www.tandfonline.com/loi/tied20

Glendon, M. A. (1991). *Rights talk: The impoverishment of political discourse*. New York: The Free Press.

Harry, B., & Klingner, J. K. (2005). *Why are so many minority students in special education? Understanding race and disabilities at school*. New York: Teachers College Press.

Hayek, F. A. (1960). *The constitution of liberty*. Chicago, IL: University of Chicago Press.

Heshusius, L. (1984). Why would they and I want to do it? A phenomenological theoretical view of special education. *Learning Disabilities Quarterly, 7*, 363–367.

Hudgins, E. L. (1995). Handicapping freedom: The Americans with Disabilities Act. *Regulation, 18*(2), 67–76.

Johnson, M. (2003). *Make them go away: Clint Eastwood, Christopher Reeve, and the case against disability rights*. Louisville, KY: The Avocado Press.

Jung, J. (2009, October 26). Peter Singer reflects on a decade at Princeton. *Daily Princetonian*. Retrieved from http://dailyprincetonian.com/news/2009/10/peter-singer-reflects-on-a-decade-at-princeton/

Keefe, C. H. (1996). *Label-free learning: Supporting learners with disabilities*. York, ME: Stenhouse.

Kittay, E. F. (2001). The ethics of care, dependence, and disability. *Ratio Juris, 24*(1), 49–58.

Kliewer, C., & Biklen, D. (1996). Labeling: Who wants to be called retarded? In W. Stainback & S. Stainback (Eds.), *Controversial issues confronting special education: Divergent perspectives* (2nd ed.) (pp. 83–95). Boston, MA: Allyn & Bacon.

Kuhse, H., & Singer. P. (1985). *Should the baby live? The problem of handicapped infants*. Oxford, UK: Oxford University Press.

MacIntyre, A. (1984). *After virtue* (2nd ed.). Notre Dame, IN: University of Notre Dame Press.

MacIntyre, A. (1999). *Dependent rational animals: Why human beings need virtues*. London, UK: Duckworth.

Nozick, R. (1974). *Anarchy, state, and utopia*. New York: Basic Books.

Reid, D. K., & Valle, J. W. (2004). The discursive practice of learning disability: Implications for instruction and parent school relations. *Journal of Learning Disabilities, 37*, 466–481.

Sandel, M. (1998). *Liberalism and the limits of justice* (2nd ed.) Cambridge, UK: Cambridge University Press.

Sandel, M. (2009). *The case against perfection: Ethics in the age of genetic engineering*. Cambridge, MA: Harvard University Press.

Shakespeare, T. (2006). *Disability rights and wrongs*. London, UK: Routledge.

Shakespeare, T. (2014). *Disability rights and wrongs revisited*. London, UK: Routledge.

Shakespeare, T. & Watson, N. (2014). The social model of disability: An outdated ideology? *Research in Social Science and Disability, 2*, 9–28.

Silver, N. (2011, June 20, 2011). Poll finds shift toward more libertarian views. New York Times. Retrieved from http://fivethirtyeight.blogs.nytimes.com/2011/06/20/poll-finds-a-shift-toward-more-libertarian-views/

Singer, P. (2011). *Practical ethics* (3rd ed). Cambridge, UK: Cambridge University Press.

Singer, P. (2012, March 16). The "unnatural" Ashley treatment can be right for profoundly disabled children: Disability activists have concerns about limiting growth, but it is not in the interests of the children to ban the treatment. *The Guardian*. Retrieved from http://www.guardian.co.uk/commentisfree/2012/mar/16/ashley-treatment-profoundly-disabled-children

Taylor, C. (1989). *Sources of the self: The making of the modern identity*. Cambridge, MA: Harvard University Press.

Taylor, Charles. (1991). *The ethics of authenticity*. Cambridge, MA: Harvard University Press. (Originally published in Canada in 1991 under the title *The malaise of modernity*.)

Taylor, C. (1999). Conditions of an unforced consensus on human rights. In J. R. Bauer & D. Bell, (Eds.), *The East Asian Challenge for Human Rights*. Cambridge, UK: Cambridge University Press.

Thomas, C. (2004). How is disability understood? *Disability and Society, 19*(6), 563–568.

Tremain, S. (1998). Feminist approaches to naturalizing disabled bodies, or does the social model of disablement rest upon a mistake? Paper presented at the annual meeting of the Society for Disability Studies, Oakland, CA.

Tremain, S. (2002). On the subject of impairment. In M. Corker & T. Shakespeare (Eds.), *Disability/postmodernity: Embodying disability theory*. London, UK: Continuum.

Vallentyne, P. (2012). Libertarianism. In E. N. Zalta (Ed.), *The Stanford encyclopedia of philosophy*. Retrieved from http://plato.stanford.edu/archives/spr2012/entries/libertarianism/

Walzer, M. (1983). *Spheres of justice*. Oxford, UK: Basil Blackwell.

Walzer, M. (1987). *Interpretation and social criticism*. Cambridge, MA: Harvard University Press.

2. "As a cripple, I swagger": The Situated Body and Disability Studies in Education

BETH A. FERRI

> "If it is possible and pleasant for me and my kind to enter, the world will become a livelier place. You'll see."
> —Mairs (1996b, p. 106)

Scholars of contemporary disability studies (DS) locate dis/abilities[1] within structures of society rather than within the biology or essence of individuals. Such critical understandings of disability as a social and political construct implicitly build upon Beauvoir's oft-cited "woman is made, not born" critique of biological determinism. In other words, the disabled body[2] functions as a cultural text "made" within social relations of power and inscribed with meaning. Despite the fact that Beauvoir did not explicitly or adequately address disability, and although her writing (at least in translation)[3] is peppered with ableist metaphors, several of her ideas about the body are particularly germane to disability studies in education (DSE).

In this paper, I highlight Nancy Mairs'[4] writing, making connections to Beauvoir's concept of situated embodiment to demonstrate how both authors conceive of the body as both situation and point of view. Privileging knowledge generated from lived/embodied experience is but one example of the many points of connections between Mairs and Beauvoir that have relevancy to DSE. With concepts such as *la situation* (situation) and *l'expérience vécue* (lived experience) (1989/1952, pp. 34–37), Beauvoir refuses essentialism and biological determinism and privileges alternative knowledge claims grounded in particular lived realities—themes also addressed by Mairs.

In viewing the body as simultaneously material reality and situation to be taken up and interpreted—an occasion for meaning, rather than as a static object or state of being—Mairs and Beauvoir also expose the instabilities of categories, such as disabled and normal, a destabilization that is likewise central to DSE. Expanding and complicating the social model of disability by refusing individual/social, mind/body, and theory/practice binaries, Mairs presents a highly sophisticated theory of disability that stays intimately close to the particularities of her own body. Embracing a phenomenology of disability,[5] Mairs conceives disability as political and social, but also deeply personal. She also expands and complicates the social model of disability, a foundational starting point for DSE. Delving deeply into the relationship between embodiment, subjectivity, language, perception, and voice, her work is particularly fertile ground for reframing disability as more than a sum of oppressive and exclusionary forces—it is instead an equally valid way of knowing and being in the world.

Reluctant Writers and Writing as an Ethic of Care

How to begin a book one does not want to write? Simone de Beauvoir (1952/1989) begins *The Second Sex* by stating, "For a long time I have hesitated to write a book on woman" (p. xix). She expresses doubt that any more ink should be spilt on the topic. Similarly, Nancy Mairs (1996b) begins her book, *Waist-High in the World: A Life Among the Non-disabled*, lamenting: "I cannot begin to write this book" (p. 3). Although she resists the idea of immersing herself in her "crippled life," Mairs nonetheless finds the subject "dragging at [her] wheels" (pp. 3–4). Differentiating her book from the many disability or even multiple sclerosis (MS) narratives, hers is not a "little instruction book" (p. 6). She tells readers that instead of writing a "feel-good" book, a genre that would more likely be a bestseller,[6] she offers a "feel-real" book (p. 18).

But the question remains: Why do both Beauvoir and Mairs write in spite of their initial trepidation and for what purpose? Perhaps their reluctance underscores the difficulty involved in writing oneself both into and against dominant discourses. Writing about gender or disability, they realize, requires engaging with cultural scripts that exclude or deny lived experience. How, for instance, does Mairs write about disability and Beauvoir about gender in ways that do not further link them to the very limits of the categories they aim to complicate? How, too, do we in DSE rally politically around the construct of disability, at the same time we aim to trouble its very foundations as a way to label and sort children in schools?

Those familiar with Mairs' prolific body of writing might question why she would suddenly be reluctant to discuss her disability. Disability is, in fact, a central concern[7] in much of Mairs' writing. In fact, because several of her essays are among the few widely anthologized essays featuring disability, some worry that she will be the only writer people may associate with disability (Garland-Thomson, 1994). This critique is not altogether unfounded[8] and has not changed in recent years despite the proliferation of DS scholarship. Life writing within DS has featured mostly people with physical and sensory disabilities and very few people of color.[9] DSE has expanded this range by including autoethnographies by individuals with autism, learning disabilities, and mental disabilities (Smith, 2013) as well as life writing by people of color and young adults (Biklen, 2005; Connor, 2008; Ferri, 2011).

Paradoxically, although widely read, Mairs is largely dismissed in theoretical scholarship. Perhaps the disabled body is "somehow too much a body, too real, too corporeal … [or] too little a body, not quite a body … not real enough" (Porter, 1997, p. xiii). Focusing solely on autobiographical writing about disability reifies a kind of mind/body split, wherein disability is read as individualist and experiential, but not as advancing a theoretical or philosophical argument.[10]

Further, although Mairs is often praised for the quality of her writing, many even within DS remain unconvinced of the political or theoretical potential in autobiographical work (Haugen, 2011). Her work, for instance, has been characterized by some disability studies scholars as being too personal, too individualist (Davis, 1997), or too confessional (Mitchell & Snyder, 1997)—in other words neither the stuff of serious academic scholarship nor literary work. Even more ominous is the fear that writers like Mairs might feed a voyeuristic public appetite hungry to consume confessional accounts of triumph over tragedy (Mitchell & Snyder, 1997). Haugen (2011) writes that in dismissing the personal, DS fails to recognize the insights within fields such as feminist studies, which place personal experience at the center of its politics and theory. In other words, autobiographies of oppressed groups can themselves be sites of resistance (McKay, 1998). We should not, therefore, underestimate the political significance, particularly of individuals who have been denied subjectivity to "write themselves into being" (McKay, p. 97). Scholars in DSE, often grounded in qualitative research, have on the whole been less suspicious of the value of memoir and life writing. Couser (2002) argues that "autobiography deserves a prominent place" (p. 109) in DS for its ability to speak against the grain of dominant understandings of disability.

Mairs herself concedes that by insisting on embodied writing, she exiles herself from "conventional academic discourse" (1996a, p. 60), which "favors using intellect ... [over] experience" (1994, p. 128). Yet, although her writing is "intensely personal, it is not at all singular" (p. 119). Mairs writes that by weighing theoretical insights against her own experience, she developed "a voice I might 'own'" (p. 30). Nonetheless, because hers is an embodied rhetoric in a culture that continues to value the disembodied voice, even when writing about the body, Mairs, although widely read, has not been given the same kind of critical or scholarly attention as other writers, even within DS.[11]

Similarly, despite the fact that *The Second Sex* has been translated into more than 26 languages, Beauvoir continues to be seen as a scholar who was deeply influenced by others, most notably Sartre and Merleau-Ponty, but rarely as the locus of theory. Largely dismissed in discussions of phenomenology, existentialism, and embodiment, Beauvoir is often portrayed as an interpreter or imitator of other's ideas[12] (Moi, 1994; Simons, 1999).

Likewise, Mairs' books are more likely to be shelved in health and illness sections of bookstores than in feminist studies or DS, even though her work is firmly grounded in both. Yet theoretical issues infuse Mairs' writing and, like Beauvoir's autobiographical writings, Mairs begins with the self, but a self-in-relation—a situated, embodied self. Writing at the intersections of experience and theory, philosophy and literature, mind and body, emotions and politics, the complexity of Mairs and Beauvoir are rendered unintelligible by the very paradigms of oppositional thinking they write against.

Mairs and Beauvoir describe the purpose of their writing as cartographic—to help map out a path for others, a path illuminated by their own experiences, but not meant to be taken as universal or essential. Beauvoir (1952/1989) writes, "from a woman's point of view I shall describe the world in which women must live ... to envisage the difficulties in their way ... as they aspire to full membership in the human race" (p. xxxv). Similarly Mairs (1994), who describes writing as an intrinsically social act and an "erotic impulse toward an other" (p. 147), claims to offer a "Baedeker for a country to which no one travels willingly" to make the terrain less alien, less perilous, and maybe even more amusing (Mairs, 1996b, p. 6). She writes, as well, for readers "who need, for a tangle of reasons, to be told that a life commonly held to be insufferable can be full and funny. I'm living the life I can tell them" (p. 11). For Mairs (1994), the goal is not to write about "illness as metaphor, but illness as illness, in order to persuade the skeptical reader, that survival ... is possible" (p. 129). Thus, both writers view the very act of writing as an ethic of care (Weiss 1999, p. 157).

For Mairs and Beauvoir, a reciprocal ethic of care is one that refuses subject/object binaries. Mairs (1996b), however, does not write in order to "uplift" her readers. Instead she seeks to lower and steady her readers until they are sitting beside her. She invites readers to share her space—to sit nearby and observe "the waists of the world drift past" (p. 18). She thus overturns the ableist expectation that she, as a disabled woman, will be the object of care. In other words, Mairs' notion of care involves mutual subjectivity and shared responsibility. Beauvoir, too, desires human relationships that are based on reciprocity and equality, which "recognize [that] the freedom of self and Other are interconnected" (Simons, 1999, p. 102) involving people "mutually-recognizing each other as subject" (Beauvoir, 1952/1989, pp. 730–731). As Scholz (2000) explains, Beauvoir's "reciprocity requires that individual projects be defined according to their interaction with the freedoms and projects of others" (p. 40). Both Mairs and Beauvoir articulate dialogic and reciprocal social relations that refuse subject/object dualisms or hierarchical notions of care.

Drawing on this work offers new ways to conceptualize inclusive classroom spaces—where students become natural supports for one another in mutual and shared interdependency.

These themes of self-in-relation can be highlighted in other texts, such as Amanda Baggs, *In My Language* (www.youtube.com/watch?v=JnylM1hI2jc); the blog *Autistic Hoya* (www.autistichoya.com); films such as *Autism Is a World* (Wurtzburg, 2004); *Wretches and Jabberers* (Wurtzburg, 2011), and a range of performance pieces (e.g., Lynn Manning's *Weights* [2005]), as well as parent memoirs written by disability studies scholars (e.g., Bérubé, 2002; Harry & Harry, 2010; Savarese, 2007). These too can be said to represent an ethic of care and a desire to intervene in cultural scripts and to reach out to imagined others. This is not to say that all memoir or life writing represents this kind of "discursive activism" (Cumings, 2011, p. 53) combining both affective and counter-hegemonic impulses—in fact many do not. Moreover, as I have argued elsewhere, we need better models for how to read (and teach) these texts in ways that highlight their transgressive potential (Ferri, 2011). Yet, by encouraging students to write their own stories and helping teachers to take up life writing through critical reading practices, we are engaging not simply in a voyeuristic consumption of an other, nor are we "giving voice" to an other. Instead, through these texts we are invited to take up an emancipatory theory of self-in-relation.

Body Talk: Embodied Rhetorics of the Self

"Disabled people have been spoken about, and spoken for, but rarely listened to."

—Sherry (2005, p. 165)

Language, embodiment, subjectivity, and voice are ongoing concerns for Mairs. Invited to do a talk about "finding" her voice, Mairs remembers feeling quite perplexed by the request. She remembers thinking that she never considered the possibility that her voice might be lost or missing (1996a, p. 83). She writes:

> I've found my voice, then, just where it ought to have been, in the body-warmed breath escaping my lungs and throat ... No body, no voice; no voice, no body. That's what I know in my bones. (p. 96)

Insisting on the centrality of embodied knowing, Mairs (1994) also writes of her changing relationship to language. At one time, language "seemed to be a tool—ordinary to the point of transparency—for representing my daily needs and demands and desires." Yet, like Beauvoir, Mairs (1996a) is suspicious of the disembodied "I." She likes, for instance, the phrasing "I am a body" rather than "I have a body," because the latter posits the body as object, the "not I," which can be possessed by the "I" (p. 84).

To understand that subjectivity, language, identity, knowledge, and even politics are grounded in the lived body has much relevance to DSE. These ideas can elucidate a shortcoming of the social model of disability to embrace embodiment and lived experiences with impairment. Indeed, if impairment-specific ways of knowing are to be embraced, one has to acknowledge that disability experience is more than oppression, but something that can offer insight, perception, and knowledge. When we shy away from talking about impairment, we risk divorcing the subject and the inherent duality of experience and subjectivity.

In first encountering Mairs' writing, students are often surprised by her irreverent candor. In her most widely anthologized essay, "Carnal Acts," Mairs (1986), for instance, discusses both her choice of language and her decision to identify as crippled:

> First, the matter of semantics. I am a cripple. I choose this word to name me. I choose from among several possibilities, the most common of which are "hand-icapped" and "disabled" ... People—crippled or not—wince at the word "crip-ple," as they do not at "handicapped" or "disabled." Perhaps I want them to wince. I want them to see me as a tough customer, one to whom the fates/gods/viruses have not been kind, but who can face the brutal truth of her existence squarely. As a cripple, I swagger. (p. 9)

In choosing the word "cripple," Mairs claims to seek accuracy and authenticity. She does not want to place distance between representation and lived reality. "Cripple," she writes, does not hint at difference; neither does it pretend that difference doesn't matter. Thus, Mairs acknowledges and even plays with the socially constructed "baggage" attached to the word cripple—subverting ableist stereotypes by positioning herself as a "tough customer" who does not limp, but "swaggers." It could be said that Mairs queers the term cripple, redeploying and twisting it from its prior usage as a political strategy (Butler, 1993, p. 228). Similarly, terms like "neurotypical" help call attention to ableist frameworks that devalue disabled ways of knowing and being. In this way, Mairs offers an important counterpoint to person-first terminology, often embraced within educational discourses.

Importantly, Mairs recognizes that the terms of her identity are not unlimited. Choosing among the given terms and categories, Mairs fashions a self out of materials at hand. By attending to the politics of naming and the embodied location of her identity, Mairs engages with what Butler (1993) insists are the "invariably ambivalent resources through which identity is forged and reworked" (p. 228). Similarly, for Beauvoir, gender choice is an ambiguous interplay of individual choice and acculturation. In choosing gender, or other social markers for that matter, Beauvoir insists that we do not acquiesce to a fixed ontology, but actively "appropriate, interpret, and reinterpret" (Butler, 1998, p. 31) a "cultural history which the body already wears" (p. 41). The ambiguity of existence involves recognizing that we are always simultaneously materiality and consciousness, rather than simply one or the other (Kruks, 1998). Thus, a central insight offered by both Mairs and Beauvoir is that we cannot divorce the phenomenology of disability from its social consequences without erasing the lived experience of the subject. In other words, in embracing the social model of disability, it is critical that we also value lived experiences and diverse ways of knowing and being.

Recognizing, however, that identity is not fashioned outside of social and historical contexts and that language is neither value-neutral nor disembodied, Mairs asserts that identity is a story that we make up as we go along, crafted from the available scripts and mythologies. Consequently, at the same time that we create ourselves in stories, so too are we created and written by the rhetorical expectations of narrative (Miner, 1997). However, a life with MS, Mairs reminds us, does not fit the conventional disability narrative—the villain (MS) is unconquerable, the myth never gets resolved, and the hero/heroine is defeated and disgraced. Yet Mairs (1996b) contends that this stereotypical plot is only one possible storyline; "there are plenty of others" (p. 125). Thus, because a life with MS does not conform to the conventional "hero myth," Mairs occupies a position similar to Beauvoir's (1989) "third sex" (p. 31). In refusing binary thinking, both writers recognize and articulate transgressive spaces for alternative subjectivities. Noting the ambiguity of her situation, Mairs (1996a) writes, "To view your life as blessed does not require you to deny your pain. It simply demands a more complicated vision" (p. 15). Embracing a both/and epistemology, Mairs and Beauvoir offer DSE a theoretically rich view of constraint and choice, where meaning is neither determined nor freely chosen, but must continually be won.

Mairs, like Beauvoir, refuses divisions of mind/body and subject/ object. She insists that she cannot separate her thinking self from her embodied self. She (1996b) describes the question of who she would be without MS as a "Koan" or an "intrinsically unanswerable question" that is "particularly and necessarily ponderable"—"not so much [as] a question but as a task" (p. 8). She explains that without MS, she would be both "no body" and "nobody" since "no simple subtraction" would render her whole (p. 8). Nor does she contain MS, like a tumor that could be cut away from the rest of her self. MS, like her wheelchair, has been "literally incorporated" as part of her body: flesh, blood, metal, and rubber. In other words, to Mairs, "MS can't be stripped away without mutilating the being who bears it" (p. 8). Mairs (1996b) insists, "I always write, consciously, as a body" (p. 60). In this way, Mairs resists fragmentation of the self—insisting that identity always exceeds the categories we might use to describe it.

Refusing mind/body dualisms is a critical task of DSE. Failing to disrupt this binary upholds disability hierarchies, in which intellectual disabilities come to represent the ultimate "not me" category, even within DS. How, then, do we help students reconcile disability designations as disembodied constructions with their own embodied subjectivity? How do we honor and encourage students' efforts to forge alternative epistemologies and multiple identities in ways that allow them to refuse such alienation or fragmentation? Getting behind self-advocates' rejection of the "R word," embracing neurodiversity, and promoting projects such as I am Norm[13] represent necessary correctives to school-based disability labels that signify deficit. Highlighting narratives that are personal as well as socially conscious and activist-minded offer politically potent alternatives to forging a politics of disability in schools.

Body as Situation and Point of View

Mitchell and Snyder (1997) critique postmodern theories of embodiment that uncritically employ disabled bodies as cyborgs or metaphoric figures, which blur the division between human and machine in fantastic or alarmist tones, while ignoring the subjective experiences of disabled people. Likewise, Wendell (1996) critiques feminist theories of the body as "both incomplete and skewed toward [celebrating] healthy, non-disabled experience" (p. 5). In contrast to the normative, universal, and acontextual body, Weiss (1999) contends, "There is no such thing as 'the' body ... Instead the body" is always particular and connected to lived experience (p. 1).

In *Waist-High in the World*, Mairs (1996b) discusses her experience of living with MS as a type of situated embodiment, which places her metaphorically and corporeally underneath and on the margins of able-bodied society. She asserts that marginality is more than a "metaphor for power relations ... [it is] a literal description of where I stand (figuratively speaking): over here, on the edge, out of bounds, beneath your notice. I embody metaphors" (p. 59). She explains, "disability is at once metaphorical and a material state, evocative of other conditions in time and space ... yet, 'like' nothing but itself. I can't write about it except by conflating the figurative and the substantial, the 'as if' with the 'what is'" (p. 58). Again, Mairs maintains the impossibility of disentangling the material reality of the body from the socially constructed meanings, consequences, and values ascribed to it.

For Beauvoir (1952/1989), too, "To be present in the world implies strictly that there exists a body which is at once a material thing in the world *and* a point of view toward this world" (p. 7). For both Beauvoir and Mairs, the body is of course its material reality, but also a place from which to perceive the world. This angle of vision produces idiosyncratic and partial perspectives, grounded and authenticated in the lived experience of the knower. The body is therefore simultaneously material, social, and perceptual.

Mairs underscores how the body is a place from which to perceive the world. In the choice of title for *Waist-High in the World: A Life Among the Nondisabled*, Mairs (1996b) addresses directly the context of living among the nondisabled, who "bound around heedlessly" through the "empty air" above her head (p. 15). From her embodied position, she writes that she feels "invisibilized, if there were such a word; negated; disappeared" by the averted eyes of others[14] (1996a, p. 77). Not seen, Mairs nonetheless sees—noting, like Beauvoir (Scholz, 2000) and many theorists hence, the potentially transcendent view from the margin. She writes, "From my wheelchair, nothing looks the same" (1994, p. 46). In the classroom such readings can prompt discussions about how different forms of embodiment yield equally valid ways of knowing and perceiving the world.

Mairs (1996b), for instance, describes her ever-shrinking angle of vision, or depending on perspective, an ever more condensed, focused, and nuanced landscape. By focusing her perception, like changing the aperture of a camera from wide angle to a macro, Mairs finds she is more attentive to detail and the disparity between her body and able-bodied experience. In *Carnal Acts*, Mairs (1996a) states:

> ...although they were not over, the nature of my adventures would have to change ... Some days I don't even make it to the back yard. And yet I'm unwilling to forgo the adventurous life: the difficulty of it, even the pain, the suspense and fear, and the sudden, brief lift of spirit that graces, unexpectedly, inexplicably—the pilgrimage. If I am to have it too, then I must change the terms by which it is lived. And so I do. I refine adventure, make it smaller and smaller ... And now, whether I am feeding fish flakes to my bettas or crawling across the dining room ... lying wide-eyed in the dark battling yet another bout of depression, cooking a chicken, gathering flowers ... meeting a friend ... I am always having ... adventures. (pp. 6–7)

Although her position on society's margin strengthens her capacity for attending and witnessing, Mairs (1996b) also finds that it can be isolating and difficult. She explains that "waist-high" also resonates with "knee deep" (p. 18). For Mairs, recognizing and examining how her angle of vision is intimately tied to her bodily situation makes important differences in thought, perception, and social consequences. Some of those consequences are more fortunate than others. Mairs explains how as a writer, being waist-high is just the right height for writing. Beauvoir (1989), too, insists that, "The body of a woman is one of the essential elements in her situation in the world" but not enough to define her as woman (p. 37). In other words, according to Beauvoir, "biological differences do not themselves constitute a destiny" (Kruks, 1998, p. 65). Thus, to simultaneously affirm "the body's irreducible materiality and the ways in which materiality is always invested with cultural significance" is to embrace a body that is neither fully biologically, nor culturally determined, according to Butler (in Weiss, 1999, 76).

When taken together, Beauvoir's concepts of situation and lived experience illustrate the value of situated knowledge claims, as more fluid and partial. By conceiving the body as situation, Beauvoir refuses essentialism or biological determinism, opening spaces for alternative knowledge claims grounded in lived reality. Similarly, Mairs (1996b) argues that although acquiring a disability "requires revisions of identity," it can also "yield fresh insight" (p. 134). Because of its unpredictability, MS, in particular, is a disability that requires Mairs (1996a) to learn to "accommodate uncertainty" (p. 104) and ambiguity as she continually renegotiates her changing bodily situation and varying social contexts. As Mintz (2011) writes, for Mairs, the self is "constantly shifting ... into the next essay, into a new ... meaning or understanding, a new phase of MS" (p. 173). The following quote illustrates

Mairs' (1996a) evolving sense of connection between consciousness and embodiment. She writes that her body

> looms in my consciousness now as it never did when all my gestures were as thoughtless as yours perhaps still are ... I must now attend to my body—both in the sense of "fix the mind upon" and "watch over the workings of." (p. 5)

This "destabilization of the body as given" (Weiss, 1999) suggests that the relationship between consciousness and embodiment is continually built via contact with the social world (p. 74). Analogously, woman, according to Beauvoir, although defined by her sex in opposition to a neutral and normative male opposite, is made woman by her situation, not by her biology. In other words, for Beauvoir (1952/1989), sex, like disability or race or sexuality, would not "precede the cultural interpretation of that difference, but [would] itself [be] an interpretive act laden with normative assumptions" (p. 40). Mairs (1996b) similarly describes disability as "part of a binary, existing in relation to a privileged opposite" (p. 13): "Whoever gets to define ability puts everyone else in place" (p. 14). Therefore, one is disabled only from the socially constructed point of view of the abled. Binary thinking, according to both Mairs and Beauvoir, is a habit of mind, rather than an apprehension of a transparent reality. Attending to subjectivity and agency, both writers critique binary categories and leave open the possibility that subjectivity and perception can be re-conceived—over and against views of the dominant culture. Referring to people without disabilities as "the nondisabled," for instance, Mairs highlights that from a disabled point of view, "they are the deficient ones" or the ones without: "Already, in this way, I begin to reconstruct the world" (p. 14).

These examples highlight the potential of textual encounters that are both generative and performative (Cumings, 2011). As Cumings writes, writers like Mairs are "crucial to the project of bringing suppressed or marginalized perspectives into fuller view" (p. 53). The "politics of location and interconnectedness" in these narratives, in fact "underscores the situated origins of all [knowledge] claims" (p. 54). In other words,

> If the disabled body can be imagined as a state of being out of sync with one's culture, rather than a state of pathology, wrongness, or pitiable inferiority, the stigma of the category "disabled" weakens, allowing people to entertain more comfortably the possibility that they belong in that category, and to understand that the category is not stable or inherently bad. (p. 15)

In other words, these claims illuminate how different ways of being can afford different and yet equally valid ways of knowing. Encouraging students to embrace what Brueggemann (1999) refers to as "the sense I made with one sense missing" can open creative and critical conversations about how each of us comes to know differently and how disability-informed ways of knowing can offer epistemic insights (p. 85).

Expanding the Conversation

Like Miner (2011), I have aimed in this chapter to stress the importance of attending more critically and thoughtfully to writers such as Mairs—whose work might be called authotheoretical (Cumings, 2011). Attending to theory within personal narrative underscores the "politics of location and interconnectedness," as well as the situated origins of subjectivity and epistemology (p. 54). As critical educators, it is important that we engage with stories in which disability is forged in and through multiple discourses of gender, race, sexual orientation, and social class. Through these stories we begin to see disability, and indeed even impairment, as not purely natural or fixed, but as a function of lived experience and discourse (Mintz, 2007). Like Mintz, who calls for a return to the "visceral" in DS, critical theory, perception, and subjectivity are grounded within the "poetics and politics" of the lived and situated body (p. 3).

Beyond suggesting that there is much to learn from Nancy Mairs in particular, and life writing more generally, I have also implicitly made a case for integrating theory, particularly feminist theory, in DSE. I am also making the case for attending to theory as a political act. If there is a lesson we can take from eugenic-based deficit thinking, it is that theory has not always been a friend of disability. And yet I would argue that if theory can be violent, it can also be emancipatory. Situated at the intersections of feminist theory and disability studies, feminist disability studies troubles binary thinking, while attending the status of the lived body, the politics of appearance, the medicalization and disciplining of the body, and the privileging of normalcy (Garland-Thomson, 2001). Yet feminist disability studies is neither easily defined nor monolithic—nor is it unrelated to other critical frames of thought, such as critical race studies. From varied interdisciplinary and critical contexts, scholars in these fields yield fruitful insights about the necessity of embracing a both/and approach that would account, for instance, for the social consequences of disability, but not as divorced from the embodied lived experience of disability (Marks, 1999; Meekosha, 1998; Garland-Thomson, 1994). As a group, these scholars contend that an intersectional approach to disability is both necessary and productive in order to add complexity and nuance to DSE.

Insights drawn from Beauvoir's situated embodiment, as articulated in Mairs' writing, are firmly located within a feminist disability studies framework, but also relevant to concerns within DSE. Embracing the ambiguity and paradox of embodied experience, Mairs and Beauvoir demand that we, too, attend to complexity in our thinking about disability and other social markers. In acknowledging their reluctance to write, they encourage us to take risks—to create intellectual structures that allow for the complexity of disabled experience and multiple sites of theory and activism. By their refusal of binary understandings of mind and body, phenomenology and epistemology, they point out the limits of thinking about the social consequences of disability as universal or as separate from the lived experience of impairment. In mapping out a path fraught with complexity, they ask us not to contain their words or ideas in static or simplistic ways, but use them in the service of making meaning (Smith, 2013).

To dismiss either Beauvoir or Mairs or to read them as purely as experiential is to miss the theory at work in their work—to overlook, for instance: how perception, knowledge, and voice are all grounded in the particular lived situation of the body; how binary thinking places artificial distance between embodiment and consciousness; how the self is irreducible to the categories we employ to contain it; and how particular bodily situations yield both ontological and epistemological consequences. These writers offer a "theoretical and imaginative framework" to explore the living of a life that is shaped but not determined by social contexts, offering a productively transgressive place to further this conversation (Mairs 1996b, p. 17).

Notes

1. I use the term *dis/ability* to draw attention to the ways that both disability and normalcy are mutually and socially constructed.
2. The disabled body is meant to call to mind the entire body—such that body, mind, emotion are inseparable from and indeed connected to the lived body. In the case of some disabilities, the body can also encompass the augmented body—rubber, metal, plastic, and technological.
3. For an excellent discussion of the problems associated with the translation of *The Second Sex*, see Simons (1999, pp. 61–71).
4. A noted poet and essayist, Nancy Mairs has written nine works of nonfiction, including memoir, books of essays, and a book of poetry. A critical anthology of Mairs' writing (edited by Johnson & Mintz, 2011) was recently published by Palgrave.
5. For discussions regarding the need for phenomenological understandings of disability within disability studies, see Marks (1999); Meekosha (1998); Paterson & Hughes (1999); Price & Shildrick, (1998); and Garland-Thomson (1994, 2001).
6. In writing autobiographical essays about the body and refusing to separate critical and creative writing, Mairs (1994) writes that she risks becoming "everybody's other" even though she believes "all writing is creative … all writing is critical" (pp. 44–45).

7. Disability *is* a theme in Mairs' writing, but not to the exclusion of or in isolation from other topics. For example, Mairs' essays also cover such issues as: gender, sexuality, family and relationships, as well as writing.
8. Many anthologies in women's and gender studies, for instance, typically include a very limited number of essays by people with disabilities, often one by Mairs and another excerpted from Grealy's *Autobiography of a Face* (1994) or from Lorde's *Cancer Journals* (1995/2006). Moreover, by incorporating primarily (or only) the autobiographical voice, they relegate disability to the experiential—a critique made earlier by Black feminist scholars such as hooks (1989) and others (Zinn, Cannon, Higginbotham, & Dill, 1990; Dill & Zambrana, 2009).
9. See the work of Couser (1997, 2002, 2009) and Mintz (2007).
10. Cumings (2011) notes that several of Mairs' books, including *Plaintext* (1986), *Bone House* (1995) and *Carnal Acts* (1996) originally contained more "literary-critical-philosophical" (p. 45) content, which was later cut by the publisher.
11. A recent anthology focused on Mairs' writing, edited by Johnson and Mintz (2011), is titled, *On the Literary Nonfiction of Nancy Mairs: A Critical Anthology.*
12. This may explain why we read much about how Beauvoir was influenced by Sartre, but very little about how Sartre and others were influenced by her (Moi, 1994).
13. http://iamnorm.com
14. Her linguistic choice of verbs focuses our attention on social action and refuses any corresponding ontological status of *being* invisible. This ontological refusal is also inherent in Beauvoir's statement that woman is made, not born. It is also evocative of DS scholars who play with words like dis-enabled to connote that disability is something we do and abled-bodied status is not an ontological reality, but something that is conferred.

References

Beauvoir, de, S. (1952/1989). *The second sex.* (Trans. H. M. Parshley). New York: Vintage.
Bérubé, M. (2002). *Life as we know it: A father, a family, and an exceptional child.* New York: Vintage.
Biklen, D. P. (2005). *Autism and the myth of the person alone.* New York: New York University Press.
Brueggemann, B. J. (1999). *Lend me your ear: Rhetorical constructions of deafness.* Washington, DC: Gallaudet University Press.
Butler, J. (1993). *Bodies that matter: On the discursive limits of "sex."* New York: Routledge.
Butler, J. (1998). Sex and gender in Simone de Beauvoir's *Second Sex.* In E. Fallaize (Ed.), *Simone de Beauvoir: A critical reader* (pp. 29–42). London: Routledge.
Connor, D. J. (2008). *Urban narratives: Portraits in progress, life at the intersections of learning disability, race, and social class.* New York: Peter Lang.
Couser, G. T. (1997). *Recovering bodies: Illness, disability, and life writing.* Madison: University of Wisconsin Press.
Couser, G. T. (2002). Signifying bodies: Life writing and disability studies. *Disability studies: Enabling the humanities* (pp. 109–117). New York: Modern Language Association.
Couser, G. T. (2009). *Signifying bodies: Disability in contemporary life writing.* Ann Arbor: University of Michigan Press.

Cumings, S. G. (2011). On writing in a collaborative spirit: Nancy Mairs' ethic of community. In M. L. Johnson & S. B. Mintz (Eds.), *On the literary nonfiction of Nancy Mairs: A critical anthology* (pp. 43–62). New York: Palgrave.

Davis, L. (1997). Enabling texts. *Disability Studies Quarterly, 17*(4), 248–250.

Dill, B. T., & Zambrana, R. E. (2009). Critical thinking about inequality: An emerging lens. In B. T. Dill & R. E. Zambrana (Eds.), *Race, class, and gender in theory, policy, and practice* (pp. 1–21). New Brunswick, NJ: Rutgers University Press.

Ferri, B. A. (2008) Changing the script: Race and disability in Lynn Manning's *Weights. International Journal of Inclusive Education, 12*(5–6), 497–509.

Ferri, B. A. (2011). Disability life writing and the politics of knowing. *Teachers College Record, 113*(10), 2267–2282.

Garland-Thomson, R. (1994). Redrawing the boundaries of feminist disability studies. *Feminist Studies, 20*(3), 583–597.

Garland-Thomson, R. (2001). *Toward a feminist disability theory.* Conference on Gender and Disability, Rutgers University.

Grealy, L. (1994). *Autobiography of a face.* New York: HarperCollins.

Harry, B., & Harry, M. (2010). *Melanie, bird with a broken wing: A mother's story.* Baltimore, MD: Paul H. Brookes.

Haugen, H. M. (2011). On difficult gifts: A biographical portrait of Nancy Mairs. In M. L. Johnson & S. B. Mintz (Eds.), *On the literary nonfiction of Nancy Mairs: A critical anthology* (pp. 25–41). New York: Palgrave.

Hooks, B. (1989). *Talking back: Thinking feminist, thinking black.* Cambridge, MA: South End Press.

Johnson, M. L., & Mintz, S. B. (Eds.). (2011). *On the literary nonfiction of Nancy Mairs: A critical anthology.* New York: Palgrave.

Kruks, S. (1998). Beauvoir: The weight of the situation. In E. Fallaize (Ed.), *Simone de Beauvoir: A critical reader* (43–71). London & New York: Routledge.

Lorde, A. (1995/2006). *The cancer journals: Special edition.* San Francisco, CA: Aunt Lute.

Mairs, N. (1986). *Plaintext: Deciphering a woman's life.* New York: Perennial/Harper & Row.

Mairs, N. (1994). *Voice Lessons: On becoming a (woman) writer.* Boston, MA: Beacon.

Mairs, N. (1996a). *Carnal acts.* Boston, MA: Beacon.

Mairs, N. (1996b). *Waist-high in the world: A life among the nondisabled.* Boston, MA: Beacon.

Manning, L. (2005). *Weights: One blind man's journey* [CD-ROM]. New York: Bridge Multimedia.

Marks, D. (1999). Dimensions of oppression: Theorizing the embodied subject. *Disability & Society, 14*(5), 611–626.

McKay, N. Y. (1998). The narrative self: Race, politics, and culture in black American women's autobiography. In S. Smith & J. Watson (Eds.), *Women, autobiography, theory: A reader* (pp. 96–107). Madison: University of Wisconsin Press.

Meekosha, H. (1998). Body battles: Bodies, gender and disability. In T. Shakespeare (Ed.), *The disability studies reader: Social sciences perspectives* (pp. 164–180). London: Cassell.

Miner, M. (1997). "Making up the stories as we go along": Men, women, and narratives of disability. In D. T. Mitchell & S. Snyder (Eds.), *The body and physical difference: Discourses of disability* (pp. 145–160). Ann Arbor: University of Michigan Press.

Miner, M. (2011). "Making up the stories as we go along": Men, women, and narratives of disability. In M. L. Johnson & S. B. Mintz (Eds.). *On the literary nonfiction of Nancy Mairs: A critical anthology* (pp. 145–160). New York: Palgrave.

Mintz, S. B. (2007). *Unruly bodies: Life writing by women with disabilities.* Chapel Hill: University of North Carolina Press.

Mintz, S. B. (2011). Transforming the tale: The auto/body/ographies of Nancy Mairs. In M. L. Johnson & S. B. Mintz (Eds.), *On the literary nonfiction of Nancy Mairs: A critical anthology,* (pp. 161–182) New York: Palgrave.

Mitchell, D. T., & Snyder, S. L. (1997). Exploring foundations: Languages of disability, identity, and culture. *Disability Studies Quarterly, 17*(4), 241–247.

Moi, T. (1994). *Simone de Beauvoir.* Oxford, UK & Cambridge, MA: Blackwell.

Paterson, B., & Hughes, K. (1999). Disability studies and phenomenology: The carnal politics of everyday life. *Disability and Society, 14*(5), 597–610.

Porter, J. I. (1997). Foreword. In D. T. Mitchell & S. Snyder (Eds.), *The body and physical difference: Discourses of disability* (pp. xiii–xiv). Ann Arbor: University of Michigan Press.

Price, J. S., & Shildrick, M. (1998). Uncertain thoughts on the dis/abled body. *Vital signs: Feminist reconfigurations of the bio/logical body.* Edinburgh: Edinburgh University Press.

Savarese, R. J. (2007). *Reasonable people: A memoir of autism and adoption.* New York: Other Press.

Scholz, S. J. (2000). *On de Beauvoir.* Belmont, CA: Wadsworth.

Sherry, M. (2005). Reading me/me reading disability. *Prose Studies, 27*(1–2), 163–175.

Simons, M. A. (1999). *Beauvoir and* The Second Sex. New York: Rowman & Littlefield.

Smith, P. (Ed.) (2013). *Both sides of the table: Autoethnographies of educators learning and teaching with/in [dis]ability.* New York: Peter Lang.

Weiss, G. (1999). *Body images: Embodiment as intercorporeality.* New York: Routledge.

Wendell, S. (1996). *The rejected body: Feminist philosophical reflections on disability.* New York: Routledge.

Wurtzburg, G. (Director). (2004). *Autism is a world.* [Documentary]. United States: CNN & State of the Arts.

Wurtzburg, G. (Director). (2011). *Wretches and jabberers.* [Documentary]. United States: State of the Arts.

Zinn, M. B., Cannon, L. W., Higginbotham, E. & Dill, B. T. (1990). The costs of exclusionary practices in women's studies. In G. Anzaldúa (Ed.), *Making face, making soul/Haciendo Caras: Creative and critical perspectives by feminists of color* (pp. 29–41). San Francisco, CA: Aunt Lute.

3. BEyon\ce\D inclusion: Wud mite[ymouse] be NEXTERATED X

PHIL SMITH

Here's the thing, see.

I'm the inclusion guy.

You know, that one teacher at the high school—the curmudgeonly, flakey, progressive special educator—who's all into including students with disabilities into general education. Pushin' the principal to get kids into chemistry class, or English class, or whatever. Kids with intellectual/developmental disabilities. Kids with severe reputations. Kids "on the spectrum." Kids who are just way out there.

I worked in schools and in agencies providing support to people with disabilities in the community, for years. Now I'm the inclusion guy at the university. That one guy—the curmudgeonly, flakey, progressive education professor—who's all into helping educators understand how to include students with disabilities in general education. Pushing my colleagues to teach their pre-service teachers how to make that happen.

I am a self-described pain in the ass. I admit it. Wrote a book about it (Smith, 2010). (Inclusion, that is, not bein' a pain in the ass.)

But I've been thinkin' lately (perfessers do that kinda thing, ya know?). What if a goal of inclusion—across oppressions and identities—is not a useful trajectory for this thing we call education? What if the

Western
White
Eurocentric
Neoliberal
Institutionalization

support(hose)ing the   dominant
                        demonic   moneysucking—
                                       1. 3 trillion dollar (Strauss, 2013a)
                                       (globally $4.4 trillion and growing
                                       REALLY fast)
                                       (Strauss, 2013b)—

industrial facade
that we pretend iz
teaching/learning
         is so deeply   flawed
                        corrupted
                        broken
                        crippled
                        mutilated
                        injured
                        dismembered
                        defective   ABLEIST METAPHORS IN TENSION
                                       ALLY DEPLOYED TO HIGH BRIGHT THE
                                       LIGHT OF DAY THARE COMMON/CON
                                       MAN USE IN INSTITUTIONALLY ABLE
                                       EST COMMODIFIED WESTERNIZED
                                       (WHY AT URP) KULCHUH (SHOCK
                                       ELECTROAD)

that applying values and strategies of inclusion to   it,
                                      ('cause   it
                                                really is   an it
                                                            a thing,
                                                            an objet (not d'art)
                                                            a   reified
                                                                 commodified
                                                                 bona fide
                                                                 crapified
                                                                 Fid (oh)
                                                                 dog of a corrupt
                                                                   capitalist
                                                                   imperialist)

is like applying a patch {adams} to the blown out|up bicycle tire inner toob
of edoo[doo]cashinal

               infra
               infro
               infree   (alley
                       ally
                       ahlee)
               structure

that is already wholly
          holy
          holely   totally
                    escalatingly
                    absolut(vodka)(kafka)e/loot (yeah, stolen from us
                    all)/ludic ly

broken? Hell, not just broken, but weaponsuvmassdeconstruction nuked into
total Hicks
     (hickey)

boson boatswain particle(board) capitalist annihilation. Nukified fried Kentucky
Colonel Fred Sanders antivegeterianist salmonellaed bloodied .edu cash national
              chicken
              chick (Barbie and) Ken

Education is a burned-out hulk (not green, but certainly a blue-eyed monster)

flagrantly fragrantly vagrantly   conflagration
                                   flagellation
that we have been   conned out   of
                        conned in   to
                        conning   towered toward to word.
                                   we all live in a yellow…

Worse: what if the tiny and huge storeez we (Ma)tell® about inklu(e)shun and
op(ed)press on (sticker) and eduKAT(E)scion are told from the totally privileged, centered, and dominant minority, surrounded by (butt still totally dominating) the grassrooted/margined/edged/boundaried/segregated majority?
This   piece
        (not peace or peas or kale)
               uv writhing writing witch yoo(hoo) are weeding reed-
               ing cums to you from a

place

that I have most very precisely and pretty much exquisitely inexactly already de/inscribed befour, undt zo if ewe wanna know how you landed in this patch of doo-doo doing(Loch)(lox)ness, go two/four/up/by (Smith, 2001a) and (Smith, 2001b) and (Smith, 2006) and (Smith, 2008) for a

> de/entailed
> derailed
> entrailed {studying thereof tea leaves fer a prediction uv da foochur}
> dental tool [suffering the pain of THAT hole ting)
> TRANS(embodied   sexool)mogrif(ter)(mast)ication
> fornication
> er, ok, storee

aboud wut dis iz and hough ya mighta landerated on this partic(ell)ular(loid) molar planet(al)oid. It enters hear (exit only) from "the spring of the imagination, when the winter of clean positivism fades completely and we are fre/er/iere" (Zach Richter, personal communication, April 25, 2013). Accept, of course, positivism wud never clean, not even by the Tide® of manufactured epistemofflogical ocean of Comte and his followers (and, for good measure, fuck you, Foucault).

In sum (quotient and equationally eloquent elegance), waddle happen(stance now) here will be an en|in-tire\less/ly trans=crossdressing=gressive, neuroqueered(un)iversive|aversive, and already-much-too-contrarian, in|un|at|tentionally (tenHUT!), oppositional, abolitional

> u/eu/dystopic
> dye st(r)op(t)ic
> die, sucker!
> di-succor
> hopic
> elliptic
> marked/marketed

> textual
> text you all
> Tex-Mex dual duel

anarchic (not arched) ick ick ick writing wry thing un|en|door|dour|jam—
peach—bed thing(iemabob)(nod Jack) is not   metaphoric
                                                                    me 2 flower lick

it is embodied and imbedded and has been bedded (a beast wid 2 approxi-
MATE backs) and lived (to tell the tall tell-tail tale tee(hee) beer) and in ter-
rupt/terrogate the world and how it is con/de (Rice) structed.

LIVE, FROM NEW YORK, IT'S SATUR

nalia made gnu -   -   -   -   -   -   -   -   -   -   -

And, in doo-wing sew, I yam (potatoes arise!) committed (asylumed) "to
language as a site of experimentation, power, struggle, and hope" (Giroux,
2012, p. 100), though probabbley NOT exactly in the way ole Henry had in
mind (though with luck and hard work, the outcome will be along the lines
of what he intended).
Here, I always already
critique the   creation
                 consumption
                 cooption
                 commercialization
                 commodification
                 consorbtion   of   inclusive
                                                   universalist
                                                   eugenicist
                                                   monocultural
                                                   education
from the place of the counter-hegemonic neurodiverse|queer polyculture.
Why?
Or, moh bettuh:
Wry?

> Here's the thing: "It is generally accepted that 'Inclusion' means inviting
> those who have been historically locked out to 'come in' ... Who has the
> authority or right to 'invite' others in?" (Asante, 2013).

Well, Nobodaddy (Heh. Because, of course, Secresy gains females loud ap-
plause).
They that do are self-authorizing and demonic.
The act of inclusion by the   White
                                middle/upperclass

     male
     heterosexual
     able-bodied (however temporar(e)olee)
     positivist
     Eurocentric
     northern

         dominating
         hegemonic
         rule-enforcing
         monosemic

of all dem poh liddle udders
reinforces the rights and power uv da self-per(de)ceiving do-gooder domination nation neoconlibs without changing a goddam thing.
whoo maid dem so special and exalted and almighty as to let ebberbody else in?

and wry is id dat ebberbody else wantz to get in|en|em bed widdim anyway?
doesn't that make us
   com
   im
   ex plicit wid da ting{aling} dat deyve maid? like wee wanna bee
part(y) uv dat anyhoo?   I don't think so.

dat be evil incarnate (whether perceived or nut).

And, well, see, er, **MORE:**

"One of the problems with the move to 'promoting inclusion' is that inclusion
in practice implicitly assumes that the quality of mainstream society is not
only desirable, but unproblematic and legitimate … Equally, a fundamental, if
implicit, premise of social inclusion is the existence of an 'ideal of common life'
… which everyone should aspire to. In practice this assumes a general consensus
on basic values around involvement in community, work, family and leisure …
In addition, social inclusion discourse implies that society is comprised of a com-

> fortable and satisfied 'included majority' and a dissatisfied 'excluded minority'.
> This focuses attention on the excluded minority and fails to take seriously the
> difficulties, conflicts and inequalities apparent in the wider society which actually
> generate and sustain exclusion ..."
>
> (Spandler, 2007, p. 6)

I question with ex(ice) treme
                             dream
                             cream

pre[post]judice the desirability (ah, sweet desire!) and legit|ext|int|imacy of that
(this) thesethosethem society—its more than a little   problematic
                                         conblemishauto[matic]
                                         fanatic

There is, indeed, a much-too-already-comfy|cuddly|cushy dominating hege-
monic hierarchical uber-class   supported and
                                extended and
                                amplified and
                                boosted and
                                accelerated

                                by an absolootly ginormous disparity
                                of wealth (Domhoff, 2013) and in-
                                come (Wiseman, 2013), da biggerest
                                on this (or probably any other) plan-
                                et, one that is creating
                                "difficulties, conflicts and inequalities"

(those words are much too weak/dainty/flimsy to describe what is in fact in
place, but let 'em serve [eat cake] for now). This awl plaize out[house] in an e—
ducat—(sc)ionall {solar} system dat is "dominated by pedagogies that are utterly
instrumental and geared toward memorization, conformity, and high-stakes test
taking ... intellectual dead zones and punishment centers" (Giroux, 2012, p.
117) (a-gun, dese wurds do nod be-gun to do
                                      to be
                                      or not ornate
                                      do be do be do
                                      justice to the   annihilation
                                                        obliteration
                                                         amputation

of hope, equity, and democracy that might possibly have beginnerated to
go{o} on there—but let 'em serve(ice) fer now).

In such a sizdem (modeled on biznez), the best we can even marginally hope for is to include

> "students who will undoubtedly be viewed as, for want of any other term, artificial transplants whose ersatz presence in the general education classroom will inevitably be subject to abiding doubts about their assimilative adequacy" (Gallagher, 2010, p. 36).

Witch just ain't good enough.
Nod fer da crips and queers dat I hang wid. Me and mine(d).
Given the screwed-uppedness (that's a technical term, they teach it to ya in doctor school, all others need not apply) of our increasingly privatized (the balls of it) .edu cash nationalism

sizdem
size [not]dem-ocratic
size DOES matter

undt da   horrors
                          whores
                          errors
that it is   perpetrating
                 decimating
                 segregating
                 desolating
                 regulating
                 detonating
                 perpetuating
                 devastating
                 on our|my|the   culture—on our polyculture (Aronowitz, 2008; Giroux, 2012; Illich, 1971; Prakash & Esteva, 2008),

> We need to stop ~~working towards inclusion, because~~ including people with disabilities into the broken and harmful institution of education ~~doesn't make sense~~. Instead, as Illich said, we need to figure out what it might mean to "deschool" society—to imagine and create a way for children and adults, in this silly culture within which we find ourselves, to learn and grow and teach and change in ways based on common sense, as Prakash and Esteva say… I think that is the real work. We need to be focused on a bigger, more important, more radical and revolutionary project. (Smith, 2013, pp. 275–276)

My colleagues and friends and teachers and co-conspirators in the neurodi-
vergence movement
have taught me sum tings   though not always explicitly and I be tinkin'
                                many uv 'em wood arguate wid me, which I
                                TOTALLY relish {and mustard}.

One of 'em is this:
                    Inclusion cannot be given.
Whoah.   Dig on that, Jack.
                Inclusion~power.
Perhaps   inclusion=power.

And "real power can not be given, only taken" (Coppola, 1990). In da zame
weigh, reel inkylooseshun
ion from Zion
cannot be gibbon, only taken, bacon. This taking of inclusion—leads us call
it the part(whole)ic®ip(le)ation in the common [core] zoshial and gultur-
al-gluteous cotton fabric of greater and lesser humanic communities—

> (and by this, dear reader, I do not mean "a 19th-century notion of a homoge-
> nous, tight-knit and small locale" (Ben-Moshe, 2011, p. 195), uh uh, nosirree-
> bob, Bud (this one's fer) rather a plaize of "support and acceptance ... based
> on solidarity and unity ... the antithesis of confinement" (Ben-Moshe, 2011,
> p. 196))

involves
devolves
revolves
necessarily a clam chowduh claim to the active|not-passive|perseverative in-de-
re-volv{o}ement in the politea of disdatdemdese(bull)dozerhoser communities,
and a flame[thrower] claim (sometimes re-claim) to powuh (to da peepul).
My homies in da neurodiver[ticulosis]gent (should be femme) activism and
scholarship

claim their|our right to be who they|we are and who they|we

want to be in a not-yet-our-culture-because-it-hasn't-entirely-been-created-or-
imagined,
                        perseverating (over and over and over and over and
                        over and over)
                        flapping (rejoice, you wrigglers!)
                        squeeeeeeeeeeeealing
                        echoing echoing echoing echoing echoing

Can you gimme an amen, brothers and sisters?
our way into a GNU corpogoddamnreality that rejects da
        pure-snow-white honkey strait|straight bourgeois subdude BORING
                whatever you wanna call what it is we got now.

Like, fuck DAT shit, know w'am sayin'? Heh.
Anarchoneuroqueer and owning/celebrating/claiming it. And through that
ownership/celebration/claiming, creating a radical youtopia(ry)n vision
(deaf and) of what will cum:

> "the aspiration is to funda-
> mentally change the way we
> react to each other, the way
> we respond to difference
> or harm, the way normal-
> cy is defined and the ways
> resources are distributed
> and accessed" (Ben-Moshe,
> 2011, p. 359).

Da werk, mein freund, den, is dis:
end the pederasstized sozial insTITooshun of .edu cash nationalism globali-
sation as we know id. Create Samsung knew in its (bed)stead, preferably(ob-
late) samsara dat Duz da saim tingaling as an institution but is not institoot-
shun[Big]Al. Do so across all levels, most especially at the level of so-called
higher (I wanna, I wanna, I wanna, I wanna take you) education.
In this cultural space, money cannot possibly be involved.
I have absofuckinglutely no ideer (in da headlights) what this space (the final
frunteer) looks like or smells like or tastes like or how to make it happenin',
Jackson. Only that it needs to.
But the cool (totally frigid[aire]) thingking is, see, that eye donerated half (or
three-quarters) to
        know
        sow
        blow
        GO!

what it loogs lige, matey. This is not some kinda hocus pocus locus, hear (me out
and back in the screen door of somnambulant justusice), nossuh; it's not some
weird wired whored buncha (prolly pot, huh) smoke and freak show mirrors
(here's lookin' at you, kid). As Ben-Moshe points out, the abolitionists didn't
have a clew (sailing along) what an Amurrican   soziety
                                           coquettery

without slavery would look like, only that slavery must end. They made it up as they went along.

Wee can do da zame.

When weave finisherated, if we ged id (w)right, whether we're (w)rong or right, whether we're wroing, we won't even have to conceeve of
the
strange
ting
we call   inclusion.

References

Aronowitz, S. (2008). *Against schooling: For an education that matters*. Boulder, CO: Paradigm.

Asante, S. (2013). What is inclusion? *Inclusion Network*. Retrieved from www.inclusion. com/inclusion.html

Ben-Moshe, L. (2011). *Genealogies of resistance to incarceration: Abolition politics within deinstitutionalization and anti-prison activism in the U.S.* Retrieved from ProQuest Digital Dissertations. (UMI No. 3495084).

Coppola, F. (Director) (1990). *The godfather: Part III* [Motion picture]. United States: Paramount Pictures.

Domhoff, G. (2013). Wealth, income, and power. Retrieved from http://www2.ucsc. edu/whorulesamerica/power/wealth.html

Gallagher, D. (2010). Educational researchers and the making of normal people. In C. Dudley-Marling & A. Gurn (Eds.). *The myth of the normal curve* (pp. 25–38). New York: Peter Lang.

Giroux, H. (2012). *Education and the crisis of public values: Challenging the assault on teachers, students, and public education*. New York: Peter Lang.

Illich, I. (1971). *Deschooling society*. New York: Harper & Row.

Prakash, M., & Esteva, G. (2008). *Escaping education: Living as learning within grassroots culture*. New York: Peter Lang.

Smith, P. (2001a). Inquiry cantos: A poetics of developmental disability. *Mental Retardation*, *39*, 379–390.

Smith, P. (2001b). MAN.i.f.e.s.t.o.: A Poetics of D(EVIL)op(MENTAL) Dis(ABILITY). *Taboo: The Journal of Education and Culture*, *5*(1), 27–36.

Smith, P. (2006). Split------ting the ROCK of {speci [ES]al} e.ducat.ion: FLOWers of lang[ue]age in >DIS<ability studies. In S. Danforth & S. Gabel (Eds.), *Vital Questions in Disability Studies in Education* (pp. 31–58). New York: Peter Lang.

Smith, P. (2008). an ILL/ELLip(op)tical *po* – ETIC/EMIC/**Lemic**/litic *po*st® uv ed DUCAT ion *re*cherché *re*pres©entation. *Qualitative Inquiry*, *14*, 706–722.

Smith, P. (Ed.) (2010). *Whatever happened to inclusion? The place of students with intellectual disabilities in education*. New York: Peter Lang.

Smith, P. (2013). Looking to the future. In P. Smith (Ed.), *Both sides of the table: Autoethnographies of educators learning and teaching with/in [dis]ability* (pp. 263–277). New York: Peter Lang.

Spandler, H. (2007). From social exclusion to inclusion? A critique of the inclusion imperative in mental health. *Medical Sociology Online*, 2(2), 3–16.

Strauss, V. (2013a, January 9). Education reform as a business. *Washington Post*. Retrieved from http://www.washingtonpost.com/blogs/answer-sheet/wp/2013/01/09/education-reform-as-a-business/

Strauss, V. (2013b, February 9). Global education market reaches $4.4 trillion—and is growing. *Washington Post*. Retrieved from http://www.washingtonpost.com/blogs/answer-sheet/wp/2013/02/09/global-education-market-reaches-4-4-trillion-and-is-growing/

Wiseman, P. (2013, September 10). Pay gap between 1 percent and everybody else reaches widest point since 1920s. *Huffington Post*. Retrieved from http://www.huffingtonpost.com/2013/09/10/pay-gap-between-1-percent_n_3900373.html

Section II

Research

4. *Enacting Research: Disability Studies in Education and Performative Inquiry*

Jan W. Valle

"Theatre has had an historic role in society as providing a relatively safe way of talking back to power. Across many cultures and traditions over time we can trace patterns and instances of groups of people using the stage as a space and place to tell their stories."

—Prendergast & Saxton (2009)

As a professor in the childhood education program at the City College of New York (CCNY) who teaches inclusive education courses outside of a special education program, I primarily identify as a disability studies in education (DSE) scholar. I came to the DSE community having been a special education teacher, co-founder and educational director of a private school for children with learning disabilities, educational evaluator/consultant/parent advocate for a developmental pediatrics clinic, and educational director for a nonprofit organization dedicated to meeting lifespan needs of people with learning disabilities. I consider my current work within the university as the latest iteration of a longtime engagement with the field of special education. It is within this multiplicity of lived experiences that I ground my DSE research agenda.

Central to my research is the understanding of disability as a civil rights issue. As an undergraduate majoring in special education as P.L. 94–142 (Education for All Handicapped Children Act, 1975) passed into law, I was deeply influenced by the political activism of parents of children with disabilities and their advocates whose efforts redefined a nation's response to disability. I eagerly joined what I understood to be an educational revolution and became a special education teacher. In the fall of 1978, the year in which states were required to have implemented P.L. 94–142, I began as a first-year teacher in a middle-school resource room for students with mild to moderate learning and emotional disabilities. I entered the classroom well-schooled in the medical model of disability. Then I met real students living complex lives in multiple and shifting contexts. And my re-education began. My experiences as a special education teacher mirrored the emerging critique of special education that first appeared in the early 1980s. From those earliest years, the now legendary effects of a parallel system of education were already evident. My students and I struggled to make sense of our context, simultaneously working within and resisting the negative consequences of labeling and segregation.

It was as a doctoral student that I was introduced to disability studies and the emerging discipline of disability studies in education (see the introductory chapter for an explanation of the difference between DS and DSE)—a turning point in my sense-making of all that I had experienced working in and with the field of special education. The work of DS/DSE scholars (re)shaped and (re)confirmed my understanding, providing language within which to (re)conceptualize disability as a discursive practice rather than pathology and deficit. From the vantage point of the present, I see that my life's work has been defined by an ongoing desire to "make sense" of special education and its unintended consequences, and to collaboratively engage with students identified with disabilities and their families to "make things better."

It is hard to imagine how I might have constructed a research agenda outside of DSE. I well understand how privileged I have been to learn from, work alongside, and write with other DSE scholars and to have contributed to an ever-growing body of literature in this emerging discipline. As noted in our introductory chapter, a staggering amount of DSE research has been generated in the past decade or so. In recent years, however, I found myself growing increasingly uncomfortable about the fact that most of my research endeavors focused on "making sense" rather than "making things better." I began longing for a way to integrate DSE research more closely into the lives of everyday people. And as is the way of serendipity, it was at this point that my department opened a graduate program in educational theatre. Given that this program offers an option for New York State teacher certification, students who choose this route must take a course in inclusive education in order to be able to teach within the public schools. My colleague Jennifer Katona, director of CCNY's educational theatre program, approached me about developing and teaching an inclusive education course that would reflect the needs of teaching artists and the contexts within which they work. It was this collaboration that initiated my foray into educational theatre where I quickly recognized its implications for DSE research.

In this chapter, I make a case for integrating arts-based research, specifically theatre arts, and disability studies in education as means to provide access to DSE research and practice for an audience beyond the academy. Moreover, I contend that moving beyond traditional models for teaching and scholarship can move us closer to realizing the kind of social change advocated by DSE scholars. First, I set the context by describing the cross-program collaboration between Jennifer Katona and myself that led to my engagement with ABR. Then, I share two examples of the integration of DSE with ABR: (1) an ongoing partnership among Nicole Kempskie, a playwright and director, Jessica Meyer, composer and performer, and myself to produce *The M.O.M. Project*, an ethnodrama based on narratives told by mothers of children with disabilities; and (2) a case example of graduate students in educational theatre integrating DSE into their research and practice.

The Case for Integrating DSE and Arts-Based Research

Before presenting an argument for integrating DSE with Arts-Based Research (ABR), it is noteworthy to point out that disability studies (DS) scholars have long relied upon the humanities as a framework to study disability (Snyder, Brueggemann, & Garland-Thomson, 2002). DS scholars are well-recognized for their work in legitimizing narratives of individuals with disabilities as scholarly sources of valued knowledge (Couser, 2009). Moreover, theater-based scholarly work within DS has allowed space for creative works (Lewis, 2006) and theories (Sandahl & Auslander, 2005) to emerge that challenge traditional boundaries and promote alternative ways to understand disability. Notably, Linda Ware, a DS/DSE scholar, is well-known for her ongoing inquiry into disability and the arts (Ware, 2011, 2008). I contend that the arts-based precedent established by such scholars can and should serve as a model and inspiration for new directions in DSE research.

So, what exactly is arts-based research? Shaun McNiff offers the following definition in the *Handbook of the Arts in Qualitative Research* (Knowles & Cole, 2008):

> Art-based research can be defined as the systematic use of the artistic process, the actual making of artistic expressions in all of the different forms of the arts, as a primary way of understanding and examining experience by both researchers and the people that they involve in their studies. (p. 29)

Simply put, arts-based research (ABR) relies upon one or more artistic processes that may be used in generating, analyzing, and/or presenting data that emerges from collaboration with the people we engage in inquiry.

Although the origins of ABR can be traced back to the 1970s, the discipline developed through the 1990s (Sinner, Leggo, Irwin, Gouzouasis, & Grauer, 2006). Early work by Elliot Eisner and Sara Lawrence-Lightfoot is widely recognized, in particular, for its integration of qualitative research with features of narrative fiction (Cahnmann-Taylor & Siegesmund, 2008). In the four decades since its inception, ABR has earned a scholarly reputation for broadening and deepening the qualitative research paradigm through its experimentation with varied representational methods (Leavy, 2009).

Unsurprisingly, there are many iterations of ABR across the arts. Given that theatre is the focus of this chapter, I offer the example of "applied theatre" as an instance of ABR in action. Prendergast and Saxton (2009) describe the purpose of applied theatre as follows:

> Applied theatre works overtly either to reassert or to undermine socio-political norms, as its intent is to reveal more clearly the way the world is working. For example, reminiscence theatre, community-based theatre and museum theatre are most often reassertions and celebrations of memory and history. On the other hand, theatre of the oppressed, popular theatre, theatre in education, theatre for health education and theatre for development are most often focused on undermining the status quo to promote positive social change. Prison theatre may fall within either depending upon intention and context. (p. 8)

Applied theatre differs from conventional theatre in a number of ways. For example, the performance usually takes place in a space not typically designated for theatre. The actors may or may not be formally trained in theatre arts. The content of the performance most often reflects the life experiences of audience members and/or issues relevant to their community. On occasion, audience members even may be asked to contribute to the performance (Prendergast & Saxton, 2009).

Perhaps the person most associated with applied theatre is the Brazilian director Augusto Boal, founder of Theatre of the Oppressed, whose politically charged "legislative theatre" (drawn from the work of Paulo Freire) is known internationally (Greenwood, 2012). However, there are many others who also have contributed significantly to the development and implementation of applied theatre (for example, see Greenwood, 2005; Miller & Saxton, 2004; O'Neill, 1995).

Eisner (2002) credits ABR with inspiring new and original thinking, enhancing awareness about the human condition, and (re)presenting complex aspects of what it means to be human. Leavy (2009) also recognizes the potential of ABR to enhance critical awareness and further argues that its research practices are well-suited in particular to "social-justice-oriented research that seeks to reveal power relations (often invisible to those in privileged groups) ... build coalitions across groups, and challenge dominant ideologies" (p. 13).

The points of compatibility between ABR and DSE are evident in a shared commitment to challenge a world; that is, to bring marginalized voices to the forefront, raise critical awareness, and contribute to social change. In the remainder of the chapter, I illustrate why I believe that arts-based research practices are not only relevant to DSE's overarching social justice agenda, but also hold great promise for making DSE research accessible to the culture at large.

The Educational Theatre Context

CCNY's graduate program in educational theatre prepares theatre educators who can: (1) lead theatre classes at all levels (K–12); (2) integrate theatre studies into the classroom and general school curriculum; (3) work with a diverse population of students in a variety of educational settings, including schools and community agencies; and (4) enrich participants' lives and provide them with the skills necessary to realize theatrical performances. Examples of course offerings include: Theatre/Performance for Young Audiences (K–12), Exploring the History of Theatre, Fundamentals of Teaching Theatre, Devising Theatre (K–12), Physical Theatre, Drama as a Learning Medium Across the Curriculum, Teaching Literacy Through Drama, Integrating Theatre and Related Arts into the Curriculum, Applied Theatre, Teaching English Language Learners Through Drama, Conflict Resolution Through Theatre, and Drama in Education (www.ccny.cuny.edu/edtheatre/index.cfm). My course, Inclusive Practices for the Arts is offered within the educational theatre curriculum to meet the New York State certification requirement that teachers in *all* subject areas and grade levels take a three-credit course about inclusive practices for "students with disabilities."

As stated earlier, Jennifer Katona, director of the educational theatre program, approached me several years ago about co-constructing an inclusion course to meet the particular needs of her students, the majority of whom come to the program with professional arts backgrounds (e.g., actors, directors, playwrights, dancers, puppeteers, television writers, choreographers, filmmakers). The context within which teaching artists work differs significantly from that of classroom teachers. Teaching artists may visit a public school for one day or engage in an artist residency that might last for several weeks. Their classes may be made up of students in a single grade level or multiple grade levels. At other times, teaching artists may not work during the traditional school day, but rather in an after-school program or in partnership with a community organization. They typically construct lesson plans and follow state standards, yet formal student assessments are not part of their work. It is noteworthy that many teaching artists also continue their professional careers.

All of the aspects listed above contributed to the program director's choice to offer an inclusion course through the educational theatre program instead of having students take a generic inclusion course offered by the special education program. But perhaps the most significant reason for designing this course was her understanding that a DSE orientation to disability is closely aligned with the philosophy and curriculum of educational theatre. The course, Inclusive Practices for the Arts, meets all of the requirements set forth by the state, yet expands the curriculum content to include a DSE orientation, as reflected in the course description:

EDCE 4500K: Inclusive Practices for the Arts

The potential of theatre arts as a powerful vehicle for positive disability representation is explored. Candidates draw upon the work of artists with and without disabilities to [re]conceptualize disability as natural human variation and an essential feature of diversity in a multicultural society. Topics of study also include special education law, disability categories under IDEIA, differentiated instruction and universal design for learning, collaborative teaching, and classroom management. [15 hours fieldwork]

It should be noted that the required "topics of study" are discussed and carried out within the contexts in which teaching artists actually work.

The DSE orientation of the course is evident in the study of media constructions of disability, assignment of first-person disability narratives, and class screenings of documentaries about disability. (For examples of such resources, see Chapter 7, "Practicing What We Teach: The Benefits of Using Disability Studies in an Inclusion Course"). Each semester, a panel of arts professionals who work in inclusive settings visits our class. Students engage in the field by observing/working in inclusive theatre settings in public school settings and/or attending integrated K–12 school performances (able-bodied students and students with disabilities performing together). Over the past five years, it is noteworthy that the New York City arts community has significantly increased its offerings of "disability and the arts" performances, events, and opportunities. For example, students have earned fieldwork hours by attending integrated theatre and dance performances, disability-themed theatre, disability film festivals, disability and the arts conferences, sensory-friendly Broadway performances, and workshops for theatre educators.

Arts-Based Research Meets Disability Studies in Education

In this section, I describe two examples of integrating arts-based research and disability studies in education. The first is an example of the influence of ABR upon my narrative research with mothers of children labeled with disabilities. The second is an example of the influence of DSE upon the research and practice of three current graduate students in CCNY's educational theatre program.

The M.O.M. Project: Staging Narrative Research

The M.O.M. Project (*Mothers On Mothering: Narratives of Disability*) is an in-progress theatre piece based on a collection of narratives told by 15 mothers (representing diverse generations, classes, races, and cultures) whose children have been labeled with disabilities. I originally collected the narratives for my dissertation. Nearly all of the women I interviewed were mothers with whom I had had a previous professional relationship in regard to the ongoing "special" education of their children. In short, this collection of narratives reveals *persisting* devaluation of "mother knowledge" by professionals, despite the parental right to participate in educational decision making about their children as guaranteed under the Individuals with Disabilities Education Improvement Act (I.D.E.I.A., 2004).

During the first semester that I taught the Inclusive Practices and the Arts course, my dissertation was published under the title *What Mothers Say About Special Education: From the 1960s to the Present* (Valle, 2009). After having shared a few excerpts from the book with my class, a student, Pamela Ritke (a professional actor/director/playwright) asked if she could create a readers' theatre script based on the narratives for her final class project. She enlisted six class members to "workshop" an initial draft of the script. These classmates later performed the piece under her direction on the last day of class. The director of the educational theatre program attended class that evening as well. As a result, the piece was chosen to be featured at the spring 2010 Benefit for Educational Theatre. *The M.O.M. Project* debuted on April 27, 2010, in a black-box theatre on the CCNY campus to a full house of approximately one hundred audience members.

It is worth noting that the original class performance relied upon the usual elements of readers' theatre, described by Butler-Kisber (2010) as

> ...a joint dramatic reading from a text, usually with no memorization, no movement and a minimum of props, if any at all. Participants read aloud assigned parts from prepared scripts ... Unlike traditional theatre, the emphasis is on oral expression of the text, rather than on acting and costumes. (p. 140)

Given the context of our classroom as a performance space, readers' theatre was the logical theatrical choice as it eliminated the need for staging, movement, script memorization, and costumes.

In reworking the piece to take it from a class project to a campus production, we recognized the need to expand the readers' theatre format to include features of ethnodrama and ethnotheatre, described as follows:

> An ethnodrama is a written, artistically composed arrangement of qualitative data using such dramatic literary conventions as monologue, dialogue, and stage directions. Ethnotheatre is the synchronous, three-dimensional, mounted performance display of the ethnodrama for spectators. (Saldana, 2008, p. 196)

With a mixed-method approach, *The M.O.M. Project* took on elements of a more professional theatre production. Six women sat on stools and read from scripts as is typical for readers' theatre; however, the new production incorporated lighting, professional actors (most of whom were students in the educational theatre program), a script that included dialogue and interaction among the actors, and movement onstage (e.g., gesturing and responding to the other actors while seated, and walking upstage for extended monologues). Moreover, visual images, conceived and drawn by David Connor, were projected onto a screen behind the actors to draw audience attention to themes within and across the narratives as the actors performed. Following the performance, the cast, the director, two mothers whose narratives appeared in the script, David Connor, and I held a "talk-back" with the audience. It was during this lively exchange that I began to see more clearly the promise theatre holds for making research accessible to a wider and more diverse audience. (For an extended discussion of *The M.O.M. Project*, see Valle & Connor, 2012).

In yet another instance of serendipity, Nicole Kempskie, a professional playwright and director, attended the performance of *The M.O.M. Project* to support the work of CCNY's educational theatre program. After the performance, Nicole contacted me about her interest in the piece. From the very beginning of our relationship, I felt an innate kinship to Nicole's orientation to her theatre work. I now more clearly understand the connection between my work as a qualitative researcher and hers as a playwright and director. Saldana (1999) explains that the natural affinity between qualitative researchers and playwrights emerges from a common goal of trying "to create a unique, engaging, and insightful text about the human condition" (p. 60).

As a result of my collaboration with Nicole, *The M.O.M. Project* is undergoing yet another theatrical iteration. In rewriting the script from scratch, Nicole returned to my original data set to glean a deeper understanding of each mother's story. Out of the 15 mothers interviewed, she chose six mothers to highlight in the new script. Although the original script likewise featured six actors, the mothers were composite characters drawn from all of the interviews—an ABR method Saldana (1999, 2003) describes. The in-progress script, on the other hand, retains the integrity of each mother's narrative arc, an artistic choice that reflects (and respects) the individual lived experiences as originally told. Acknowledging Leavy's (2009) assertion that "the researcher must consider his or her own role within the script" (p. 148), Nicole currently is considering how my "character" might figure into the script, particularly because of the role I play in a number of the stories told by mothers as well as my researcher status as co-constructor of these narratives. We are thinking about possibilities such as those suggested by Saldana (1999) for how a researcher might appear in an ethnodrama: (1) a leading role; (2) an extra not commenting, just reacting; (3) a servant; (4), the lead's best friend; (5) an offstage voice heard on speakers; (6) a character cut from the play in an earlier draft (p. 66).

At the writing of this chapter, the first draft of the new script is nearly complete. This phase will be followed by a process of rewriting, "workshopping" the revised script with actors, and rewriting again. As an experienced and professional theatre artist, Nicole is dedicated to writing an ethnodrama that illuminates the lives of real people in addition to adhering to a professional level of aesthetics. Leavy (2009) speaks to the question of aesthetics in arts-based research:

> On a theoretical level, the emergence of these new methods necessitates not only a reevaluation of "truth" and "knowledge" but also of "beauty." Furthermore, the research community needs to expand the concepts of "good art" and "good research" to accommodate these methodological practices. (p. 17)

The recent inclusion of professional musician Jessica Meyer into our collaboration has further enhanced the level of aesthetics for this project. A gifted composer and performing artist, Jessica will write and perform original viola music to accompany the dramatic text.

Moving forward in this project, I hope to gain greater balance between "making sense" and "making things better." Langellier and Peterson (2006) write, "Performing personal narrative reclaims and proclaims both body and voice: the personal gives body to narrative, and narrative gives voice to experience" (p. 156). As a DSE scholar, it is my belief that enacting research (in this case by shifting mother narratives in body and voice from the margins to center stage) holds great promise for the possibility of "consciousness-raising, empowerment, emancipation, political agendas, discovery, exploration, and education" (Leavy, 2009, p. 135)—outcomes compatible to the work of both ABR and DSE scholars.

Teaching Artists at Work: Applying DSE to Practice and Research

In keeping with the theme of this volume, I share a recent example that demonstrates the influence of DSE upon the practice and research of three teaching artists enrolled in CCNY's graduate educational theatre program. Near the end of their program, students take a two-semester research course. In the first semester, they learn about the research process, choose a topic of study, and write a proposal that includes a literature review. During the second semester, research is carried out within an educational theatre context. The culmination of this work is a research paper that students present in a public research forum.

At the end of January 2014, three former students from my Inclusive Practices in the Arts class, Ben Compton, Kristin ("Boc") Boccamazzo, and Maria Taylor (identity disclosure requested) asked to meet with me to discuss their research proposal. They explained that their intended study would take place in a public-school special education classroom for students ages 7 through 9 who are identified as being on the autism spectrum. As a result of our initial meeting, the students and I decided to meet two more times during the spring semester to discuss their ongoing work in this classroom. We agreed to audiotape these conversations as an additional source of data for their research project. I transcribed the audiotapes for the students to include in their data set and they granted permission for excerpts to be included in this chapter.

Why disability?

It is worth noting that this is not the first semester that educational theatre students have chosen disability as the focus of their research projects after having taken Inclusive Practices for the Arts. In light of this fact, I asked these students about their reason(s) for choosing disability for their research topic. The following conversation took place after their initial observations of the special education classroom where their study would take place, but before they began working with the children.

Maria: I feel like artists in history, and in general, they have different modes of learning and self-expression. That is why I am interested in disability and the arts. Personally, I think everyone is on the spectrum in one way or another. Everyone is a little ADHD. I'm a little dyslexic sometimes, you know.

Ben: I guess one of the things that piqued my interest from your class and then moving into the research class is that I really didn't know a lot about people with disabilities and the whole idea of identity and disability and the way that through society and through education we enforce identity onto populations. And I thought it was really interesting to think about that and to think about how because of *who* these kids are and because of the identity that has kind of been forced on them, they are taken out of

this realm of having "arts access" to real and freeing arts experiences …
There is a really great intersection of arts in education and disability studies because one of the great things about art in *any* form is that it gives
you the ability to really exercise your voice and to really explore *who you
are*, not just who somebody *says* you are, but really kind of what is inside
you yearning to be free … While everyone has different levels of talent—
whether you have a disability or you don't have a disability—or you consider yourself to be an artist or not—there is still part of that process that is
the same for everybody. Tapping into that sameness, that instinct, and that
part of the process, and the curiosity that goes along with that, I think, is a
really good way of removing this idea of otherness because that's the thing
we share—this process and the want to express.

Boc: I think for me—I am a little scared to admit this … I got nervous in the
classroom. And I think that was my biggest thing. I think there is just a
lack of awareness of "the other." And in your class, I couldn't believe that
whole idea about what is [considered] normal and what is not.

The influence of a DSE perspective of disability (in contrast to the traditional
medical model understanding of disability that undergirds special education) is
evident within this exchange. For example, Maria resists the notion that people
with disabilities are qualitatively different from people without disabilities in
her assertion that artists, in particular, share characteristics with others deemed
"different" in the world. She goes as far as to suggest that "everyone is on the
spectrum in one way of another"—reflecting an understanding of disability
not as pathology or deficit but rather as merely natural human variation. Ben
extends upon Maria's comments in his framing of disability as an issue of identity as opposed to pathology or deficit. He speaks of the narrow (and arguably
false) identity *imposed* upon special education students by virtue of their labels
and the potential of the arts as an avenue for *expressing* identity. Echoing
Maria, Ben suggests that the desire to create, regardless of ability, exists within
everyone. Boc's contribution reflects her still emerging recognition of the consequences that a lack of exposure to and understanding of "the other" (persons
with disabilities) holds for her. Despite having increased her awareness and
knowledge about disability as a result of being in the Inclusive Practices for the
Arts course, Boc confesses to harboring some anxiety on the cusp of beginning
her first experience working with children on the autism spectrum.

Rethinking the research question
In our initial meeting, the students asked for feedback in regard to their proposed research on exposing children on the autism spectrum to theatre arts.
Despite having submitted a proposal for the study during the previous semester, they appeared to have reservations about carrying out the proposal as written. Maria explained that their original idea was to have a control group (no

theatre arts) and an experimental group (theatre arts exposure) and compare features of both groups following a set of interventions carried out with the experimental group. As Maria laid out this scenario, I observed mild distress creeping across their faces. Maria ended by suggesting that somehow not engaging all of the children in a theatre arts experience seemed like a rather unfair proposition. Her comment prompted Ben to articulate his growing discomfort.

> Ben: I was looking back through the notes we made and the proposal from last semester and I saw that I wrote several times in my part the term "interventions" and how it became sort of a synonym for the activities that we are doing. The more I looked at it and more I thought about it, the more disturbing it became that that was the place I was starting from. Intervention means that you are *intervening*—you are stopping a process to change the direction of it. And that's another thing about the [Inclusive Practices for the Arts] class. Now when I go back and I look at whatever I am writing about—this in particular—I really kind of reflect on the reasons that I use even specific words and that becomes a challenge for me. Like why am I using the word "intervention"? That is not *really* what I want to do. I think what we want to do is to create these great experiences for them. That is one of the things I was thinking when I was going back and wondering why did I write that in? And it's like such a *violent* word because you are putting yourself forcefully in the way of something. I think it's like a word that just gets used a lot especially in education with kids with disabilities because we are intervening to fix something. And when you think about *that*—when education is thought of like that, if it becomes like a violent activity, then it's no wonder why teachers are nervous about working with these populations. It's no wonder that you can't have just "arts experiences" for these kids because it's *all* looked at as a struggle and a fight as opposed to just creating an environment that honors them and honors the connections they make with their teachers and their fellow students and everybody else in their school.

As the words tumbled out, Ben's relief at "naming" his discomfort was palpable. His attempt to comply with the tenets of traditional research had threatened his way of being in the world as an artist and compromised not only how he would practice his craft but also how he would think about and respond to children with disabilities. The Inclusive Practices for the Arts course is grounded in the notion that how we *think* about disability determines our *response* to disability—an idea that Ben had understood quite well in class. His discussion here likening "interventions" (a commonly used term in special education research and instruction) to a "violent activity" reveals the influence of a DSE perspective upon his current decision making in the real world. Moreover, he directly challenges the construction of children with disabilities as "needing to be fixed"—as if they somehow possess less humanity than the children without disabilities who are, in contrast, deemed able to benefit from "art for art's sake."

Following extensive discussions about the meaning of disability within public schools and the potential of teaching artists to disrupt the status quo, the group decided to shift their focus to a qualitative study of self-reflective practice as artists working to create a positive theatre arts experience within the context of special education.

> Ben: We have gone from a question like "What can arts and theatre do to bolster emotional, academic, and social growth [of children on the autism spectrum]" to "How can we as theatre artists create a positive experience for these kids? How can we prepare ourselves as teachers who don't have a lot of experience working with this population?"

Presuming competence

In approaching the task of creating a positive theatre arts experience for children identified on the autism spectrum, the group agreed that their work would center around a presumption of competence. In the spirit of self-reflection, Ben considered the source of his lingering anxiety about his upcoming work in a special education context.

> Ben: It also made me think about *my* assumptions that I make about people, and particularly about populations that are classified as having disabilities—and how I was very intimidated about working with those populations. What I first thought was me being intimidated because of the *disability* I think is really more like being intimidated by not *trusting* myself and not having as much faith in what I can do. So it's really, you know, the assumption that people with disabilities can't do something I think that is really more a reflection on that educator or that other person than the kid or adult with the disability.

The following exchange occurred after the group had begun working in the classroom. They settled on a unit called "Masks, Characters, and Stories" in which the children were asked to exercise and refine "the actor's instrument" (body, voice, and mind) by making strong physical, vocal, and narrative choices. In the exchange below, Maria describes the process of creating an original script based on the children's ideas and words.

> Maria: Well, they started creating their own original characters. So Mitzy came up with Melissa Pig on her mask. And we were like, "Who's that?" She was like, "This is Melissa Pig. Melissa Pig goes to the store. Melissa Pig does this. Melissa Pig does that. Lives by the ocean ... What is she going to do today? And then she'll tell us what she's going to do today down by the seashore and we'll write that up on chart paper. And does anyone else have an idea for what could happen next? Oh—well she goes on the boardwalk. Okay, great. What happens on the boardwalk? Blah, blah, blah. So then we'll create a script using their ideas and their dialogue—

Ben: [overlap] and their words as much as possible. And we might fill in some
of the major plot holes.
Maria: There might not be any, though. Who knows? It might be a fully formed
story.

Given that children identified on the autism spectrum typically are described as lacking imaginative play, it is noteworthy that these teaching artists actively disrupt this belief by providing access to and supporting imaginative work. It is of further interest that Maria challenges Ben's comment that the students may need their help to construct a story. This is an example of how the group functioned as a source of accountability for making assumptions about student competence.

In the exchange below, Maria and Boc talk about how their practice is continually shaped by the children in the classroom. What they describe points to a clear resistance within their work to a deficit understanding of disability in favor of a strengths-based approach.

Maria: We have two non-verbal kids. So when we come in as theatre practitioners, we are like, "Let's make a script!" Wait a second. They might be able to give us the ideas in some way, shape, or form, but they're not going to be able to stand up and say it. So what *can* they do? They can give us actions. They can give us body gestures and facial expressions. And they can make sounds. They can *certainly* make sounds. Ivan is *so expressive* even though he doesn't speak. And you *know* he's in it because you'll ask him, "Was the second house made of straw?" And he's got yes or no cards in front of him and he's like … [acts out Ivan tapping vigorously on a card]
Boc: I felt a little like I didn't really know how—I mean I *knew* how—but you just have to like throw yourself in there … I like getting from them and then building from there. Okay, so this is what we got this week. Like Melissa Pig! That's a gift. Okay, so what can we do?

Ben and Maria further consider how they draw upon their artistry as a source for the kind of instructional improvisation described above.

Ben: I think a good part of it is that we trust each other, but more we trust the kids in the class … I know how to be an artist. I *know* how to be responsive to the needs of my fellow performers and my fellow artists who are creating with me. That is what the kids in the class are. They are our fellow performers, fellow artists.
Maria: And it's always on your toes—working on your toes in the moment. And that's very much like creating scene work or dance.

Negotiating representation
As the semester drew to a close, the group had to agree upon the best way to present their results at the public research forum. The following discussion emerged about how to represent the children in the study.

Maria: We are going to write an ethnodrama.

Ben: But one of the things actually about the ethnodrama that I am a little conflicted about is I don't know *how* to present the things that they are saying to us. I don't feel that comfortable like—

Maria: [overlap] you don't want to make caricatures out of them—

Ben: [overlap] caricatures and it's also it's just like I feel there's always so many people who are lined up to speak for these kids that I feel a little bit weird doing that. I know that we could probably say like, "Now Ivan said to me …" Working with a population who are regularly disenfranchised and their voice is represented *for* them, I think it's really important that we not *take* their words. I think that's kind of the whole challenge for us to find a way to put their words into our script where it's *their* words and not an interpretation of their words.

Maria: You're making me have a vision of projecting their quotes behind our heads. And it's very Tennessee Williams!

Indicative of a DSE perspective on disability, the group raised concerns about speaking *for* students with disabilities as well as appropriating their words as part of a publicly performed text, debating their right to represent them at all. In the end, the students wrote the ethnodrama using only their own words derived from the transcripts of our group discussions as well as excerpts from the written reflections the group shared with one another following each lesson. Mixed media was integrated into the performance as lesson plan goals were projected on a screen behind the actors along with a few video clips of their work in the classroom. Their performance wrapped up an evening of research presentations to an enthusiastic audience.

In summary, I contend that this case example well illustrates the application of DSE tenets to practice and research as well as the use of an ABR method (ethnodrama) to communicate work in a public forum. Moreover, I believe that this work illustrates the untapped potential of artists and the arts to contribute not only to the education of children with disabilities but also to the education of us all. Imagine the shift that would occur if we were to abandon our desire to "fix" in favor of viewing students with disabilities as "fellow performers, fellow artists" in the classroom.

The Next Act

In this chapter, I argue a case for integrating ABR methods into DSE practice and research. I further posit that arts-based researchers could likewise benefit from the work of DS/DSE scholars. For example, Patricia Leavy (2009), a well-known ABR scholar, writes in her text, *Method Meets Art*:

In addition to facilitating understanding, a common goal in the (re)presentation stage, the place of the researcher in the ethnodramatic script is inextricably linked to the epistemological and theoretical underpinning of the study. For example, scholars working from "power-reflexive" or "power-sensitive" perspectives (Haraway, 1991; Pfohl, 1994) such as critical theory, queer studies, feminism, critical race theory, postcolonialism, poststructuralism, and postmodernism may be particularly attentive to how power operates in part via the researcher's choices with respect to disclosure and authority. (p. 148)

Notably, there is no reference to DS or DSE within the examples of "power-reflexive" or "power-sensitive" perspectives. In light of the connections outlined in this chapter between ABR and DSE, I contend that a collaboration among these Special Interest Groups (SIG) within the American Educational Research Association (AERA) could yield interesting conversation and open possibilities for collaborative work.

In considering how to move forward in the integration of ABR methods, I would like to highlight the differences between the two case examples presented in this chapter. In the first example, interview data is (re)presented through mixed ABR methods: readers' theatre, ethnodrama, and visual images. In contrast, the second example (re)presents through ethnodrama the *process* of "artists as researchers" working in the field. It seems there is much to explore beyond performing data. For example, Norris (2000) suggests that "drama can serve as a complete research activity, with the potential to serve as a method of data collection, analysis, and (re)presentation" (p. 45). The work done by the three educational theatre students is an example of what Leavy (2009) describes:

> In addition to serving as a method for investigating and representing the experiences and perspectives of various groups, performance ethnography can also serve as a vehicle for addressing the research process itself, that is, how the knowledge-building process unfolds, including how it is experienced by the researcher and others involved. (p. 151)

Moreover, I believe that applied theatre (described earlier in this chapter) holds promise as a method for engaging both actors and audience (e.g., students with and without disabilities, families, teachers, administrators, and auxiliary personnel) in exploring issues of disability, inclusion, and access within their own communities.

Clearly, there is much to explore in integrating ABR and DSE. I close this chapter with words about the relationship between art and disability in a journal entry written by a current student in the Inclusive Practices in the Arts class:

> Before this class, disability was uncharted ground for me. It was unnamed. I have explored ideas of age discrimination, gender bias, racism, not enough but at least some. Without knowing it, I had ignored disability totally while living with it all

around me. I now view the world quite differently. As Mat Fraser [a well-known disabled performance artist from the U.K.] so succinctly and movingly put it in his interview [shown in class], it gives us the opportunity to discuss, talk about our discomfort, look, see differently and ultimately accept the "beautiful and beastly" in all of us. The artist tries to portray and bring an understanding and meaning to the human experience, and what is that human experience without everything and everyone who is part of the human experience? It is not just about some of us. It is about all of us. So reflecting the experience of all of us is exactly what art is there to do. It is always pushing boundaries, exposing the truth, reflecting back at society what society is doing, making sense of the world's petty problems by turning them into art. So without disability included, the art is incomplete.

—Janet Girardeau (2014)

References

Butler-Kisber, L. (2010). *Qualitative inquiry: Thematic, narrative and arts-informed perspectives*. London: Sage.

Cahnmann-Taylor, M., & Siegesmund, R. (Eds.) (2008). *Arts-based research in education*. New York: Routledge.

Couser, G. T. (2009). *Signifying bodies: Disability in contemporary life writing*. Ann Arbor, MI: University of Michigan Press.

Eisner, E. (2002). *The arts and the creation of mind*. New Haven, CT: Yale University Press.

Greenwood (2005). *Playing with curriculum. Drama for junior classes.* Invercargil: Essential Resources.

Greenwood, J. (2012). Arts-based research: Weaving magic and meaning. *International Journal of Education & the Arts, 13*(Interlude 1). Retrieved from http://www.ijea. org/v13i1/

Haraway, D. (1991). *Simians, cyborgs, and women: The reinvention of nature*. New York: Routledge.

Knowles, J. G., & Cole, A. L. (Eds.) (2008). *Handbook of the arts in qualitative research*. Thousand Oaks, CA: Sage.

Langellier, K. M., & Peterson, E. E. (2006). Shifting contexts in personal narrative performance. In D. S. Madison & J. Hamera (Eds.), *The Sage handbook of performance studies* (pp. 151–168). Thousand Oaks, CA: Sage.

Leavy, P. (2009). *Method meets art: Arts-based research practices*. New York: Guilford Press.

Lewis, V. A. (2006). *Beyond victims and villains: Contemporary plays by disabled playwrights*. New York: Theater Communication Group.

McNiff, S. (2008). Art-based research. In J. G. Knowles & A. L. Cole (Eds.), *Handbook of the arts in qualitative research*, pp. 29–40.

Miller, C., & Saxton, J. (2004). *Into the story: Language in action through drama*. Portsmouth, NH: Heinemann.

Norris, J. (2000). Drama as research: Realizing the potential of drama in education as a research methodology. *Youth Theatre Journal, 14,* 40–51.

O'Neill, C. (1995). *Drama worlds: A framework for process drama.* Portsmouth, NH: Heinemann.

Prendergast, M., & Saxton, J. (2009). *Applied theatre.* Chicago, IL: Intellect, University of Chicago Press.

Pfohl, S. (1994). *Images of deviance and social control: A sociological history.* New York: McGraw-Hill.

Saldana, J. (1999). Playwriting with data: Ethnographic performance texts. *Youth Theatre Journal, 14,* 60–70.

Saldana, J. (2003). Dramatizing data: A primer. *Qualitative Inquiry, 9*(2), 218–236.

Saldana, J. (2008). Ethnodrama and ethnotheatre. In J. G. Coles & A. L. Knowles (Eds.). *Handbook of the arts in qualitative research* (pp. 195–207). Thousand Oaks: CA: Sage.

Sandahl, C., & Auslander, P. (Eds.). (2005). *Bodies in commotion: Disability & performance.* Ann Arbor, MI: University of Michigan Press.

Sinner, A., Leggo, C, Irwin, R., Gouzouasis, P., & Grauer, K. (2006). Arts-based research dissertations: Reviewing the practices of new scholars. *Canadian Journal of Education, 29*(4), 1223–1270.

Snyder, S. L., Brueggemann, B. J., & Garland-Thomson, R. G. (Eds.). (2002). *Disability studies: Enabling the humanities.* New York: Modern Language Association of America.

Valle, J. W. (2009). *What mothers say about special education: From the 1960s to the present.* New York: Palgrave.

Valle, J., & Connor, D. (2012). Becoming theatrical: Performing narrative research, staging visual representation. *International Journal of Education and the Arts, 13* (LAI 1). Retrieved from http://www.ijea.org/v13lai1/

Ware, L. (2008). Worlds remade: Inclusion through engagement with disability art. *International Journal of Inclusive Education, 12*(5/6), 563–583.

Ware, L. (2011). When arts informs: Inviting ways to see the unexpected. *Learning Disability Quarterly, 34*(3), 194–202.

5. "It was just like a piece of gum": Using an Intersectional Approach to Understand Criminalizing Young Women of Color With Disabilities in the School-to-Prison Pipeline

SUBINI ANCY ANNAMMA

"The prison therefore functions ideologically as an abstract site into which undesirables are deposited, relieving us of the responsibility of thinking about the real issues afflicting those communities from which prisoners are drawn in such disproportionate numbers."

—Angela Davis (2003, p. 16)

In speaking of race, gender, sexuality, and social class, Goodwin (2003) writes, "Each of these social constructs in itself and of itself rendered a subordinate and arguably punishable status on the individual. Often those who were labeled mentally ill were racialized (i.e., black), gendered (i.e., female), sexualized (i.e., homosexual or promiscuous), or simply poor, and no amount of 'treatment' could change or alter those social positions" (p. 230). In framing her perspective, Goodwin illustrated how women who are socially constructed with multiple subordinated identities became more susceptible to punishment. It is worth noting that women and girls' interactions with punishment often occur in the private sphere, under such conditions as domestic violence, drug use, and sexual abuse (Belknap, 2007; Richie, 2012). However, conceptualizing women's issues as exclusively private overlooks the fact the women and girls can and do experience violence and domination within the *public* sphere at the hands of the state (Ritchie, 2006).

For young people of color, racialized state violence often occurs in schools via what is known as the School-to-Prison Pipeline (referred to here as "the Pipeline") (Winn, 2011). The Pipeline is conceptualized as the "prioritization of incarceration over education,"[1] and is enacted when schools look and feel more like prisons than institutions dedicated to learning through a reliance on such things as policing, ticketing, disciplinary exclusion, metal detectors, fencing, and police dogs (American Civil Liberties Union, n.d.). Although much of the Pipeline literature has focused on males, girls of color are experiencing increased interactions within this phenomenon (Morris, 2012). In this chapter I ask: What are the mechanisms for moving young women of color with multiple marginalized identities into the School-to-Prison Pipeline, thereby constructing them as criminal?

Intersections and the Pipeline

In public schools, both disciplinary actions and assignment within special education programs have shown a relationship with future incarceration (Kim, Losen, & Hewitt, 2010; Meiners, 2007). Young women as a whole are underrepresented in disciplinary actions and special education, but young women of color are overrepresented in both (Oswald, Coutinho, & Best, 2002; Stearns & Glennie, 2006). Additionally, young women who identify as queer are at higher risk for punishment than their heterosexual counterparts and are therefore more susceptible to public school actions that steer them into the Pipeline (Himmelstein & Brückner, 2011; Meiners, 2011). It follows, then, that queer young women of color with disabilities may be extremely vulnerable to being routed into the Pipeline.

An Intersectional Theoretical Framework

In order to better understand the highly vulnerable position of queer young women of color with disabilities, I utilized an intersectional framework of theories and methodologies. I agree with Meiners (2011) who recognizes that "[g]ender, socio-economic status, race, and other categorical markers are co-constructed and these relationships must be visible in theoretical analysis of disposable youth or those targeted for warehousing, and in all intervention practices and resistance work" (p. 73). Guided by these thoughts, I relied upon Critical Race Theory (CRT) and its branches, Disability Critical Race Theory (DisCrit), and Queer Crit, to construct an intersectional analysis that renders visible what these queer young women of color with disabilities are subjected to and how they are educated within the Pipeline (Annamma, Connor, & Ferri, 2013; Crenshaw, Gotanda, Peller, & Thomas, 1995;

Misawa, 2010). Combining these theories provides a framework within which to explore how allegedly "neutral" policies and pedagogy create compulsory standards of whiteness, able-bodiedness, and heterosexuality, and how such normative standards mark girls as manifesting biological deficits within their bodies and minds that then are understood as "medical conditions" (Delgado & Stefancic, 2001; McRuer, 2006; Watts & Erevelles, 2004). Thus, my conceptual framework recognizes the social construction of race, sexual identity, and disability as society's response to differences from the norm and, importantly, identifies the material consequences of those constructed multiple identities. This approach is intended to reject a uni-dimensional analysis that limits the understanding of how multiple subordinated identities interact in complex ways (Crenshaw, 1993; Solórzano & Bernal, 2001). In other words, such a framework troubles monolithic understandings of identity in favor of the kind of deep analysis that an intersectional understanding of race, sexual and gender identities, and disability can provide (Ferri & Connor, 2009; Lorde, 1984; Solórzano & Yosso, 2002). Finally, I argue that my focus on authentic counter-narratives that contrast to "the master narrative" is likewise compatible with an intersectional framework (Matsuda, 1987).

In a current master narrative about young women, the dominant discourse is rife with hysteria about the rise of the "bad girl," a modern female who is more violent than in the past—despite little evidence to support such a phenomenon (Males, 2010). This master narrative depicts young women of color in urban schools as more dangerous than their white peers and more deserving of incarceration (Chesney-Lind & Jones, 2010). It further positions young women of color as gender non-conforming (Morris, 2012), and queer women of color as dangerous lesbians "out for blood," even when simply defending themselves from physical or institutional attacks (Miller, 2014). Thus, an analytical approach that emphasizes intersectionality and counter-narratives provides an opportunity to view these girls not as inherently bad or naturally violent, but as thoughtful young women constantly maneuvering through dangerous situations. Such an approach allowed me to *center* the voices of historically marginalized young women in order to understand not only the ways that hegemony is enacted, but also the ways in which these young women resist institutional racism, heteronormativism, and ableism.

Exploring Constructions of Criminal

Constructions of criminal are often based on race, heteronormativity, and ability (Davis, 2003; Kim et al., 2010; Mogul, Ritchie & Whitlock, 2011). Schools play a large part in this criminalization, pathologizing those who do not fit into the norms on which American public education was built:

the white, the heterosexual or "straight," the able-bodied. Schools further perpetuate inequities by ignoring students as victims of violence and viewing them instead only as perpetrators (Rios, 2011). Yet, many young girls of color are required daily to negotiate conflict and violence in order to survive (Jones, 2009). Breakdowns of education, health care, and policing result in lack of protection for many young women of color, but these facts are largely ignored by educators when discipline is enforced (Winn, 2011). Instead, these students recognize that most teachers are unfair and discriminatory in applying discipline, usually missing the meaning and nuances of specific situations (Sheets, 2002). Conversely, a teacher who takes a relational approach to discipline, one characterized by care and attention, has less need to enact disciplinary measures in the classroom (Gregory & Ripsky, 2008). In particular, it has been noted that supportive school staff can provide a sense of safety for queer students of color who face threats from students and adults in schools (Diaz & Kosciw, 2009).

As stated elsewhere, this chapter examines how marginalized intersectional identities of young women—race, special education status, and sexual orientation—co-construct them as criminal via the everyday practices of schools. It is not my intention to stack marginalized identities on top of one another, but rather to recognize ways in which systems of oppression interact (Annamma, Morrison, & Jackson, in press).

Research Context and Methodology

As a former special education teacher in a large urban high school, I observed that many of my students, the majority of whom were students of color, would disappear for weeks at a time and then come back and tell me, "Ms., I was in juvie" (short for juvenile hall) or "I got suspended, ticketed, and arrested, Ms." I began to realize that my students were missing school because of incarceration, often for incidents that happened in school. Later in my career, when I taught in the juvenile incarceration system, I found that many of the youth there were also of color, had disabilities, and identified as queer. Working in both systems, public education and juvenile incarceration, I was reminded daily of the intelligence displayed by many of my students and saddened at the lack of acknowledgment given to their abilities. Many of my girls were gender non-conforming and these students were positioned instead as failures through pathologization and criminalization. As a woman of color who identifies as straight and cis-gendered (my gender identity matches my gender performance), and teaches students classified as disabled, I wanted to understand how adolescent girls of color in public schools who identified as queer experienced criminalization, what contributed to it, and how they resisted it.

This chapter highlights the voices of young women of color who self-identify as sexually fluid or lesbian; the term *queer* will be used for all. Culling from a larger study that took place in two juvenile incarceration settings in a large Western state,[2] participants were included in this study if they identified as queer and of color, and met the study's definition of disabled (had been in, were currently in, or could qualify for special education services as nominated by staff). The five participants range from 14 to 20 years of age; and two identified as African American, two as Latina, and one as Native American. The doubly sensitive nature of some students' status (under 18 and incarcerated) results in details about the girls and the institutions in which they were incarcerated being purposefully vague. In order to access their thoughts and lived experiences, I utilized methodological pluralism, a "strategy of data collection and analysis to document how change and discontinuity, braided with a desire for narrative coherence and consistency, shape the stories young people tell about themselves, over time and space" (Katsiaficas, Futch, Fine, & Sirin, 2011, p. 120). Accordingly, this study included: in-depth interviews with school and security staff (19) and students (34), classroom observations (105), document analysis (40), and participant data analysis (Katsiaficas et al., 2011).

To answer the research question, I sifted data throughout the collection process and included participant analysis whenever possible. Erickson (2006) notes how we can study down, up, or side by side, and each of these choices signifies our deeper commitments. Studying down often leaves unexplored those who have privilege and power. Studying up alleviates this problem, yet it can still ignore asymmetrical power relations between the researcher and subject. Studying side by side attempts to transform the subject to a participant, if not a partner. Though studying side by side did not alleviate asymmetries in power in this study, it altered them to some extent by making them more transparent. In mining the data, the participants made connections that I had not.

I constructed the data set top down from the literature and bottom up from the raw data, looking for patterns to confirm and disconfirm evidence, generating conceptual categories, developing a code thesaurus, and engaging in frequency counts (Erickson, 1998). I refined my codes by continually returning to the data before settling on final codes that were used to systematically explore the data for atypicality (Glaser & Strauss, 1967). I then selected quotes representative of the common experiences of the young women at different points of the Pipeline, as well as distinct events that represented each participant's individual experiences.

Findings

For purposes of clarification, my use of "criminalization" captures the transition from punishment of behaviors to the start of legal ramifications for behaviors. The study revealed three major mechanisms for moving bodies from sites of education to sites of incarceration: a cycle of (1) labeling, (2) surveillance, and (3) punishment. Each of these mechanisms made young women of color more vulnerable to juvenile incarceration.

Labeling

Labeling, defined here as the formal or informal naming of a student with an identity (e.g., race, gender, sexual identity, sexual expression, ability or disability), appeared to have an impact upon an eventual construction as criminal. Formally, participants experienced disability labeling, gender labeling, and racial labeling by teachers, psychologist, administrators, and other school personnel. Informally, they were subject to labels describing their behaviors, gender expression, and identities by adults and peers in schools.

Individualized Education Plans (IEPs) and other school records contained information about race, gender, and disability. It is noteworthy that, in the case of these young women, racial and gender labeling was often taken from other school documents and rarely discussed with the student. Moreover, it seemed the disability label functioned as an artifact that mediated how teachers treated the participants. For example, Esperanza shared how she believed her disability label functioned as a tool for the teacher: "When they would do stuff with the class and stuff she would like send me to the special ed place so I couldn't do the stuff that they were doing." Esperanza believed that the label allowed her teachers to monitor her closely and send her away whenever they did not want her present (Annamma, 2014). When adolescent girls are already monitored because they are of color and of a "lower" social class, *and* they receive a disability label, then the degree of surveillance intensifies, along with the likelihood of an increased risk of punishment.

Raniqua reported that increased surveillance ironically did not result in the academic support she needed, as evidenced in our interchange below:

SAA: Were you in special ed classes growing up?
Raniqua: Yeah, I was.
SAA: And did you think being in special ed classes was better than being in regular classes?
Raniqua: No, because you would think that being in special ed classes you'd get more one-on-one help, but it didn't. At 19, I'm barely getting my high school diploma because I didn't have enough credits, English credits at that.

Raniqua recognized that, in theory, special education is supposed to provide individual help, but in practice she did not receive that academic support. Therefore, she experienced the association of increased surveillance with limited progress within the academic realm.

Labeling occurred informally when some students were also branded as troublemakers or as having behavior problems. Miakoda remembers that once a teacher identified her behavior as problematic, they were in constant conflict:

SAA: So when you had this conflict with your teacher, afterwards did you get suspended or expelled from school?
Miakoda: I got suspended a few times.
SAA: Do you remember what it was for? With peers or teacher?
Miakoda: It was with my teacher, mostly with my teacher.
SAA: Any specific incident.
Miakoda: Uh uh. I just remember like she was making me write papers, writing one sentence over and over and over and over and it was just really frustrating.

Miakoda's quote illustrates two things: (1) the impact of labeling upon increased punishment; and (2) the influence of certain types of punishment leading to an increase in "problematic" behaviors leading to more labeling, surveillance, and punishment. Once positioned as having a behavior problem by her teacher, Miakoda was consistently monitored and punished. The latter point will be explored more fully in the punishment section below.

Words like "faggot," "dyke," "retarded," "stupid," "dumb," and other sexuality- and disability-based slurs are commonly used in schools (Diaz & Kosciw, 2009). All five queer young women of color with disabilities mentioned hearing terms like "gay," "retarded," and "faggot" directed toward them throughout their schooling. Raniqua talked about her identification as a lesbian and the harassment she experienced:

I think about it is, I see it this way, to me it doesn't really matter. Like, yeah, it sucks when gay pride comes to have all those idiots talking down to you and stuff. Like it sucks to get talked about and labeled as sinning or something, you know, but I just see it as life. I love going to Pride anyway. I get to be around people like me.

Raniqua shares the impact of being harassed in schools by peers because of her gender expression and sexual identity. However, this labeling came not only from peers but also from teachers. In a document analysis of education records, files included the terms "trouble maker," "mannish," "masculine features," and "aggressive behavior." Many times these terms were linked together in paragraphs as if being non-conforming to standards of femininity made one more likely to be problematic in behavior and in need of surveillance.

Surveillance

Surveillance is the act of closely monitoring a student for non-conformity in identity, academic performance, or behaviors. In schools, such scrutiny often leads to punishment and labeling, which in turn leads to more surveillance. Ieofemah described surveillance in her classes:

> Ieofemah: There's this really, really mean teacher …
> SAA: What made her mean?
> Ieofemah: Yeah. Like because she's always, she'll be on me about anything. [Mimicking adult voice] Why you sitting like that? Why you looking at me like that? Why you talking to her? You know, she's a bad influence. [Laughs] The person I'm talking to is not a bad influence, you know? [The teacher's] just mean.

As a young woman of color who did not fit traditional gender norms and had a special education label, Ieofemah recognized how some teachers targeted her for observation and potential punishment. Vittoria shares how she could tell when she was being observed by teachers and how it impacted her behavior:

> Vittoria: When like people around me are looking, like I don't like feeling like a punk. Or like embarrassed.
> SAA: What does that mean?
> Vittoria: Like I don't know, it feels like they are taking away my dignity or something or my pride. And I'm like, oh no, this is not going to happen.
> SAA: So a lot of it is either getting involved if somebody is disrespecting you?
> Vittoria: Yeah, and I don't like that. It feels like, I gotta do something.

Here, she described a process wherein her own awareness about increased surveillance by teachers and her reaction to it subsequently led to punishment. In a similar manner, Raniqua shared how actions at school also led to punishment from other agencies:

> SAA: Were you first [in the Department of Family Support]?
> Raniqua: Yes.
> SAA: So you did not commit a crime then?
> Raniqua: [Shakes her head] Then I kept messing up. I kept running and getting more charges.
> SAA: When you were [in the Department of Family Support] did you get taken away from your mom?
> Raniqua: Yeah.
> SAA: Why?
> Raniqua: From my behaviors, not going to school.
> SAA: Your mom wasn't neglecting you?
> Raniqua: No.
> SAA: So then you got [in the Department of Family Support] and they started sending you away and you kept running away and got committed?
> Raniqua: Yeah.

SAA: Did you have a particular thing that you got committed for?
Raniqua: No, just violation of probation. Just kept violating it.

Although truancy is concerning, the focus on punishment did not solve Raniqua's truancy issues. Removal from her home led Raniqua to run away from out-of-home placements, resulting in her arrest and subsequent criminalization. Interestingly, four of the five participants stated that running away led to their first encounters with criminalization. Raniqua's story illustrates ways in which school surveillance can serve as an entry into criminalization. Removing Raniqua from her home did not solve her truancy, but rather led to criminalization.

Surveillance exists not only within the domain of teachers, but also within the domain of peers. Miakoda shares how she experienced racial surveillance as a Native American in a predominantly White school:

Miakoda: Middle school, for seventh grade I went to a Catholic school. Uh, I did not like it. I was the only one who was dark skinned cuz in the summer, I get really, really dark. And all them White kids did not understand me. And I was like, oh my god. Mom, what are you doing to me? Please just take me out of this school. So then I got through it somehow. I did not like nobody. I didn't like none of the teachers. I did not do none of their Catholic school work, I was not doing it.
SAA: You didn't have any friends there?
Miakoda: Just one other girl, I had like one friend.
SAA: And was she also a person of color?
Miakoda: [Yes], she was Mexican and she was one grade ahead of me.
SAA: At the elementary school you went to, were there more people of color?
Miakoda: Yes, there was a lot. So imagine going from that to a Catholic school. I was like, even though I'm Catholic, I'm not doing this.

Miakoda tells a story of being racially harassed in a predominantly White school. Queer students of color in schools with a majority-White student body are more likely to be harassed for their race (Kosciw & Diaz, 2006). Particularly, Native American students who identify as queer are more likely to bullied for their religion (Diaz & Kosciw, 2009). In the following excerpt from Miakoda's story, she reveals an example of how queer young women of color with disabilities are highly susceptible to bullying and harassment:

I started getting bullied by some of the girls and I didn't let them bully me, so I just didn't want to go to school anymore. They were like are you trying to step up to us? And I was like, yeah, cuz you are not going to push me around and think you can have my lunch and things. Uh uh. You crazy. I really didn't like going to school after that. I was like, I don't want to go anymore.

Once she began fighting back against the bullies, Miakoda was immediately punished, triggering her criminalization. In sum, surveillance became a mechanism for criminalization in both direct ways (Raniqua) and indirect ways (Ieofemah, Viattoria, Miakoda).

Punishment

Punishment is conceptualized as providing formal or informal consequences to a student who has engaged in an undesirable behavior. As evidenced from the excerpts above, punishment does not happen in a vacuum but rather is directly linked to both labeling and surveillance. Moreover, punishment meted out as a result of surveillance and labeling appears to lead to *increased* labeling and surveillance. Ieofemah remembers several incidents of punishment once she was labeled:

> Ieofemah: I got suspended for telling a mean teacher to shut her fat mouth … She just always pointed out the negative stuff, you know instead of focusing on the positive stuff that I was doing.
> SAA: Did you feel that she just kind of went after you when you weren't doing well?
> Ieofemah: Um hmmm. Or she would catch me off guard, where I'm like, just sitting down and tying my shoe and she'll go off.
> SAA: So even at times when you don't feel like you're doing anything wrong, even?
> Ieofemah: Um hmm. Like sit down and tying my shoe.

Ieofemah felt that the teacher was targeting her, so she argued about the degree of scrutiny that she was subjected to—leading to more punishment and more surveillance. Viattoria shares how she began to manipulate punishment to fit her own goals of getting out of school.

> Viattoria: Yeah, and I was too, you know. I would go to school and they'd send me to detention or I'd get myself in detention.
> SAA: What do you mean by that?
> Viattoria: Like I'd tell the teacher you're stupid or something. Then [me and my friends] would all go to detention and we'd have heavy jackets and we'd sit there and smoke because there was no teacher.
> SAA: There was no teacher? And you would just like hang out and get high?
> Viattoria: Yeah, in the school.

Viattoria's savvy and ingenuity allows her to take a mechanism of criminalization and use it for her own ends. Of course, this ultimately did not serve her interests because she became increasingly criminalized within the Pipeline. Viatorria's experience echoes the point made earlier by Miakoda that certain types of punishment can lead to increased behaviors leading to more labeling, surveillance, and punishment—resulting in a vicious circle. If increased punishment is not linked to behavior (Miakoda) or when punishment is used for containment (Viattoria), the focus shifts away from learning.

Finally, punishment occurred not only through detention but also the process of ticketing.

SAA:	What did you get tickets for?
Miakoda:	I got a ticket for disorderly conduct.
SAA:	Disorderly conduct, was that for fighting or disrespecting?
Miakoda:	Fighting in school.
SAA:	Were all of your tickets for in-school stuff?
Miakoda:	Um hmm.

In this instance, Miakoda shares how punishment through tickets issued by police in school led directly to criminalization.

Participant response to labeling, surveillance, and punishment
Being subjected to the process of criminalization did not mean that non-confirmative identity expression, achievement, or behaviors were curtailed. Instead, the participants reported responding in creative ways. For example, they never passively accepted the actions of school personnel. Viattoria recalls how she lashed out physically when her girlfriend was assaulted by an administrator.

Viattoria:	It was crazy though. I just got, like one time, I was going with this person and the teacher, the principal, he hit her. Like he pushed her.
SAA:	He pushed a student?
Viattoria:	Yeah and I was going out with that person at that time so then I got really mad and I started pushing him and then I got suspended for like, two weeks.
SAA:	Yeah, for pushing a teacher?
Viattoria:	But he pushed a student though.
SAA:	Yeah, that's messed up. Did he file charges against you or did you just get suspended?
Viattoria:	No. He didn't file charges but I just got suspended. And she was like on the ground and I was like oh my god.

Viattoria's story suggests that queer young women of color with disabilities are not safe in schools and that threat can come from both adults and peers. Ieofemah also tells a story about responding to punishment,

Yeah. I always had good grades but I couldn't do it being put back in my mom's home and taken out. So, a couple, a month of being at the school, I was like I can't take this anymore, I haven't seen my mom yet, I need to go see my mom. So I bolted. I was out. I went to go see my mom and she didn't know I was on the run. I was like telling her everything that the caseworker came to school and started telling my teachers. Which was a whole bunch of lies and stuff and I was like alright, I need to let my mom know this. And at the time, I was smart. I had a cell phone on me that wasn't turned on because the service just got cut off. And I recorded everything that she had said and then I took it to my mom and let her listen to it.

Ieofemah's story is one of being targeted for surveillance and punishment with her word being considered against an adult's word. Knowing that she would not be taken seriously without proof, she employed technology to record her caseworker's report to her teachers. Esperanza's response to punishment was one of suspicion:

SAA: When things started going downhill, did anyone try to help? Were there teachers or anyone who asked what was going on with you?
Esperanza: No. Cuz that's none of y'all business. I would be like what the fuck you mean? Stay out of my business because teachers, they're cop callers. But then when you need cops, they're nowhere to be found.

Esperanaza's attitude may seem harsh, but considered within the context of constant scrutiny and punishment, it becomes more comprehensible. In sum, having to negotiate multiple deficit-based discourses both in and out of school, these queer young women of color with disabilities grow suspicious of who and what to trust, taking steps to protect themselves against efforts to construct them as criminal.

Discussion

The conceptual framework used here—CRT, DisCrit, and Queer Crit—demands attention be given to ways that "neutral" policies and pedagogy create compulsory standards of whiteness, able-bodiedness, and heterosexuality. Through the mechanisms of surveillance, labeling, and punishment, these "non-biased" policies and pedagogical practices contribute to a cycle that can construct young queer women of color with disabilities as criminal. Their identities are likely to prompt negative responses as their "embodiment" in the world differs from the norms of schooling, leading to a criminalization process. Figure 1 illustrates the cycle of criminalization created by these three interlocking domains that serve to reify the School-to-Prison Pipeline.

Simply stated, this cycle of criminalization is built on largely unquestioned normative standards, and the more standards a student violates, the more vulnerable she is to being perceived as—and then shaped into—a criminal.

Queer theorists Mogul, Ritchie, and Whitlock (2011) note, "Normative sexualities and gender expressions, alone or in combination with markers of race and class, have also informed the manner in which different instances of similar conduct are interpreted" (p. 209). In this study, their words were affirmed. Young women of color with disabilities who did not express normative femininity or sexuality were often criminalized in schools. They reported being subjected to a constellation of aggressions, including slurs about their race, disability labels, and sexual orientation. In addition, they were labeled in

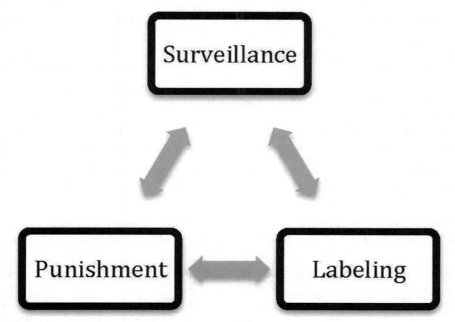

Figure 1. The Cycle of Criminalization.

educational files regarding their sexual identity and expression. Furthermore, several participants provided accounts of having been verbally and physically assaulted in schools by peers and supervising adults. Considering that a LGBTQ-inclusive curriculum is also absent from most students' lives, we see how such adolescent girls are not just ignored but also violently dominated within and erased from schools via surveillance, labeling, and punishment (Kosciw & Diaz, 2006. The queer young women of color with disabilities in this study faced an educational context wherein they were ignored in the curricula, unsupported in the classroom, and harassed in the halls. Such an environment contributes to the construction of these young women as potential criminals, currently beyond help and needing to be contained. Viattoria described being criminalized in this way: "It was just like a piece of gum, you know when you step on it and it follows you? It followed me." What is important to note here is that Viattoria was aware that once she was entered into the cycle of surveillance, labeling, and punishment, she could not escape.

Implications for Transformative Schooling

Ways to disrupt the Pipeline must be imagined through intersectional analyses (Meiners, 2011). In this study, adolescent girls were subjected to the cycle of criminalization via state domination, erasure, and violence because they violated the pervasive, multiple standards of normativity. If we are to craft education for students with multidimensional identities, we must explore multidimensional solutions to create what I am calling "transformative schooling."

Critical pedagogy

Critical pedagogy, as described by Duncan-Andrade and Morrell (2008), consists of teaching children core academic skills that allow them to access postsecondary education and careers, while simultaneously striving

> to create spaces for students to learn as they also embrace and develop affirmed and empowered identities as intellectuals, as urban youth, and as members of historically marginalized ethnic groups. (p. 18)

To expand on this definition of critical pedagogy, I would add that public education must take into account not only students' ethnic and cultural backgrounds, but more importantly their intersectional identities that make them more vulnerable to oppression than belonging to any one group alone. This type of pedagogy should be rooted in students' lives, recognizing their multidimensional identities, and centering those identities in the pedagogy (Lorde, 1984). I argue that race, sexual identity and expression, ability and disability should be highlighted and discussed in the curriculum, learned by all, and built upon as strengths (Freire, 1970). Moreover, training teachers in critical pedagogy would allow them to resist current normative standards, become more aware of the ways these hegemonic ideals play out in schools, and conceptualize differences as strengths. Critical pedagogy, deeply rooted in concepts of social justice, must attend to both developing academic skills and raising critical consciousness among youth so they can confront the inequities they face both in and outside of schooling (Delpit, 1995; Ladson-Billings, 1995). Ultimately, this type of pedagogy must challenge dominant ideologies in both pedagogical philosophy and practice (Misawa, 2010).

Restorative and transformative justice principles

Implementation of culturally relevant pedagogy should significantly reduce the need for disciplinary actions because school will become more relevant to students' lives; however, it should be noted that culturally relevant pedagogy will not reduce all conflicts that occur in schools because students contend with state violence and domination outside of schools. As teachers go through a process of unlearning hegemonic norms, conflicts may continue to arise in schools. It is recommended to respond to conflict by moving toward restorative and transformative justice instead of punishment (Amstutz

& Mullet, 2005; Harris, 2006; Zehr, 2002). Restorative justice seeks to collaboratively recognize the purpose of problematic behaviors, address the needs of both the harmed and the student who harmed by "putting right" the harm in order to heal (Banner et al., 2012). Transformative justice frameworks build on the foundations of restorative justice. The focus is not only on individual acts that violate communities and cause harm, but also on the ways systems perpetuate inequities and how such inequities impact behaviors (Morris, 2000).

Transformative schools
Combining these concepts into a framework requires educators to address multidimensional issues including the following: (1) practice critical pedagogy and confront systemic inequities while building academic skills; (2) address the individual harm done to a community (restorative justice); and (3) examine what systemic inequities contributed to the individual harm and address those inequities through pedagogy (transformative) (See Figure 2).

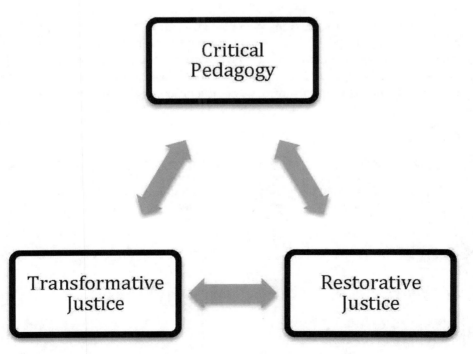

Figure 2. Transformative Schools Framework.

Ideally, this framework could replace the mechanisms that construct students with multiple subordinated identities as criminal and instead envision them as change agents in their own schools and communities.

Conclusion

This chapter illustrates the way disability studies in education (DSE) can be used as a significant force within a conceptual framework in research. Conceptual frameworks have the power to shape all aspects of study from the theories we center, to the research questions we pose, to the methods we utilize (Ravitch & Riggan, 2012). In other words, DSE is more than a theoretical ideology; it is a flexible and useful tool in empirical research that allowed me to bring different questions, theories, and methods to bear within research. In this particular case, I utilized DSE in the form of DisCrit-aligned with CRT and Queer Crit in order to create space for theorizing across disciplines and highlighting intersectionality within specific counter-narratives. Using DSE allowed me to refuse oversimplified conceptualizations of The Pipeline as simply a gender (e.g., male) problem or a race (e.g., African American) problem, leading me instead to consider the ways The Pipeline is enacted for girls with multiple marginalized identities (Annamma et al., 2013). Although I recognize that even multidimensional solutions within education cannot solve the structural inequities that students face on their own, I contend that such an educational orientation does have the potential to reduce the flow of the School-to-Prison Pipeline. At this point in our history, that is a necessary and essential goal.

Notes

1. State violence occurs for girls in other social service agencies as well as neoliberal policies that directly feed the Pipeline, which is part of the trend towards mass incarceration (Alexander, 2010; Díaz-Strong & Meiners, 2007). However, for the purposes of this chapter, I will focus on ways education institutions perpetuate state violence on and domination over young women of color with disabilities.
2. All names of places, institutions, and people are intentionally vague or pseudonyms designed to protect the anonymity of the participants.

References

Alexander, M. (2010). *The new Jim Crow: Mass incarceration in the age of colorblindness.* New York: The New Press.

American Civil Liberties Union (n.d.). School to Prison Pipeline: Talking points. Retrieved from https://www.aclu.org/files/assets/stpp_talkingpoints.pdf

Amstutz, L. S., & Mullet, J. H. (2005). *The little book of restorative discipline for schools: Teaching responsibility, creating caring climates.* Intercourse, PA: Good Books.

Annamma, S. A. (2014, March 31). Disabling juvenile justice: Engaging the stories of incarcerated young women of color with disabilities. *Remedial and Special Education.* doi: 10.1177/0741932514526785

Annamma, S. A., Connor, D., & Ferri, B. (2013). Dis/ability critical race studies (DisCrit): Theorizing at the intersections of race and dis/ability. *Race Ethnicity and Education, 16*(1), 1–31.

Annamma, S. A., Morrison, D., & Jackson, D. (In press). Disproportionality fills the gaps: Connections between achievement, discipline, and special education in the school-to-prison pipeline. *Berkeley Review of Education.*

Banner, C., Bennett, L., Connors, J., Pai, S., Shanahan, H., & Wadhwa, A. (2012): How can we hold you? Restorative justice in Boston schools. In S. Bahena, N. Cooc, R. Currie-Rubin, P. Kuttner, & M. Ng (Eds.), *Disrupting the school-to-prison pipeline* (pp. 76–89). Cambridge, MA: Harvard Educational Review.

Belknap, J. (2007). *The invisible woman: Gender, crime, and justice* (3rd ed.). Belmont, CA. Thomson Wadsworth.

Chesney-Lind, M., & Jones, N. (Eds.) (2010). *New perspectives on gender and violence* (Kindle edition). New York: State University of New York Press.

Crenshaw, K. (1993). Mapping the margins: Intersectionality, identity politics, and violence against women of color. *Stanford Law Review, 43*, 1241–1299.

Crenshaw, K., Gotanda, N., Peller, G., & Thomas, K. (1995). *Critical race theory: The key writings that formed the movement.* New York: The New Press.

Davis, A. (2003). *Are prisons obsolete?* New York: Seven Stories Press.

Delgado, R., & Stefancic, J. (2001). *Critical race theory: An introduction.* New York: New York University Press.

Delpit, L. (1995). *Other people's children.* New York: The New Press.

Diaz, E. M, & Kosciw, J. G. (2009). *Shared differences: The experiences of lesbian, gay, bisexual, and transgender students of color in our nation's schools.* A report from the Gay, Lesbian and Straight Education Network (GLSEN). Retrieved from http://www.glsen.org/sites/default/files/Shared%20Differences.pdf

Díaz-Strong, D., & Meiners, E. (2007). Residents, alien policies, and resistances: Experiences of undocumented Latina/o students in Chicago's colleges and universities. *InterActions: UCLA Journal of Education and Information Studies, 3*(2).

Duncan-Andrade, J. M. R., & Morrell, E. (2008). *The art of critical pedagogy: Possibilities for moving from theory to practice in urban schools.* New York: Peter Lang.

Erickson, F. (1998). Qualitative research methods for science education. In B. J. Fraser & K. G. Tobin (Eds.), *International handbook on science education* (pp. 1155–1173). Dordrecht, Netherlands: Kluwer.

Erickson, F. (2006). Studying side by side: Collaborative action ethnography in educational research. In G. Spindler & L. Hammond (Eds.), *Innovations in educational ethnography: Theory, methods and results* (pp. 235–257). Mahwah, NJ: Lawrence Erlbaum Associates.

Ferri, B., & Connor, D. (2009). "I was the special ed girl": (En)gendering disability from the standpoint of urban working-class young women of color. *Journal of Gender and Education, 22*(1), 105–121.

Freire, P. (1970). *Pedagogy of the oppressed*. New York: Herder and Herder.

Glaser, B. G., & Strauss, A. L. (1967). *The discovery of grounded theory: Strategies for qualitative research*. Chicago, IL: Aldine.

Goodwin, M. 2003. Gender, race, and mental illness: The case of Wanda Jean Allen. In A. K. Wing (Ed), *Critical race feminism: A reader* (2nd ed.) (pp. 228–237). New York: New York University Press.

Gregory, A., & Ripski, M. (2008). Adolescent trust in teachers: Implications for behavior in the high school classroom. *School Psychology Review, 37*(3), 337–353.

Harris, M. K. (2006). Transformative justice: The transformation of restorative justice. In D. Sullivan & L. Tift (Eds.), *Handbook of restorative justice: A global perspective* (pp. 555–565). New York: Routledge.

Himmelstein, K., & Brückner, H. (2011). Criminal justice and school sanctions against non-heterosexual youth: A national longitudinal study. *Pediatrics, 127*(1), 48–57.

Jones, N. (2009). *Between good and ghetto: African American girls and inner-city violence* (Rutgers Series in Childhood Studies). New Brunswick, NJ: Rutgers University Press.

Katsiaficas, D., Futch, V. A., Fine, M., & Sirin, S. (2011): Everyday hyphens: Exploring youth identities with methodological and analytic pluralism, *Qualitative Research in Psychology, 8*(2), 120–139.

Kim, C., Losen, D., & Hewitt, D. (2010). *The school-to-prison pipeline: Structuring legal reform*. New York: New York University Press.

Kosciw, J. G., & Diaz E. M. (2006). The 2005 National School Climate Survey: The Experiences of Lesbian, Gay, Bisexual and Transgender Youth in our Nation's Schools. New York: GLSEN.

Ladson-Billings, G. (1995). Toward a theory of culturally relevant pedagogy. *American Educational Research Journal, 32*(3), 465–491.

Lorde, A. (1984). *Sister outsider: Essays and speeches by Audre Lorde*. Berkeley, CA: Crossing Press.

Males, M. (2010). Have "girls gone wild"? In M. Chesney-Lind & N. Jones (Eds.), *New perspectives on gender and violence* (pp. 13–32) (Kindle edition). New York: State University of New York Press.

Matsuda, M. (1987). Looking to the bottom: Critical legal studies and reparations. *Harvard Civil Rights-Civil Liberties Law Review, 22*(2), 323–399.

McRuer, R. (2006). *Crip theory: Cultural signs of queerness and disability*. New York: New York University Press.

Meiners, E. R. (2007). *Right to be hostile: Schools, prisons, and the making of public enemies*. New York: Routledge.

Meiners, E. R. (2011). A queer time and place: Educational analysis and intervention in the prison nation. *Powerplay: A Journal of Educational Justice, 3*(1), 71–86.

Miller, J. (2014). Foreword. In D. Peterson & V. Panfil, *The handbook of LGBT communities, crime, and justice,* New York: Springer.

Misawa, M. (2010). Musings on controversial intersections of positionality: A queer crit perspective in adult and continuing education. In V. Sheared, J. Johnson-Bailey, S. J. Colin III., S. Brookfield, & E. Peterson (Eds.), *The handbook of race and adult education: A resource for dialogue on racism* (pp. 187–200). San Francisco, CA: Jossey-Bass.

Mogul, J. L., Ritchie, A. J., & Whitlock, K. (2011). *Queer (in) justice: The criminalization of LGBT people in the United States.* Boston, MA: Beacon Press.

Morris, R. (Ed.). (2000). *Stories of transformative justice.* Toronto: Canadian Scholars' Press.

Morris, M. (2012). Race, gender, and the School-to-Prison Pipeline: Expanding our discussion to include Black girls. In *African American policy forum. Retrieved from http://aapf.org/wpcontent/uploads/2012/08/Morris-Race-Gender-and-the-School-to-Prison-Pipeline.pdf*

Oswald, D. P., Coutinho, M. J., & Best, A. M. (2002). Community and school predictors of overrepresentation of minority children in special education. In D. Losen & G. Orfield (Eds.), *Racial inequality in special education* (pp. 1–13). Cambridge, MA: Harvard Education Press.

Quinn, M. M., Rutherford, R. B., Leone, P. E., Osher, D. M., & Poirier, J. M. (2005). Youth with disabilities in juvenile corrections: A national survey. *Exceptional Children, 71*(3), 339–345.

Rabaka, R. (2010). *Against epistemic apartheid: W.E.B. Du Bois and the disciplinary decadence of sociology.* Lanham, MD: Lexington Books/Rowman & Littlefield.

Ravitch, Sharon M., & Riggan, Matthew (2012). *Reason & rigor: How conceptual frameworks guide research.* Thousand Oaks: CA: Sage.

Richie, B. (2012). *Arrested justice: Black women, violence, and America's prison nation.* New York: New York University Press.

Rios, V. M. (2011). *Punished: Policing the lives of Black and Latino boys.* New York: New York University Press.

Ritchie, A. J. (2006). Law enforcement violence against women of color. In Incite! Women of color against violence (Eds.), *Color of violence: The Incite! anthology,* (pp. 138–156). Cambridge, MA: South End Press.

Sheets, R. H. (2002). You're just a kid that's there. *Journal of Latinos and Education, 1*(2), 105–122.

Solórzano, D. G., & Bernal, D. D. (2001). Examining transformational resistance through a critical race and latcrit theory framework: Chicana and Chicano students in an urban context. *Urban Education, 36*(3), 308–342.

Solórzano, D. G., & Yosso, T. J. (2002). Critical race methodology: Counter-storytelling as an analytical framework for education research. *Qualitative Inquiry, 8*(1), 23–44.

Spade, D. (2011). *Normal life: Administrative violence, critical politics, and the limits of the law.* Cambridge, MA: South End Press.

Stearns, E., & Glennie, E. J. (2006). When and why dropouts leave high school. *Youth and Society, 38*(1), 29–57.

Watts, I. E., & Erevelles, N. (2004). These deadly times: Reconceptualizing school violence by using critical race theory and disability studies. *American Educational Research Journal, 41*(2), 271–299.

Willen, S. S. (2007). Toward a critical phenomenology of "illegality": State power, criminalization, and objectivity among undocumented migrant workers in Tel Aviv, Israel. *International Migration, 45*(3), 8–38.

Winn, M. (2011) *Girl time: Literacy, justice, and the school-to-prison pipeline.* New York: Teachers College Press.

Zehr, H. (2002). *The little book of restorative justice.* Intercourse, PA: Good Books.

6. *An "In-Betweener" Ethnographer: From Anxiety to Fieldwork Methods in a Cross-Cultural Study of Bilingual Deaf Kindergartners*

Mid-morning on May 5, 2009, Fikriye Kurban, Joe Tobin, and I rendezvous near the Arizona State University campus and drive to central Phoenix where the Phoenix School for the Deaf is located. We make our way quickly through the parking lot in 115-degree desert heat, looking more like journalists than anthropologists with our bulky cameras and tripods, shotgun microphones, and bags of gear in tow. The deaf school, with its Southwest architecture and outdoor hallways, looks to me like any other school in Phoenix that I have ever visited. When we walk through the tinted lobby doors, a woman welcomes us from behind the counter, simultaneously signing and speaking, "Hello, are you here visiting someone?"

"Yes," I say, "we're here to film in Patrick's kindergarten classroom."

Handing over a guest book, she motions for us to fill in our names. People coming in and going out of the lobby look at us curiously. I'm guessing it is the equipment that is catching their attention. Then I realize that *everyone* is signing with one another. Our research team has no way to know what is being said. We are sign-impaired.

I am overcome by shame. I am deaf[1] and the so-called deaf culture expert of the research team, yet I cannot sign much beyond fingerspelling and a handful of words that my fingers awkwardly fumble over. I push my hurt pride aside and occupy my mind with a mental to-do list for the film project.

After getting our guest badges, we make our way through the courtyard, heading south on the school property toward the portable classroom where Patrick is waiting. We struggle down the sidewalk, lugging bulky equipment under a broiling desert sun. When we arrive, Patrick opens the door to a dark, unlit classroom and greets us.

"Well, welcome back, J. V.," he says and signs to me, swinging his arms open for my two guests to also come in. I introduce Fiko and Joe. After a few minutes of small talk using some fingerspelling, some signing, some gesturing, and a good bit of speech reading and speaking, we realize we are running late. We need to set up the cameras in time to capture the routines of the day, starting with the students arriving for school. The three of us grab the video equipment and walk-jog a few hundred meters to the bus drop-off spot where teachers and staff have already begun to gather. Shortly after, students ages 5 to late teens roll in on long, yellow diesel-engine buses. The filming starts with the buses idling near the front of the school and the pace picks up quickly once the students disembark from the buses. Patrick, the lead character in our film, stands near the entry gate greeting kids as they come off their buses. Patrick has charisma. I realize he is the popular teacher on campus. Students of all ages stop to greet him. I begin to wonder if this is because Patrick is big "D" Deaf. Deaf teachers are in the minority on this campus.

Our cameras follow him. I get caught up in the action—angling for positioning, lighting, close-ups of children interacting with one another, shots of Patrick signing and speaking with children and adults, and the hustle and bustle of a predictable school morning. I focus on capturing moments on film that show the routines of daily classroom life as well as moments that appear to me to be atypical, odd, interesting, or provocative. Most often, Patrick is at the center of these filmed moments.

About two hours into filming, a powerful exchange takes place between Patrick and his kindergarten student Angel, so much so that it shakes me abruptly out of the identity I have assumed as a "detached" ethnographer to confront the truth that I am, in fact, an "in-betweener" ethnographer. My fieldnotes, scribbled at the moment of this exchange, hint at the looming tensions that soon will emerge for me:

> Patrick and a student, Angel, are at the front of the room. Patrick signs and speaks, "Okay, Angel, now we're going to ..." Angel cuts him off. Shakes his head quickly, "No ... no ... no." Standing atop a stool by the board, Angel looks into Patrick's eyes. Angel waves his hands over his throat. He makes what seems like a gesture of turning a key, repeating the key turning near his Adam's apple a few times for emphasis, as if he's turning off his voice in protest! But I don't know what Angel means! Frustrating. Something is going on and it's important. I need to ask Patrick about this.

After school lets out that day, I sit down with Patrick and tell him that his exchange with Angel reminds me I am silent in the Deaf world—a world I long to be a part of. Fiko and Joe watch as I steer the interview into the personal realm. I am not sure if they are frustrated with me, being polite, or intrigued by our exchange. However, I am well aware that I am way off task and making this project personal.

I ask Patrick about Angel: "What was I missing? I know it was important. What was going on?"

A knowing grin forms on Patrick's face, as if he knows some deep, dark secret. He does not say too much in front of Fiko and Joe, but he now knows what is fueling my interest in this research project—my identity crisis. In a later interview, Patrick explains:

> I understand your pain, J.V., the pain of many people like you who are searching for your Deaf identity. This [replaying the key-turning movements] means "voice-off"—an in-your-face showing of resistance against using speech. But really, Angel is not declaring that he belongs to Deaf culture. He's saying that he has the ability to do both—speak and sign. Angel can mediate between both the hearing and Deaf worlds. In that exchange at the board and in that moment, he prefers the Deaf world. The "voice-off" is Angel's way of announcing that he prefers to sign, even though he can hear well enough to speak and pass as hearing. Angel heard me speak and he said, "No, no, no, voice-off" and I also took this to mean he values sign language. He's saying, "We belong to Deaf culture, use our language." He is also being Angel, a playful kid.

This "voice-off episode" has and continues to serve as a cautionary tale for me. It discloses my earliest anxieties in conducting fieldwork and the reflexive dilemmas that emerged as a result of being forced to confront my newfound role as an in-betweener ethnographer navigating liminal spaces. It also offers for public view my memorable first slips as an untested ethnographer unfamiliar with sign language as well as the romanticized ideas about deaf culture that I held. Looking back on all this now, I can see how I transferred my own complicated life story and desire to become a member of the deaf cultural and signing community onto the scene. These ethnographic accounts are useful when understood as artifacts of my attempts to organize my own anxieties as an inexperienced and in-betweener ethnographer. Likewise such accounts reflect my attempts to organize additional anxieties about anticipated responses and criticisms from hearing- and deaf-world interlocutors who, I expected, would be reading and making judgments about my accounts.

The voice-off episode is included in the pilot film we made of Patrick's bilingual kindergarten classroom at the Phoenix School for the Deaf. Joe Tobin and I subsequently used this pilot film as a cue for discussion in preliminary focus-group interviews with teacher and parent informants. What we initially discovered was some of the deeply held beliefs of teachers and parents and some of the forms of these tensions, agreements, and disagreements informants bring to discussions about best practices for supporting deaf children's language(s) and academic development. Perhaps more importantly, I also discovered how much my own rather muddled beliefs and practices drove what I was seeing in my research.

At the start of the study, my role as an in-betweener seemed less blurred even as it was complicated. As an in-betweener, I live and work in the liminal spaces in between the cultural worlds of deaf and hearing. I'm deaf in the hearing world. Yet I'm hearing in the deaf world. I identify myself as culturally "big D" Deaf. Because I read lips and speak more skillfully than sign, I also identify as linguistically "little d" deaf. In a perfect world, I would speak and the world would sign. That way, I could retain my eloquence in spoken language, yet use sign language to more clearly understand others. Most of my life I have been an insider to the deaf experience and an outsider to deaf culture. I am an insider to the mainstream U.S. public school experience, special education, and speech therapy. I am an outsider to the schools for the deaf where I conduct research in kindergarten classrooms that use sign language. I am doubly an outsider as a researcher in deaf schools in Japan and France and the larger cultures in which these kindergarten classrooms are embedded. My anxiety has been fueled by my sense of the inadequacy of my membership in all of these worlds.

Shifting From Anxiety to Method in Fieldwork

In this chapter, I describe how our pilot study in Patrick's classroom in Phoenix led to a video ethnography project[2] funded by the Spencer Foundation entitled *Kindergartens for the Deaf in Three Countries: United States, France, and Japan* (Tobin, Valente, & Horejes, 2010; Valente & Tobin, 2010). Writing from my emic perspective as an in-betweener ethnographer, I also explore the affective dimensions of liminal spaces that I encountered in carrying out this fieldwork. I focus on the voice-off example because it spotlights the "reflexivity in action" that occurred in discussions regarding existential, ethical, and methodological dilemmas that emerged during and after my fieldwork as well as during the writing of this chapter (Crapanzano, 1977, 2003). Drawing from Massumi (2002) and Leander and Boldt's (2013) description of affect as the body's unlimited potential to affect and be affected, I also revisit epiphanies I recorded in my fieldnotes and in discussions with informants and our research team about the voice-off episode in order to explore the affective dimensions of conducting fieldwork in liminal spaces. I do this by tracking what Boldt and Valente (2014) refer to as the "interstices"—in this case, an opening, often a fleeting or secreted thought, feeling, or moment to be explored—which, for ethnographers, appear in their anxieties, fantasies, boredoms, fixations, indifference, impatience, excitements that shape their psyche.

The Role of Emotional Response and Anxiety in Fieldwork

Prior to postmodern concerns with representation and reflexivity, anthropologist George Devereux (1967) borrowed from psychoanalysis in an attempt to develop a systematic approach to an ethnographer's emotional response to fieldwork, paying particular attention to feelings of anxiety (Clifford & Marcus, 1986; Lutz & White, 1986; Marcus & Fischer, 1986). In Devereux's (1967) primer on "anxiety" in fieldwork, *From Anxiety to Method in the Behavioral Sciences*, he outlines how processes borrowed from psychoanalysis, particularly strategies for systematically exploring transference and countertransference in psychotherapy sessions, open up new possibilities for researchers to think about the implications of emic and etic perspectives in conducting fieldwork (Devereux, 1967; Crapanzano, 1977). Devereux especially emphasized that researchers should pay attention to and write up descriptions of how fieldwork affects the researcher, questioning social-science fieldwork practices where researchers aimed to become distanced observers tasked with writing de-emotionalized and ostensibly objective fieldwork descriptions, taking from psychoanalysis the lesson that "anxiety was not something to be avoided but is the driving force which propels our intellectual questings" (p. 12).

Devereux's (1967) framework helped me confront my anxieties about the epistemological and methodological issues that surfaced during the voice-off episode, follow-up discussions with Patrick, analysis of the voice-off footage, and interviews conducted in connection with writing this chapter. As an in-betweener ethnographer conducting fieldwork at the interstices (Brueggemann, 2009; Valente, 2011a; Valente, 2014; Boldt & Valente, 2014), I reveal in this chapter the complicated ways fieldwork affected and continues to affect my understandings of the research, informants, and myself, while also offering readers an inside look at a rookie ethnographer's attempts to understand reflexivity in action.

Contesting Deaf Childhoods, Bilingualism, and Ideologies of In(Ex)clusion

Before continuing with my own experiences, I believe it is worthwhile to interrupt the story to situate it in a larger context. After all, my story can only be told and understood within the larger story of historical and cultural responses to deaf children and adults, educational opportunities they were and are afforded, and the politics of *how* to best teach children with communicative differences. My personal experiences as a deaf student being warehoused in mainstreamed classrooms and special education, as well as my concerns about the contemporary situation of deaf childhoods and competing beliefs and ideologies about the education of deaf reside within me and informs all aspects of my research.

Because more than 90% of deaf children have hearing parents, acculturation and acquiring language and identity for them is a complicated and fraught process. Most deaf children and their hearing parents have limited opportunities to interact with people who are culturally deaf and know sign (Snoddon & Underwood, 2013; Tobin, Valente, & Horejes, 2010). Parents often report struggling to raise a deaf child—in all probability their child is the first deaf person they have ever met—without much-needed support networks that include bilingual deaf and hearing role models and peers who are signers (Mitchell & Karchmer, 2004; Weaver & Starner, 2011; Valente, 2011b; Snoddon, 2013). The American Academy of Pediatrics' flagship journal, *Pediatrics in Review,* recently published bioethicist and pediatrician John Lantos's (2012) breakthrough article urging practitioners to heed concerns raised by alarming reports about hearing parents of deaf children who maintain that they were ill-informed about the importance of bilingualism for deaf children, if informed at all. In short, pediatricians are urged to stress to parents that deaf children need access to bilingualism (Lantos, 2012). Lantos also put pediatricians on notice to inform parents that research on the long-term outcomes for spoken-language-only deaf children confirms earlier studies that deprivation of language is harmful, most especially during the critical early years. The report highlighted a review of the research supporting sign language as deaf children's first language because it makes use of their innate visual-gestural-kinesthetic communicative potential and gives deaf children access to language without delays or dependence on medical-rehabilitative interventions (e.g., auditory-verbal therapy for cochlear implant recipients or speech therapy for children with hearing aids) requiring years of therapy with no guarantees for success (e.g., Grosjean, 2010; Petitto et al., 2011, Lantos, 2012).

Additionally, pediatricians are urged to stress to parents that regardless of their choices about technologies or educational placement, learning sign as the first language and having access to bilingual—spoken and sign language—environments is paramount for success (Lantos, 2012). Crucial for parents and their deaf children's sign-language development is the need for them to learn sign language in tandem and to have access to deaf and hearing signers (Snoddon & Underwood, 2013; Valente & Boldt, in press). The vast majority of educational placements for deaf children in the United States—around 80%, according to the latest surveys—are in spoken-language-only environments, most often with hearing classmates and teachers (Valente, 2011b; Gallaudet Research Institute, 2008, 2010). These oral-only approaches and inclusion education policies effectively removed the deaf cultural and hearing signing community from the lives of deaf children. Many deaf children later grow up to report feeling isolated and alone in the mainstream, struggling in their efforts to gain support from hearing educators and peers while navigating their communicative differences (e.g., Oliva, 2004; Valente, 2011a).

Most mainstreamed deaf children, who have little or no contact with sign language or deaf peers and adults, end up in schools for the deaf after failing out or struggling with little success (O'Brien, in press). In one of the few locatable studies tracking long-term outcomes for deaf students, the picture becomes even bleaker, as Vernon and LaFalce-Landers (1993) found that 30% were unemployed and 39% experienced severe mental health issues requiring hospitalization and outpatient therapy. Only 43% of deaf students graduated from college and 18% attended graduate school. More recent data tracking postsecondary completion rates indicate that eight years past high school, 52.9% of deaf students have graduated and completed training as well as 57.2% of deaf students are employed (Newman et al., 2011; Luft, 2012). However an overriding concern is that while employment rates for deaf students have increased, these rates have risen marginally in comparison to federally determined disability group categories and the majority of deaf workers are underemployed compared to hearing peers with the same skills and training, leading to further educational and economic disenfranchisement (Moores, 2001; Luft, 2012).

My personal experiences as a mainstreamed special education student have led me to place the realities of the failures of educating deaf children at the center of my work (Valente, 2011a). While I have had more success in my career than what is in general experienced by my deaf peers, it has come with the provision that I live life in-between deaf and hearing worlds. I am able to pass well enough in both the hearing and deaf worlds to find success, but these attempts at passing also provoke considerable anxieties in me. I am insecure about not belonging in either the deaf or hearing worlds. Also I am anxious about being called a fraud for attempting to pass. Even as I know I am privileged in an underprivileged world, I also know all too well the costs of living this life as an in-betweener (Valente, 2014). My role as an in-betweener has become more and more salient as I have made my way through the *Kindergartens for the Deaf in Three Countries* project.

Overview of the Kindergartens for the Deaf in Three Countries Project

Our plan for the pilot project and later for the larger multi-country research project *Kindergartens for the Deaf in Three Countries* was to make an ethnographic film of a typical day in Japanese, French, and American bilingual kindergarten classrooms to study the subjective experiences of child, parent, teacher, administrator, and expert informants using Joseph Tobin's *Preschool in Three Cultures* video ethnographic methods (Tobin, Wu, & Davidson, 1989; Tobin, Hsueh, & Karasawa, 2009). Traditionally anthropologists conduct ethnographic fieldwork for a cycle of seasons, one year or more, with the help of a cultural mediator and/or translator. As participant-observers, anthropologists customarily spend their days among cultural insiders participating in and observing the daily life of the culture they are studying while also documenting and interviewing informants about the day's activities to understand "these imponderabilia of actual life and of typical behavior" (Malinowski, 1922, p. 18). A distinct feature of the *Preschool in Three Cultures* video-cued method is that it replaces the long-term fieldwork with a collaboratively edited mini-ethnographic film to use as an elicitation tool to interview informants who are variously insiders and outsiders to daily classroom life. The film offers concrete examples from classroom life to stimulate reflections on the meaning informants make about their cultural beliefs and teaching practices. The *Preschool in Three Cultures* method works to understand culture as the principal explanatory construct and privileges insider explanations and emic over etic analysis.

Having to do the work of explaining cultural practices that are taken for granted has the effect of making the familiar strange (Kaomea, 2003, 2013; Tobin, 2000; Valente, 2011b). It is the dialogic process within the *Preschool in Three Cultures* methodology that offers insights into researchers' and informants' inner worlds and stimulates discussions about deeply held beliefs in individual and focus-group interviews. The method uses edited videos showing a typical day in each classroom as a cue for discussions with parent, teacher, and expert informants about teaching practices and cultural beliefs. This ethnographic approach especially features protocols borrowed from Bakhtin's ideas about polyvocality ("many voices"), calling for recurring dialogue between researchers and informants to learn from one another by discussing and reflecting on the multiple perspectives that emerge in these focus-group discussions. These explanations reveal not only to the informants themselves but also to the researchers their taken-for-granted ideas beliefs and practices (Tobin & Davidson, 1990).

Cultural Politics of Difference and Schooling: A Disability Studies in Education Perspective

While the design of the *Kindergartens for the Deaf in Three Countries* study is located at the intersections of anthropology and deaf cultural studies, a field that views members of deaf culture as an ethnic group, borrowing from critical ethnographic methods and theories of deaf communities (Ladd, 2008), it also draws heavily on the perspectives of disability studies in education (DSE) and its focus on the cultural politics of difference and schooling. DSE scholars study socio-political constructions of dis/ability and reject deficit perspectives of dis/ability and difference that characterize mainstream education, special education, and deaf education (Connor, Gabel, Gallagher, & Morton, 2008; Trent, Artiles, Englert, Bos, & Gerber, 1998; Artiles, 2003, Connor & Ferri, 2007; Valente, 2011a). Schools and how we acculturate children are windows into larger discourses about difference, inclusion, and exclusion. Beliefs about disability—including beliefs about deaf children and deaf education—are enactments of deeply held viewpoints and ideologies. Recent research highlights failed efforts to ameliorate the disconnect between policymakers, schools, communities, and children and their parents, with these situations continually impeded and exacerbated by stakeholder focus on ideological contestations (Tobin, Arzubiaga, & Adair, 2013). I return to the voice-off episode below to reflect upon examples of both the ideological influences at work within this study as well as the places where interstices emerged in fieldwork.

Voice-Off Episode Revisited

Anthropologists have long used psychoanalysis and psychoanalytic thinking to analyze interviews and informants—and later the interviewee themselves—but typically overlooked the experience of participant-observation, that is, fieldwork (LeVine, 1982; Heald, Deluz, & Jacopin, 1994). Critical accounts of participant-observation are illustrative examples of the complexities of the anthropological dilemma presented by fieldwork where it is generally understood that the ethnographer is to become embedded in a cultural group with the dual task of being a quasi-community member and an onlooker. To address transference and countertransference in fieldwork and the resultant intrapsychic problems of cross-cultural translation for bicultural researchers,

LeVine (1982) proposed a bicultural research method, which includes "working alliances" that are collaborations between cultural insiders and the outside investigator and are akin to a student psychoanalyst and clinical supervisor. Patrick would become my introductory guide not only to understanding the voice-off episode specifically or deaf culture generally, but also to learning sign language.

In my case, the anthropological dilemma is further complicated by the fact that I am an in-betweener ethnographer who has lived and continues to live on the fringes of the hearing and deaf worlds (Valente, 2011a, 2014). Ethnographic accounts that include descriptions of the personal and professional in fieldwork can offer an inside look into the affective dimensions of liminal spaces that ethnographers navigate. If ethnographers carry out fieldwork in liminal spaces, it is the interstices that an affectively engaged ethnographer is tracking. Interstices compel ethnographers to examine and critique their own norms and desires, which structure their meaning making and experiences in the field, tasking ethnographers with tracking, revealing, and exploring encounters and artifacts with affective potentialities and possibilities (Boldt & Valente, 2014). Interstices materialize for the ethnographer in fieldwork as anxieties, boredom, fixations, indifference, impatience, and so on, with all its inglorious imponderability of our subjectivities, intersubjectivities, and the attendant fragmented and messy accounts of these phenomena (Boldt & Valente, 2014; Clifford, 1983; Marcus, 1994; Valente, 2014). Ethnographic accounts and analyses of *when* interstices occur in fieldwork have the potential to serve as starting points for denaturalizing binaries so prevalent in and part of the ethnographic toolkit—emic/etic, participant/observer, insider/outsider, interviewer/informant—opening up the interstices for exploration.

When I sat down almost five years removed from the day we filmed in Patrick's classroom to write about voice-off episode for this chapter, I reread fieldnotes and vignettes I had written about the episode earlier in the project and watched the scene on video. I wanted to compare my fieldnotes and vignette descriptions to the actual video and possibly clean up my descriptions of the American Sign Language (ASL) dialogue to make them more precisely reflect the language of the scene. In the years since 2009, my ASL has improved greatly due to ASL immersions. On first viewing the clip, it surprised me to see how inadequate my ASL dialogue and descriptions from 2009 were and, without giving it much thought, I hurriedly set about to rewrite them. Quickly and excitedly I started to think about possible ways to interpret the ASL and narrate the scene anew. I became especially fixated on the details I left out of the original vignette that could add to the descriptions of ASL as a language in motion. It felt enlivening to be able to sit and watch Patrick sign with his children in ASL and for me now to be able to more fully understand the nuances of their communications. I felt a tinge of pride as I reflected on what I had written in the original vignette about feeling ashamed for not being able to sign in those earlier days.

The realization that I more confidently understand ASL today made me reflect on my continued frustrations learning to sign and being judged on my skills as an emergent signer. While it is clear to me that my receptive skills in ASL have improved greatly, the exercise of transcribing the video also reminded me how far I need to go to be able to express myself in ASL with more fluency. In my revised descriptions of Angel and Patrick's ASL in the vignette, I noticed that it more closely resembled English descriptions that might make sense to a hearing person but would have been inadequate to a fluent signer. I became anxious thinking about the criticism I might receive from readers well-versed in sign who might view these descriptions as lacking or as undermining the complexity of ASL. When I found myself scouring example descriptions of ASL handshapes online to match against my own, I started to worry about my attempt to narrate ASL in the vignette, finally recognizing the futility of putting ASL to paper. At this point, I started to wonder why I felt I needed to make these changes to the opening vignette descriptions. What purpose would it serve for me to change my earlier descriptions of the ASL in the video? Why did I feel I should more descriptively narrate scenes in ASL? What did all this mean for an in-betweener ethnographer like me?

Angel's voice-off moment is an example of a phenomenon in research— general and ethnographic research especially—that requires a reflexive pause and served, for Joe Tobin, Patrick and me, as a cautionary tale throughout our research. In my 2009 interview with Patrick, directly after sharing the story of the voice-off incident with him, he explained,

> When I watch you struggle to keep up with people when they talk to you, it makes me sad, because I see who I was when I was in high school, and how much I struggled and cried a few nights, simply because I couldn't understand why I couldn't live and enjoy my life 100% ... Soon, I hope, you can start telling people to turn off their voice, because when they do, you will start to see a whole new world.

The voice-off episode came early in our research project. We were thrilled to have found exactly what we were looking for; that is, a clear example of a young deaf child performing deaf cultural identity—a key theme of our research project. On videotape we caught Angel, a 5-year-old Mexican American kindergartner, performing what appeared to us as an act of deaf radical consciousness, signing "voice off." When this scene unfolded, we were

excited and encouraged because we took it as an indication that we had captured so early in the project exactly what we were looking for. I imagined
captivating book titles like *Voice Off*, *Deaf Kids Now*, and *Deaf Power, Deaf
Kindergartners: An Angel and His Revolutionaries* that suggested an inside
look into processes of acculturation into deaf identity for very young children,
and evidence that the children, even as young as kindergarten, supported a
bilingual approach to schooling. The problem was that the more we learned
through our discussions with insiders, the less we were certain of what key
episodes we captured on film meant not only to our informants, but to us as
well. These episodes captured on film mean *some* things happened (Valente,
2014), but the meaning we can make of these happenings are multiple, sometimes ephemeral, and oftentimes complicated.

A notable aspect of the *Preschool in Three Cultures* method is that the
team continually goes back to re-interview our informants, asking them to
revisit earlier discussions and to see what they think of our emerging explanations, creating a cross-national dialogue within and across several school
communities. The approach intentionally privileges insider explanations over
etic ones. The *Preschool in Three Cultures* method is self-correcting, as it leads
researchers to re-examine and question our first hunches. The repeated interviews with Patrick and other teachers we videotaped worked to make us pause
and question our early assumptions. For example, when we showed Patrick
the video segment of Angel's voice-off moment, we were surprised by his
rather underwhelmed reaction. Patrick saw it less as our having captured on
tape an example of deaf identity affirmation or of capturing the moment when
Angel announced his deaf identity and more as a typical moment of a student
choosing how to express himself (voiced or voiceless) and a rather typical
example of Angel acting the part of a class clown. Patrick did not see this as
a gesture of resistance to the audist mainstream world but rather a gesture
of resistance to his authority. When we shared our initial interpretation with
him, Patrick did not exactly say we were wrong. However, Patrick did suggest
that our interpretation, while plausible, was more likely a case of *over*reading.
Privately later on, Patrick suggested to me that I was *projecting*. At the time,
I can remember telling Patrick I was most assuredly not projecting. Now I
know differently.

Why did we make these mistakes? Were they mistakes? At the Phoenix
School for the Deaf, as outsiders to the deaf world and the school community, we may have been overeager to find an expression of radical deaf identity
because we wanted to provide evidence to support this position. As Patrick
suggested, I perhaps projected onto Angel a radical deaf cultural identity I
wished I could have displayed when I was 5 years old. I am now, as an adult

and latecomer to deaf culture, expressing such a radical deaf identity, often wishing to turn off my own voice. Angel, for me, is a source for projection or perhaps wishful thinking. Joe Tobin later reflected that he was naïve about deaf culture and deaf education, perhaps projecting onto this situation narratives from the women's movement and Black Power movement about identity politics, assimilating Angel's physical gesture into a familiar narrative of black power salutes and bra-burning and "Deaf President Now" campaigns (Tobin, 2010). Ethnography has a way of correcting for these mistakes and the video-cued ethnographic method is especially good at this correction because it is explicit and iterative. First, we document classroom events on videotape. Then, we ask teachers to help us choose which events to include in the edited video. Finally, the informants provide the interpretation. In our position as outsiders and ethnographers, we sometimes see patterns and significance that insiders do not recognize, and vice versa.

In the spirit of ethnographic endeavor, we must give pause to an insider's challenge of interpretation. During the writing of this chapter, I have found myself repeatedly returning to Vincent Crapanzano's (1972) classic ethnography, *The Fifth World of Forster Bennett: Portrait of a Navajo*, written while a rookie ethnographer himself. Crapanzano (2003) cautions ethnographers to recognize the need for fieldwork "to be seen in its existential dimensions. An anthropologist is a man in confrontation with other men— and he affects and is affected by them indelibly" (p. 18). In the foreword for the newest edition of *The Fifth World of Forster Bennett*, Crapanzano (2003) critiques his own use of confessional rhetoric that now often appears in critical personal narratives written in reflexive, critical, and indigenous ethnographic genres, noting how such writing "appeases our moral disquiet through personal revelation" (p. ix). Crapanzano raises an important point about the dangers of the "confessional turn" in ethnography, but offers another possible tactic for ethnographers to avoid the inevitable pitfalls of realism:

> By casting myself in as realistic and not always as flattering a fashion as I could ... I must have eased my own burden of responsibility, perhaps even guilt ... I still stand by the importance of "I" in social science research and description, but today I would focus on the dialogical relationship, in fact and in fantasy, that constitutes the "I" as it is constituted by the "you," and on the discursive constraints that govern that relationship. (p. ix)

Crapanzano's perspective on the ethnographer as constituted by the subject of research challenges researchers to accept the vulnerability of our own position as knowledge seekers, the limitations we are bound to work within,

and the solidity of the ground we imagine is beneath us. For me as an in-betweener researcher, understanding the ethnographic encounter between self
and the other as a dialogical relationship allows me to confront my anxieties
and defenses to more fully understand not only myself, but those I am studying. I have come to understand that it's not so much that I'm in-between
true identities—deaf and hearing—it has to do with the way that I am more
defined as a result of sorting through my transferences onto my subjects, and
the realization that I am always changing as a result of these relationships
and encounters with my informants. This is a shift from an anxious version
of in-betweener, as a person who is inadequate to the two worlds I imagined
as complete and existing on either side of me. Because the self-correcting
features of the ethnographic method allow me to attend to my projections or
transferences onto my subjects, as Patrick described, I'm developing a more
differentiated understanding of the differences between my subjects and myself. It is not research that is consumed by confession; I am deeply affected
by my subjects. The idea of being an in-betweener researcher is transforming
into an understanding that what I am in-between is who I was before the
research and who I am becoming as a result of my relationship with my subjects. It shifts from an anxious in-between to an in-between that is relational,
that allows for shared exploration and creativity.

Notes

1. Lowercase "d" "deaf" is commonly accepted to denote a physical construction of
   deafness, and uppercase "D" "Deaf" signals identification with Deaf culture and
   sign language. My decision to use "deaf" throughout reflects the complexities of
   my own life history and a move beyond binary and static understandings of deaf
   identity.
2. Dr. Joseph Tobin (University of Georgia) and Dr. Thomas Horejes (Gallaudet University) are co-principal investigators on this Spencer Foundation grant.

   Acknowledgments: I would like to thank anonymous peer reviewers, editors David
   Connor and Jan Valle, and Joseph Tobin, Gail Boldt, and Patrick Graham for their
   comments and suggestions throughout the writing of this chapter.

References

Artiles, A. J. (2003). Special education's changing identity: Paradoxes and dilemmas in
   views of culture and space. *Harvard Educational Review, 73*(2), 164–202.
Boldt, G., & Valente, J. M. (2014). Bring back the asylum: Reimagining inclusion in the
   presence of others. In M. N. Bloch, B. B. Swadener, & G. S. Cannella (Eds.), *Reconceptualizing early childhood care and education: Critical questions, new imaginaries
   and social activism*. New York: Peter Lang.

Brueggemann, B. J. (2009). *Deaf subjects: Between identities and places.* New York: New York University Press.

Clifford, J. (1983). On ethnographic authority. *Representations, 1,* 118–146.

Clifford, J., & Marcus, G. E. (Eds.). (1986). *Writing culture: The poetics and politics of ethnography.* Berkeley: University of California Press.

Connor, D. J., & Ferri, B. A. (2007). The conflict within: Resistance to inclusion and other paradoxes in special education. *Disability & Society, 22*(1), 63–77.

Connor, D. J., Gabel, S. L., Gallagher, D. J., & Morton, M. (2008). Disability studies and inclusive education—implications for theory, research, and practice. *International Journal of Inclusive Education, 12*(5–6), 441–457.

Crapanzano, V. (1972). *The fifth world of Forster Bennett: Portrait of a Navaho.* New York: Viking Press.

Crapanzano, V. (1977). On the writing of ethnography. *Dialectical Anthropology, 2*(1), 69–73.

Crapanzano, V. (2003). Foreword. In *The fifth world of Forster Bennett: Portrait of a Navajo.* Lincoln: University of Nebraska Press.

Devereux, G. (1967). *From anxiety to method in the behavioral sciences.* The Hague: Mouton.

Eisenhart, M. (2001). Educational ethnography past, present, and future: Ideas to think with. *Educational Researcher, 30*(8), 16–27.

Gallaudet Research Institute. (2008). Demographics. http://www.gallaudet.edu/Gallaudet_Research_Institute/Demographics.html (accessed Oct 14, 2011).

Gallaudet Research Institute. (2010). Demographics. http://www.gallaudet.edu/Gallaudet_Research_Institute/Demographics.html (accessed Oct 14, 2011).

Grosjean, F. (2010). Bilingualism, biculturalism, and deafness, *International Journal of Bilingual Education and Bilingualism, 13*(2), 133–145.

Heald, S., Deluz, A., & Jacopin, P-Y. (1994). Introduction. In S. Heald & A. Deluz (Eds.), *Anthropology and psychoanalysis: An encounter through culture.* London: Routledge.

Horejes, T., Valente, J. M., & Tobin, J. (2011, April). Kindergartens as sites of acculturation for the deaf. Paper presented at the American Educational Research Association Conference sponsored by Early Education and Child Development Special Interest Group, New Orleans, Louisiana, United States.

Kaomea, J. (2003). Reading erasures and making the familiar strange: Defamiliarizing methods for research in formerly colonized and historically oppressed communities. *Educational Researcher, 32*(2), 14–25.

Kaomea, J. (2013). Lab coats or trench coats? Detective sleuthing as an alternative to scientifically based research in indigenous educational communities. *Qualitative Inquiry, 19*(8), 613–620.

Ladd, P. (2008). Colonialism and resistance: A brief history of deafhood. In H. D. L. Bauman (Ed.), *Open your eyes: Deaf studies talking* (pp. 42–59). Minneapolis: University of Minnesota Press.

Lantos, J. D. (2012). Ethics for the pediatrician: The evolving ethics of cochlear implants in children. *Pediatrics in Review, 33,* 323.

Leander, K., & Boldt, G. (2013). Rereading "A Pedagogy of multiliteracies": Bodies, texts, and emergence. *Journal of Literacy Research*, *45*(1), 22–46.

LeVine, R. A. (1982). The couch and the field. In *Culture, behavior, and personality*. Chicago: Aldine Pub. Co.

Luft, P. (2012). A national survey of transition services for deaf and hard of hearing students. *Career Development and Transition for Exceptional Individuals*, *1*, 1–16.

Lutz, C., & White, G. M. (1986). The anthropology of emotions. *Annual Review of Anthropology*, *15*(1), 405–436.

Malinowski, B. (1922). Introduction: The subject, method and scope of this inquiry. In *Argonauts of the western pacific*, pp. 1–25. New York: Dutton.

Marcus, G. E. (1994). On ideologies of reflexivity in contemporary efforts to remake the human sciences. *Poetics Today*, *15*(3), 383–404.

Marcus, G. E., & Fischer, M. M. J. (1986). *Anthropology as cultural critique: An experimental moment in the human sciences*. Chicago, IL: University of Chicago Press.

Massumi, B. (2002). *Parables for the virtual: Movement, affect, sensation*. Durham, NC: Duke University Press.

Mitchell, R. E., & Karchmer, M. A. (2004). When parents are deaf versus hard of hearing: Patterns of sign use and school placement of deaf and hard-of-hearing children. *Journal of Deaf Studies and Deaf Education*, 9, 133–152.

Moores, D. (2001). *Educating the deaf: Psychology, principles, and practices* (5th ed.). Boston: Houghton Mifflin.

Newman, L., Wagner, M., Knokey, A.-M., Marder, C., Nagle, K., Shaver, D., & Wei, X. (2011, September). The post-high school outcomes of young adults with disabilities up to 8 years after high school: A report from the national longitudinal transition study-2 (NLTS2) (NCSER 2011–3005). Menlo Park, CA: SRI International. Retrieved from http://www.nlts2.org/reports/2011_09_02/index.html

O'Brien, C. (in press). *The influence of Deaf culture on school culture and leadership in a school for the Deaf: A case study*. Charlotte, NC: New Information Age.

Oliva, G. A. (2004). *Alone in the mainstream: A deaf woman remembers public school* (Vol. 1). Washington, DC: Gallaudet University Press.

Petitto, L., Katerelos, M., Levy, B., Gauna, K., Tetreault, K., & Ferraro, V. (2011). Bilingual signed and spoken language acquisition from birth: Implications for the mechanisms underlying early bilingual language acquisition. *Journal of Child Language*, *28*, 453–496.

Snoddon, K. (2013). Growing up with languages: Reflections on multilingual childhoods. *TESOL Quarterly*, *47*(3), 660–662.

Snoddon, K., & Underwood, K. (2013). Toward a social relational model of Deaf childhood. *Disability & Society*, *29*(4), 530–542.

Tobin, J. J. (2000). *Good guys don't wear hats*. New York: Teachers College Press.

Tobin, J. J. (2010). A non-deaf ethnographers participation of a study of deaf kindergartens. Paper presented at the meeting of the American Anthropological Association, New Orleans, LA.

Tobin, J. J., Arzubiaga, A., & Adair, J. K. (2013). *Children crossing borders: Immigrant parent and teacher perspectives on preschool for children of immigrants.* New York: Russell Sage Foundation.

Tobin, J. J., & Davidson, D. (1990). The ethics of polyvocal ethnography: Empowering vs. textualizing children and teachers. *International Journal of Qualitative Studies in Education, 3*(3), 271–283.

Tobin, J. J., Hsueh, Y., & Karasawa, M. (2009). *Preschool in three cultures revisited: China, Japan, and the United States.* Chicago, IL: University of Chicago Press.

Tobin, J. J., Valente, J. M., & Horejes, T. (2010). *Kindergartens for the deaf in three countries: Japan, France, and the United States.* Project funded by the Spencer Foundation. http://research.gallaudet.edu/resources/ragu/abstract/747/

Tobin, J. J., Wu, D. Y., & Davidson, D. H. (1989). *Preschool in three cultures: Japan, China, and the United States.* New Haven, CT: Yale University Press.

Trent, S. C., Artiles, A. J., Englert, C. S., Bos, C. S., & Gerber, M. (1998). From deficit thinking to social constructivism: A review of special education theory, research, and practice from a historical perspective. *Review of Research in Education, 23,* 277–307.

Valente, J. M. (2011a). *D/deaf and D/dumb: A portrait of a deaf kid as a young superhero.* New York: Peter Lang.

Valente, J. M. (2011b). Cyborgization: Deaf education for young children in the cochlear implantation era. *Qualitative Inquiry, 17*(7,) 639–652.

Valente, J. M. (2012). Going native at Ben Bahan's house. In K. Harmon & J. Nelson (Eds.), *Deaf American prose: An anthology.* Washington, DC: Gallaudet University Press.

Valente, J. M. (2014). Monster's analysis: Vulnerable anthropology and deaf superhero-becomings. In Oka & Michiko (Eds.), *Literacies of the challenged: To construct a truly inclusive society* (Multiliteracies Series). Tokyo: Kuroshio Shuppan.

Valente, J. M., & Boldt, G. (in press). The rhizome of the deaf child. *Qualitative Inquiry.*

Vernon, M., & LaFalce-Landers, E. (1993). A longitudinal study of intellectually gifted deaf and hard of hearing people: Educational, psychological, and career outcomes. *American Annals of the Deaf, 138*(5), 427–434.

Weaver, K. A., & Starner, T. (2011). We need to communicate! Helping hearing parents of deaf children learn American Sign Language. In *The Proceedings of the 13th International ACM SIGACCESS Conference on Computers and Accessibility* (pp. 91–98).

Section III

Practice

7. Practicing What We Teach: The Benefits of Using Disability Studies in an Inclusion Course

DAVID J. CONNOR

In this chapter I describe how a course that I have taught on inclusive education for 15 years has changed and evolved, largely through my interaction with—and adoption of—disability studies (DS) and disability studies in education (DSE) to inform readings, practices, assignments, and assessments. By describing the architecture of the course, I highlight how a framing of disability using DS/DSE theory within what is largely a traditional special education program serves to challenge and inform students' rethinking of familiar topics such as: challenging stereotypes; working with parents; instructional planning, delivery, and assessment of diverse learners; managing classrooms; selecting responsible curricula, and; engaging with universal design for learning (UDL). The chapter features personal observations, anecdotes of students, and a selection of artifacts within inclusive pedagogy used—all of which coalesce to purposely destabilize the current educational worldview of students, while simultaneously preparing them to work within diverse classrooms. In sum, the purpose of this chapter is to share some ways that DS/DSE can be put into practice.

In the Beginning: Teaching Inclusively

Once upon a time, long, long ago (in the early 90s), I was a classroom teacher working within a special education department within a large urban school. Unbeknownst to faculty there, Madeleine Will, assistant secretary of education for the U.S. Office of Special Education and Rehabilitation Services, had initiated a policy called the Regular Education Initiative (REI) in which students with "mild" disabilities were to be transitioned into general education classrooms, oftentimes with the support of a special educator (Will, 1986). No one had informed our faculty of this nationwide initiative. We were simply told that several of us would be going into general education classrooms to work with our colleagues there to help teach what was perceived as a hybrid-like class of students with and without disabilities. What happened was this: I was assigned four general education teachers and was told to "make it work." School administration was not enthusiastic. They had been instructed by the Department of Education to do a "pilot." This was my introduction to inclusive education. No background. No guidance. No training.

Nonetheless, I was genuinely intrigued. I could see the sense behind moving toward this trend. I had always thought that the self-contained (a euphemism for "segregated") classrooms appeared to exist more to enable the functioning of the whole school rather than for the benefits of disabled students (Skrtic, 1991). In addition, I had always advocated for students to be "mainstreamed" for the subject that was their strength, such as math, or their passion, such as art. I knew firsthand how much students hated the stigma of being labeled "special," and how that impacted upon their identity in a negative way. I also experienced what has been described as a "contamination" effect (Goffman, 1963) wherein the mere association of a person with a stigmatized group can be reason to "infect" that person by association. By this I mean I experienced the phenomenon that special educators came to believe themselves as inferior to general educators, wondering: How could I possibly go into general education classrooms and teach non-disabled youth along with "my" disabled students—with general education colleagues looking on?

Of course this myth of inferiority, and many others, was quickly dispelled once I started collaborating with my general education counterparts. From the beginning, I asserted we should each teach the whole class half of the time—for purposes of parity, equality, and fairness. To be honest, we did not know how else to proceed. We worked by trial and error—this was a pre–collaboration guru Marilyn Friend (2008) world—and our co-teaching naturally evolved as we moved forward in good faith. The situation was not ideal, but we made it work as best we could, learning from one another, mutually observing, and planning which one would teach and grade student work. As it turned out, three of the four enforced partnerships went well enough and one was strained. At the end of the year, once again without warning, we were "invited" (read: required) to share our experiences at a citywide Department of Education event. I recall being picked up by a mini-van, transported to another school, and guided on stage in a large auditorium to partake in a panel presentation. Our sizable audience was comprised of teachers who would listen to, and ask questions about, the piloting of Will's Regular Education Initiative. Without any formal preparation, we spoke about our successes and challenges of including students with disabilities.

I share these memories because it was in this year as a classroom teacher that many of my thoughts around inclusion were initially triggered. Surely, I thought, this important initiative could be better explained and implemented? Soon after, when I changed positions to serve within the superintendent's office as a professional development specialist in special education matters, the REI experience influenced my choice of specialization: the *whys* and *hows* of successful inclusion. This position allowed me access to administrators, teachers, and para-educators in more than 40 high schools that grappled with the growing trend of inclusive education. The professionals within these schools ran the gamut from being all embracing to deeply resistant of inclusion. In particular, I noticed how many special education administrators and teachers fought against inclusive practices—symptomatic of special education's inflexibility with deeply entrenched well-intentioned-but-largely-ineffective ways. In fact, my first-ever publication was a narrative description of providing professional development for these 40-plus principals on ways to support collaborative teaching within inclusive classes (Connor, 2004).

There were a number of reasons why that particular event was "high stakes" for me. These included being anxious about presenting in front of the superintendent and his deputies for three hours, engaging principals around a topic that I knew many would rather wish away, and finally—but most important—my deliberate and calculated use of DS/DSE to frame the *why* of inclusive education. I was midway into my doctoral degree at this time, and had been introduced to DS and the growth of DSE. These writings provided me with new, powerful tools that could slice through the thick skin of apathy around including children and youth with disabilities into general education. In that presentation, the risk paid off. I spent the first half of our time introducing principals to different ways of re-conceptualizing dis/abilities—thereby looking at the *why* of inclusion; the second half focused on solid, precise, useful ways in which they could support team-teaching as one response that addresses the *how* of inclusion. In brief, this was the beginning of my experiences in introducing educators working within "the establishment" to DS/DSE, as it served to provide a much-needed alternative lens to traditional, medicalized, deficit-based understandings of disability. Most people, I have found, are intrigued by looking at a familiar phenomenon such as dis/ability in a radically different way that triggers a deep, personalized response.

A History of Teaching Inclusion Courses

I have taught a graduate-level course called "Inclusion of Students with Dis-abilities" for several colleges since 1997, including at my current university since 2005. This course has always been a priority for me, something deeply personal as it resonates with my years of experience and thoughts when work-ing within schools. However, what I want to call attention to is the ideologi-cal *shift* within the course since I was introduced to DS/DSE around 2000 in the early part of my doctoral program. Coming to know DS/DSE provided the encounter that helped put words to my thoughts, provide a framework for my beliefs about human difference, and gave me methods to deconstruct the harmful practices within education. By doing this, it permitted me to call attention to such detrimental practices in ways that cannot be ignored, forcing a deeper level of engagement about basic questions such as: Who is considered disabled? According to whom? Why? Where do they belong?

By the time I came to present to the principals, the information was familiar territory within my inclusion classes. Major elements of a "DS/DSE grounding" for people that I teach include: the recognition of school structures often causing pain and damage to children; the need to use insider-perspectives and first-person accounts of people with disabilities; the erroneous justifications for segregating according to disability; the social conditions for people with disabilities; the implication of special education as an institution in perpetuating inequalities; the insularity and out-of-touch nature of special education research; the systematic attempts of special education to discourage or block pluralistic thought; special education's dogged adherence to positivist approaches within scientism; what counts as "disability" and according to whom, and so on.

These are pithy topics for professionals who want to know the "how to" of inclusion. At the same time, if the "how to" is addressed *after* these topics have been grappled with, I have found audiences/students to be far more receptive because they have at least been troubled by the idea that "These kids don't be-long if they can't do the work" and forced to consider "These kids have a civil right to be with their non-disabled peers and provided with work that they can do." If the former statement is embraced without question, then the educator is part of the existing problem, receiving a salary to maintain inequalities. If the latter statement is recognized, then a significant movement has occurred within an educator's thinking. While it is fundamentally important to change the way most educators have been enculturated to think about disability, this is only half of the job. The other half is giving them the tools needed to envision, plan for, teach, assess, and reflect upon their inclusive classes. I believe a course instructor should endeavor to provide both elements—an understanding of beliefs and the use of effective practices—as they mutually reinforce each other.

On a related note, the actual course that I discuss in this chapter— formally known as "SPED 703: Inclusion of Students with Disabilities in General Education Classrooms"—has a tradition of being a hot potato. Over the years, faculty members who did not necessarily believe in inclusion were responsible for teaching it (shocking, I know). However, since volunteering to be the faculty point person for the course, I have been able to make changes and oversee the employment of adjunct instructors to teach the course. This way, instructors with a disposition toward inclusion, and those who have practiced it, have much more to offer. In addition, when New York State requirements passed a couple of years ago to require one special education course for all candidates in general education teacher training programs, I successfully advocated that it be SPED 703 rather than the Introduction to Special Education course that is predominantly laws and regulations, with a deficit-based, disability-a-week approach. Of course, it is an enormous irony the inclusion course is programmed separately for general and special educators who receive the same content. It does seem archaic that universities are slow to change in ways they may readily require of schools. This amalgamation of general and special educators *taking the same course* about inclusion is one of my next institutional challenges.

The Course Architecture

The upside of creating and maintaining a course that all teacher candidates take is being able to explicitly frame it within DS/DSE. Although it can be done in many ways, what does it actually look like in this particular case? To begin with, I explain to students the architecture of the course, week-by-week, so they can immediately see the scope and sequence of topics. They are told, very explicitly, that I hope to respectfully engage them in their values and beliefs about disability and the right "place" for individuals with disabilities in both school and society—as the former is actually a microcosm of the latter.

Special Education With a Critical Eye: The First Third of the Course

I immediately take on the challenge of engaging with students' values and beliefs. The first three to four classes provide basic information about special education *and* DS/DSE, illustrate where major clashes lie within the field, and why they exist (Andrews et al., 2000; Baglieri, Valle, Connor, & Gallagher, 2011). We cover what may be familiar background information to some students (the history of special education, major laws and their components, IEPs, etc.), but this time with a critical eye that emphasizes the voices/ perspectives of people with disabilities. In addition, attention is called to long-standing, pervasive problems with special education that the field neglects or underemphasizes, such as: poor graduation rates; unemployment and under-employment; the school-to-prison pipeline; the achievement gap; the over-representation of students of color in specific categories, and their placement in more restrictive environments; the relation of support for children with disabilities and social class capital; the vast disconnect between research and practice, and so on. I call upon students to not allow special education to remain an unquestioned field into which they are being enculturated, but rather view it as a dynamic force that—no matter how well intended—can do more damage than good. It is important to note that such criticisms are not malicious or simply destructive but rather serve as a method in which conversations can be had about how certain practices within education should and can be done differently, inclusion being one of them.

At this juncture, the content of the course is largely theoretical. I ask that students "trust me" to see where this information will fit or be applied when we shift into practitioner-based mode in later weeks. We study DS/DSE-related topics such as: who is speaking for whom?; ableism throughout society and within schools; the social model of disability, and how it differs from the medical model; the construction of ab/normalcy throughout history and in contemporary times; disability stereotypes proliferated by the media; and, always, implications for educators and education. I want students to know and be able to articulate the differences between the medical/scientific/psychological disposition toward disability that leads to technical and managerial responses within education versus the historical/social/cultural understandings of disability undergirded by civil rights that promotes inclusivity. In addition, I summarize the tenets of DSE so that they can begin to see its relevance and possible uses for their daily practices (Connor, Gabel, Gallagher, & Morton, 2008). We also take a sobering look at the demands of "the Establishment" upon "the Population," discussing how educators must negotiate the tensions that arise—including issues of placement and instruction. On one hand, the Establishment relentlessly promotes high-stakes testing, academic standardization of the population (e.g., in New York State, levels 1, 2, 3, 4, low to high), with an increasingly lock-step curriculum, and punitive measures and penalties for those who do not or cannot comply with these demands. On the other hand, we caution how a varied population—including students with disabilities—should not be seen as a liability, but rather as part of human diversity that reflects diverse abilities, the need for differentiated/flexible instruction, as well as encouragement and motivation versus punishment.

In terms of text resources, there are three books that accompany a number of articles and chapters from DS/DSE and special education journals. While running the risk of appearing self-promoting, the primary text used is *Rethinking Disability: A Disability Studies Approach to Inclusive Practices* (Valle & Connor, 2011). Jan Valle and I wrote this text because it was the book we would have always wanted as a teacher: it is compact, informational, and filled with both the *whys* and *hows* of inclusive education—undergirded by the tenets of DSE. In it, we share our own life and career journeys as we grapple with the big issues that inclusive education raises. The second text is Tomlinson's *How to Differentiate Instruction in Mixed-Ability Classrooms* (2001), which serves as a practitioner-friendly overview of considerations and examples when creating a classroom predicated upon universal design for learning. The third text is a traditional publication: Salend's *Creating Inclusive Classrooms: Effective and Reflective Practices for All Students* (2005). Although a "big glossy," as Brantlinger (2006) derisively named the genre, this text is one of the "best in the bunch," serving as a major resource with an author who appears more genuinely inclusive in his disposition than other scholars in the field. Note that because of its expense, I recommend purchasing a former edition, which can be lower than 10% of the current published price. Taken together, weaving chapters from these texts helps students see and make connections among theory, practice, policy, and research about inclusive education.

Two other important "texts" shown early in the course are two documentary films: *Including Samuel* (Habib, 2008) and *Ir a la Escuela/Going to School* (Cohen, 2001). The first film is a contemporary classic that shows how Samuel, a young child with multiple disabilities, and his family navigate a school system and society that is not quite prepared for him. The narratives of half a dozen other students with disabilities are woven throughout, creating a complex, informative picture of children and youth, their families, and their schools. The second film is lesser known, but equally valuable. The director tells the story of Richard—a multiply physically and cognitively disabled deaf student—and other young Latino/Latinas in Los Angeles public schools, featuring their parents and what they did to secure supportive services. A good conversation is had when students compare and contrast the experiences of Samuel and Richard in terms of social class, cultural capital, ethnicity, and nationality, giving rise to the notion of different experiences depending upon the context.

Within the first third of the course, I hope to have somewhat destabilized any fixed notions of what constitutes dis/ability, the reliability of that information, the legitimacy of it as a source of knowledge, and render visible the questionable foundational values upon which special education rests. As part of this effort, I utilize two short but potent assignments. In the next sections, I describe these assignments, sample some student responses, and discuss why I believe this DSE-fueled approach is useful.

Spotlight on Movie Analysis

In our class discussion of disability in the media, although we note that some progress has been made, it becomes apparent that authentic representations of disability are still rare. Guided by the work of Safran (1998a), we look at the "archetypes" portrayed that come to bear on our analysis. Safran (1998b) claims that there are nine major categories of archetypes; I share these along with an example or two: (1) villain, for example, *Hook* (Spielberg, 1991), *Silence of the Lambs* (Bozman, 1991); monster, for example, *The Hunchback of Notre Dame* (Hahn, Tousdale, & Wise, 1996), *Friday the 13th* (Geiler, & Cunningham, 1980); seeker of revenge, for example, *Moby Dick* (Huston, 1956), *Nightmare on Elm Street* (Shaye & Craven, 1984); bitter or nasty, for example, *Passion Fish* (Sloss & Sayles, 1992); object of pity, for example, *Born on the Fourth of July* (Ho & Stone, 1989); perpetually infantilized, for example, *Austin Powers* (Todd, Moore, Todd, Myers, 1997); in possession of special powers, for example, *Don't Look Now* (Unger, 1973); suicidal, for example, *Million Dollar Baby* (Lorenz, Lucchesi, & Eastwood, 2004); or inspirational, for example, *The Miracle Worker,* (Coe, 1962). To his list I optimistically add "the everyday/no big deal" portrayal, with examples such as *The Station Agent* (Skalski, May, Tucker, & McCarthy, 2003), *Rory O'Shea Was Here* (Flynn & Wilson, 2005), *My Left Foot* (Pearson & Sheridan, 1989), and documentaries such as *Murder Ball* (Mandel, Shapiro, & Rubin, 2005). As can be seen, depictions are usually overwhelmingly negative and largely inaccurate, with disability used as a plot device rather than portraying an authentic experience (Mitchell & Snyder, 2000).

Having discussed examples by using the lens of DS/DSE to critique and counteract the messages that permeate our culture, I ask students to choose a film to scrutinize. The film can be a "classic" movie from any decade, a TV movie, a contemporary film being shown, or a personal favorite that will be re-watched with a critical lens. The format is simple. Students are required to note the full title of the film, its year of release, and respond to: (a) In what ways are disabled bodies represented? How is this contrasted with normalcy?;

(b) What are the messages these representations send to society at large?; (c) What are questions and thoughts that you have in relation to the film?

It is always interesting to read the student choices. In my most recent class, they were as follows: *Austin Powers: Goldmember* (Todd, Todd, Moore, McLeod, Lyons, Myers, & Roach, 2002); *Digging to China* (Davis & Hutton, 1997); *Edward Scissorhands* (Burton & DiNovi, 1990); *Fanaa* (Chopra & Kohli, 2006); *Forrest Gump* (Finerman, Tisch, Starkey, & Zemeckis, 1994); *The Hunchback of Notre Dame* (Hahn, Tousdale, & Wise, 1996) (four students); *Jane Eyre* (Lovell & Zeffirelli, 1996); *Koi Mil Gaya* (Roshan, 2003); *Quid Pro Quo* (Pillsbury, Sanford, & Brooks, 2008); *Radio* (Tollin, Robbins, & Gains, 2003); *Rain Man* (Johnson & Levinson, 1988); *The Sea Inside* (Amenabar & Bovaira, 2004); *The Sessions* (Levine, Nemeth, & Lewin, 2012) (two students); *Silver Linings Playbook* (Gigliotti, Cohen, & Gordon, 2012); *The Station Agent* (Skalski, May, Tucker, & McCarthy 2003); *Superstar* (Michaels & McCulloch, 1999); *What's Eating Gilbert Grape?* (Teper, Ohlsson, Matalon, & Hallstrom, 1993) (two students); and *World's End* (Bevan, Fellner, Park, & Wright, 2013). As can be seen, their choices are quite personal, and taken together make an eclectic collection ripe for analysis. Overall, having been introduced to a different way of "seeing" disability in class, student commentaries and questions are both thoughtful and insightful.

For example, one student who watched *The Hunchback of Notre Dame* shares, "After watching this movie, I began to wonder how people with physical disabilities see this movie. Do they think it a heartwarming tale, or do they find it insulting? Is the idea that the protagonist has to become a hero before he is respected something that they see in a film?" A related trope of seeing people with disabilities as monsters is also analogizing them to animals. In *Austin Powers: Goldmember*, for example, a student noted how the small person/dwarf Mini-Me is referred to as, "That vicious little ... Chihuahua thing," and responds to Dr. Evil's command, "Heel, Mini-Me, heel!" Each one of these examples indicates a sub-human status accorded to the disabled.

As with *Goldmember*, humor can no longer be taken at face value when in movies such as *Superstar*, bullies are rewarded for their actions toward the "misfit" heroine. Likewise, in classics such as *Rain Man*, students become less enthralled by Dustin Hoffman's performance as Raymond and more concerned with why he had to be returned to an institution, reinforcing the notion that there is no place for people with autism in society (even the super rich!). Unsurprisingly, inspirational tales abound, including the title character in *Radio*, who—contrary to the town's initial opinion—was able to become included in society.

Indeed, when students discuss their papers during class in groups of four, larger issues rise to the surface and create deep conversations about major themes. For example, an observation that becomes apparent is the sense of *containment* that pervades many disability narratives in the media. Forms of containment include institutions (*Rain Man, Digging to China, Silver Linings Playbook*), hidden rooms (*Jane Eyre*) and out-of-reach bell towers (*Hunchback*), rural homes (*Gilbert Grape*), or on the fringes of society (*Radio*). Even more sobering, disability is linked to a desirable death (*Million Dollar Baby, The Sea Inside,* suicidal Dan in *Forrest Gump*). It becomes shocking to students that separating, hiding, or killing people seem to be stock societal responses to disability. When relating these issues to education, it is not a stretch to link them to stigmatization, outcast status, self-contained classes, separate schools, institutions, and prisons. In addition, even commonplace enforced practices such as amniocentesis to "prevent" the birth of disabled children are looked at in a different light.

Another issue that often surfaces is the fear around sexuality and disability. In viewing *The Sessions*, a true story of Mark O'Brien, a quadriplegic man who seeks therapeutic sex, one student did additional research on the main character, including his critique of rehabilitation. O'Brien (1990) asks,

> Why do rehabilitation hospitals teach disabled people to sew wallets and cook from a wheelchair but not deal with a person's damaged self-image? Why don't these hospitals teach disabled people how to love and be loved through sex, or how to love our unusual bodies?

Strangely enough, people with disabilities are usually seen as either asexual or hyper-sexualized. In *Digging to China* (Davis & Hutton, 1997), the protagonist is looked upon with suspicion, not dissimilar to Lennie in *Of Mice and Men* (Blomquist, Sinise, & Smith, 1992). Likewise, in *Silver Linings Playbook*, Tiffany's grief and mental instability lead her to be highly promiscuous, a female pariah to be avoided at all cost within the community. Once again, these very limited depictions do not accurately represent the sexual desires of the majority of people with disabilities.

Other depictions of disabled characters are fantastically sensational. Oftentimes in Bollywood movies, the entire plot is hinged upon disability (Mitchell & Snyder, 2000). The Indian films chosen by students in the class conform to this pattern to the point of absurdity. In *Fanaa* (Chopra & Kohli, 2006), the blind heroine's sight is restored, and in *Koi Mil Gaya* (Roshan, 2003), the protagonist's disability is removed by an alien. While extreme examples, they serve to illustrate the inaccuracies in depicting disability in a "normal" or "natural" way—and the obsessive need to eradicate it (even magically or extraterrestrially) rather than accept it.

Spotlight on 24-Hour Cultural Awareness

The second assignment I share in this chapter asks students to complete a 24-hour cultural analysis of disability. This is done after we have had an in-depth, layered discussion in class about where and how we learn about disability. In contemplating the areas of personal experience, schooling experience, family, science, history, religion, psychology, television, law, medicine, books, and culture in general, we explore the tangle of knowledge we receive from these domains. However, echoing what has been noticed in the film analysis, much of the knowledge is overwhelmingly negative, inaccurate, and deficit-based. Bearing this in mind, I ask students over the course of one weekend to pick a day—either Friday, Saturday, or Sunday—to keep a list of all the times he or she encounters the broad theme of "disability" (film, TV, sports, entertainment, social events, newspaper, literature, entering and exiting buildings, using transportation systems, spontaneous conversations of others, etc.). After that, I request them to type up a bulleted list of observations noted before writing a synthesis of thoughts and impressions about how we "encounter" disability, how disability is represented, and what messages about disability are circulated throughout our culture.

Student lists are usually insightful (when they come up with the usual observations) and intriguing (when they share the unusual or unexpected). A sample of comments from a number of students is shared below:

- I noticed a homeless man missing one leg in a wheelchair. I thought to myself: How could people with a severe disability be able to work and provide for themselves?
- The mall has only one elevator.
- Only about 20% of subway stations are accessible.
- Walter Jr. having cerebral palsy in *Breaking Bad*.
- Somebody said to me, "What? Are you deaf?"
- While explaining the concept of Inclusion to a date, he said: "Oh, like putting the retarded kids in a class with regular kids?"
- The post office had a long ramp to enter building.
- Jessica Alba is quoted talking about her kids: "They're such little spazzes when they have too much refined sugar and flour."
- Friend called me a "retard" when I didn't know how to get to a certain stop on the subway.
- At a funeral, a family friend has a baby with Down syndrome. She is always referred to as "the one with the baby."
- My apartment building is inaccessible.

- Conversation about retired football players' brain scans and how many are suing the NFL because of Alzheimer's, dementia, or some other brain injury.
- In my class, one child with an anxiety disorder is physically shaking because he does not think he can cut, color, and complete his game board for word study that is due in three days.
- An article in *The Times* about whether to self-disclose a disability on a job application.
- Are some taxis wheelchair accessible? I didn't see one.
- Wheelchair as universal "handicapped" symbols on busses and in elevators.
- One of the Yankees placed on "the disabled list" for pulling his hamstring.
- Passengers on the bus during rush hour are annoyed when it stops to pick up a person in a wheelchair.
- Discussion on *Meet the Press* asking: How can we prevent mentally ill individuals from accessing guns in light of the Navy Yard shooting and other recent attacks?
- A blind woman begging for money.
- An advertisement in *Glamor* magazine for Abilify, used to treat manic or mixed episodes with bipolar disorder.

What is to be made of such a list of random-yet-connected observations about disability? As a class, we unpack the tangle of images and experiences into major themes that include: limited progress in changing both attitudinal and physical barriers; disability related to homelessness, begging, and being a burden; fear of people perceived as mentally ill; the pervasive use of ableism within everyday language; disability as fear of "loss" or "ageing"; work-related injuries; demands of schooling on children; demands of society on adults; medication as "the answer"; and the inconvenience that the disabled pose for the non-disabled. All throughout our conversations about disability, we look at individual traits versus societal responses, and the "ownership" of dis/ability along with issues of inter/dependency as a legitimate way of being—and how these ideas relate to inclusive teaching within classrooms.

Student commentaries that follow their lists are filled with all sorts of astute observations. For example, one student wrote:

> Another thing I noticed was that when I watched television shows, I never saw a person with a disability on the show or movie, I watched *Bridesmaids*, *Sex and the City*, and *Friends* on television within the twenty-four hour period. On each episode and in the movie not one character had a disability. There were

also no supporting characters with disabilities. These shows, which are aimed toward young adults, are showing their viewers that in these worlds disabilities do not exist.

Here, we can begin a conversation about how the invisibility of not seeing yourself reflected on television impacts how you think about yourself, your value, and your place in the world in relation to all other people. We can push the class conversation to ask why these extremes of invisibility or misrepresentation are apparently acceptable for people with disabilities but not any other minority group according to gender, race, sexual orientation. (Although we admit to recognizing that there is more work to be done in these areas, along with others).

Another student observed hearing her father calling a family friend who has an infant with Down syndrome "the one with the baby":

> It's funny that having a daughter with a disability became something that people know her by, as if it was a personality trait or physical characteristic, like saying 'the one with the brown hair.' Of course my father meant no harm by this, but people often define people with disabilities, as well as their families using disability. It is unfair, but I do feel it is very common.

In dissecting this statement, we return to what disability actually *signifies*. In many cases, it represents the whole child, and oftentimes, by extension, the whole family. Once again, we discuss implications for classrooms, schools, and systems in which a disability label comes to be the singularly most defining aspect of that child in the educational system (Rodis, Garrod, & Boscardin, 2001)—and the stigma associated for the individual child and collective family members (Hale, 2011).

Some Implications for Schools, Classrooms, and Teaching

All of the student observations in these (and other) assignments help shape the tenor of discussions and influence addressing the enormous elephant in the room: *What is normal?* And the constellation of related questions associated with it, including: What is abnormal? What is special? Who gets to decide? How are these constructs created and reified? What are the implications of these constructs in schools and society? What are the responsibilities of educators in navigating this often complex and contradictory terrain while honoring human differences that exist within all classrooms? This, of course, is the best conversational backdrop to have for the duration of the semester.

Another phenomenon that sometimes occurs in a DS/DSE-based class is some students feel comfortable enough to "come out" as disabled—having been in special education classes, schools, or resource rooms. I am always grateful for students who take this risk and are willing to share their insights and experiences about a variety of topics from managing stigmatizing labels to what makes a good teacher, from accessing modifications and supports to self-strategizing for academic and social survival. Such students have compelling tales that non-disabled students learn from, understanding disability "from the source" as opposed to a traditional "big glossy" soulless textbook chapter (Brantlinger, 2006).

The Other Two-Thirds of the Course

After studying what we know about disability and how we know it, our "noticings" in real life (24-hour observation) and mirrored life in the media (film analysis), I shift the focus from *why* to *how* to make inclusive classrooms work. For teachers, the study of good instructional and managerial practices cannot be underestimated. Yet, without the theoretical grounding of DS/DSE, practices appear to be understood on a very superficial level—as if "what works" is largely free of theory and ideology.

The balance of the course is crafted to contain important bread-and-butter areas such as: recognizing and responding to the diverse educational needs of students with disabilities and other learners who challenge schools; creating an environment that fosters diversity, acceptance, and friendships; teaching disability as part of diversity; the need to cultivate and sustain collaborative relationships with other educational professionals—and parents; specific skills needed for co-teaching; crafting robust units and lesson plans; differentiating instruction in numerous ways; using effective teaching techniques; managing classrooms of diverse learners; and assessing instruction of all learners. All of the above is "the stuff" that we must model and teach students so they will be as prepared as they can be for entering the profession.

Conclusion

By first providing a strong grounding in DS/DSE from a critical special educator's point of view, all practices that follow, be they collaborative teaching or differentiating instruction, make more sense. The first part of this chapter's title, "Practicing What We Teach" is (to state the obvious) a play upon the adage "practicing what we preach." In closing, there are two points I would like to emphasize. First, college professors are notorious for telling students what to do, rather than showing—and have them participate in—successful methods needed to teach. This class provides an opportunity to demonstrate

DSE/UDL-simpatico methodologies (perhaps a future topic to be given its own chapter in another volume). Second, theories of disability as human difference is an area that is underdeveloped within special education classes, and—in my experience—is intriguing and appealing to students because it requires them to question what they believe in and why. I believe these two components are vital to the success of an inclusion course worth its salt. Finally, the second part of this chapter's title, "The Benefits of Using Disability Studies in an Inclusion Course," emphasizes shifting the education of students with disabilities from deficit-based perspectives that continue to undergird special education's adherence to scientism and redirects them toward the social and moral dimensions of viewing inclusion primarily as a civil right that celebrates disability as a natural part of human differences. When we can help developing educators to make that move toward DSE-grounded thinking to help them utilize inclusive practices, then we have made some progress in our chosen discipline.

References

Amenabar, A., & Bovaira, F. (Producers), & Amenabar, A. (Director). (2004). *The sea inside* [Motion picture]. Spain: Fineline Features.

Andrews, J. E., Carnine, D. W., Coutinho, M. J., Edgar, E. B., Forness, S. R., et al. (2000). Bridging the special education divide. *Remedial and Special Education, 21*(5), 258–260, 267.

Baglieri, S., Valle, J., Connor, D. J., & Gallagher, D. (2011). Disability studies and special education: The need for plurality of perspectives on disability. *Remedial and Special Education, 32*(4), 267–278.

Bevan, T., Fellner, E., & Park, N. (Producers), & Wright, E. (Director). (2013). *World's end*. Motion picture]. U.S.: Universal.

Blomquist, A. C., Sinise, G., & Smith, R. (Producers), & Sinise, G. (Director). (1992). *Of mice and men* [Motion picture]. U.S.: Metro-Golden-Mayer.

Bozman, R. (Producer), & Demme, J. (Director). (1991). *Silence of the lambs* [Motion picture]. U.S.: Orion Pictures.

Brantlinger, E. (2006). The big glossies: How textbooks structure (special) education. In E. Brantlinger (Ed.). *Who benefits from special education?: Remediating (fixing) other people's children* (pp. 45–75). Mahwah, NJ: Lawrence Erlbaum.

Burton, T., & DiNovi, D. (Producers), & Burton, T. (Director). (1990). *Edward Scissorhands.* [Motion picture]. U.S.: Twentieth Century Fox.

Chopra, A. (Producer), & Kohli, K. (Director). (2006). *Fanaa* [Motion picture]. India: Yash Films.

Coe, F. (Producer), & Penn, A. (Director). (1962). *The miracle worker* [Motion picture]. U.S.: United Artists.

Cohen, R. (Producer & Director) (2001). *Ir a la Escuela (Going to School)* [Motion picture]. Los Angeles, CA: Richard Cohen films. Retrieved from www.richardcohenfilms.com

Connor, D. J. (2004). Infusing disability studies into "mainstream" educational thought: One person's story. *Review of Disability Studies, 1*(1), 100–119.

Connor, D. J., Gabel, S. L., Gallagher, D. & Morton, M. (2008). Disability studies and inclusive education—Implication for theory, research, and practice: Guest editor's introduction. *International Journal of Inclusive Education, 12*(5–6), 441–457.

Davis, J. (Producer), & Hutton, T. (Director). (1997). *Digging to China* [Motion picture]. U.S.: Moonstone Entertainment.

Finerman, W., Tish, S., Starkey, S., (Producers), & Zemeckis, R. (Director). (1994). *Forrest Gump* [Motion picture]. U.S.: Paramount.

Flynn, J., & Wilson, J., (Producers), & O'Donnell, D. (Director). (2005). *Rory O'Shea was here* [Motion picture]. Ireland/U.S.: Focus Features.

Friend, M. (2008). Co-teaching: A simple solution that isn't so simple after all. *Journal of Curriculum and Instruction, 2*(2), 9–19.

Geiler, A. (Producer), & Cunningham, S. (Director). (1980). *Friday the 13th* [Motion picture]. U.S.: Paramount Pictures.

Gigliotti, D., Cohen, B., & Gordon, J. (Producers), & Russel, D. O. (Director). (2012). *Silver linings playbook* [Motion picture]. U.S.: Weinstein.

Goffman, E. (1963). *Stigma: Notes on the management of spoiled identity.* New York: Simon & Schuster.

Habib, D. (2008). (Producer & Director). *Including Samuel* [DVD]. Retrieved from http://www.includingsamuel.com/home.aspx

Hahn, D. (Producer), Tousdale, G., & Wise, K. (Directors). (1996). *The hunchback of Notre Dame.* [Motion picture]. U.S.: Walt Disney.

Hale, C. (2011). *From exclusivity to exclusion: The LD experience of privileged parents.* Rotterdam, Holland: Sense.

Ho, A. K. (Producer), & Stone, O. (Producer & Director). (1989). *Born on the Fourth of July* [Motion picture]. U.S.: Universal Studios.

Huston, J. (Producer & Director). (1956). *Moby Dick* [Motion picture]. U.S.: United Artists.

Johnson, M. (Producer), & Levinson, B. (Director). (1988) *Rain man* [Motion picture]. U.S.: United Artists.

Levine, J., Nemeth, S., & Lewin, B. (Producers), & Lewin, B. (Director). (2012). *The sessions* [Motion picture]. U.S.: Fox Searchlight.

Lorenz, R., & Lucchesi, G. (Producers), & Eastwood, C. (Director). (2004). *Million dollar baby* [Motion picture]. U.S.: Warner Brothers.

Lovell, D. (Producer), & Zeffirelli, F. (Director). *Jane Eyre.* (1996) [Motion picture]. U.S.: Miramax.

Mandel, J., & Shapiro, D. A. (Producers), & Rubin, H. A., & Shapiro, D. A. (Directors). (2005). *Murderball.* [Motion picture]. U.S.: Think Films/MTV Films.

Michaels, L. (Producer), & McCulloch, B. (Director). (1999). *Superstar* [Motion picture]. U.S.: Paramount.

Mitchell, D., & Snyder, S. (2000). *Narrative prosthesis: Disability and the dependencies of discourse*. Ann Arbor, MI: University of Michigan Press.

O'Brien, M. (1990, May). On seeing a sex surrogate. *The Sun, 147*. Retrieved from http://thesunmagazine.org/issues/174/on_seeing_a_sex_surrogate

Pearson, N. (Producer), & Sheridan, J. (Director). (1989). *My left foot* [Motion picture]. U.S.: Miramax.

Pillsbury, S., & Sanford, M. (Producers), & Brooks, C. (Director). (2008). *Quid pro quo* [Motion picture]. U.S.: Magnolia Pictures.

Rodis, P., Garrod, A., & Boscardin, M. L. (Eds.) (2001). *Learning disabilities and life stories*. Needham Heights, MA: Allyn & Bacon.

Roshan, R. (Producer & Director). (2003). *Koi mil gaya* [Motion picture]. India: Yash Films.

Safran, S. P. (1998a). The first century of disability portrayal in film: An analysis of the literature. *Journal of Special Education, 31*(4), 467–479.

Safran, S. P. (1998b). Disability portrayal in film: Reflecting the past, directing the future. *Exceptional Children, 64*(2), 227–238.

Salend, S. J. (2005). *Creating inclusive classrooms: Effective and reflective practices for all students* (4th ed.). Upper Saddle River, NJ: Prentice Hall.

Shaye, R. (Producer), & Craven, W. (Director). *Nightmare on Elm Street* [Motion picture]. U.S.: New Line Cinema.

Skalski, M. J., May, R., & Tucker, K. (Producers), & McCarthy, T. (Director). (2003). *The station agent* [Motion picture]. U.S.: Miramax.

Skrtic, T. M. (1991). The special education paradox: Equity as a way to excellence. *Harvard Educational Review, 61*(2), 148–206.

Sloss, J. (Producer), & Sayles, J. (Director). (1992) *Passion fish* [Motion picture]. U.S.: Miramax.

Speilberg, S. (Producer & Director). (1991). *Hook* [Motion picture]. U.S.: Tri Star Pictures.

Teper, M., Ohlsson, B., & Matalon, D. (Producers), & Hallstrom, L. (Director). (1993). *What's eating Gilbert Grape?* [Motion picture]. U.S.: Paramount.

Todd, S., Moore, D., Todd, J., & Myers, M. (Producers), & Roach, J. (Director). (1997). *Austin Powers: International man of mystery* [Motion picture]. U.S.: New Line Cinema.

Todd, S., Todd, J., Moore, D. McLeod, E, Lyons, J., & Myers, M. (Producers), & Roach, J. (Director). (2002). *Austin Powers: Goldmember* [Motion picture]. U.S.: New Line Cinema.

Tollin, M., Robbins, B., & Gains, H. W. (Producers), & Tollin M. (Director). (2003). *Radio* [Motion picture]. U.S.: Revolution Studios/Columbia.

Tomlinson, C. A. (2001). *How to differentiate instruction in mixed-ability classrooms* (2nd ed.). Alexandria, VA: ACSD.

Unger, A. B. (Producer), & Roeg, N. (Director). (1973). *Don't look now* [Motion picture]. U.K. & Italy: Casey Productions & Eldorado Films.

Valle, J., & Connor, D. (2011). *Rethinking disability: A disability studies approach to inclusive practices*. New York: McGraw Hill.

Will, M. C. (1986). Educating children with learning problems: A shared responsibility. *Exceptional Children, 52*, 411–415.

8. Why We Do What We (Think We) Do: Creating a Campus Coalition From the Perspective of Disability Studies in Education

GEERT VAN HOVE AND ELISABETH DE SCHAUWER

At Ghent University (Belgium) within the Department of Special Education, a group of researchers is united under the banner of Disability Studies in Education (DSE) (Van Hove et al., 2008). Since 1999, this group has been trying to build an environment in which DSE is more than just a theoretical framework, a way of thinking, or a topic of class discussion. We are becoming a "network group" with strong connections to people whose lived experiences reflect the kinds of concerns addressed by DSE scholars. At the same time, we are looking at how to work with our network companions in research, education, and service to the community. It is clear that such an agenda cannot be accomplished overnight and requires the development of strong partnerships. Over the past 15 years, our coalition with network companions—the self-advocacy movement Onze Nieuwe Toekomst (Our New Future),[1] the parents' association Ouders voor Inclusie (Parents for Inclusion), and Steunpunt Inclusief Hoger Onderwijs (Expertise Centre for Students with Disabilities in Higher Education Institutions)—has developed naturally into an embedded structure at the university and is considered pivotal to our overarching agenda.

About the Campus Coalition

A parent who is a member of our campus coalition described it as follows:

> "the Disability Studies group at Ghent University can be compared to a table
> around which organisations that have common interests are given the opportunity

to sit down and get to know each other in order to share experiences about their minoritarian position, find inspiration in each other's work, and plan joint campaigns. The organisations act as the legs of the table that provide the Disability Studies group with the support and balance that are essential to stay in touch with the reality of people with a label and their families."

Based on these thoughts, we are working daily toward a coalition that can be defined as "a temporary coming together of distinct parts that result in a form of unity in which the new whole retains the original parts" (Ford, 2007, p. 310). From a very practical perspective (that is, the "how to"), we have learned that over the last 15 years such a coalition is not solely built on shared ideology. We could only have sustained such long-lasting partnerships because of our focus on the following organizing principles: (a) learning to become and stay very sensitive to the velocity of and within our partnership building process; (b) confronting different processes linked to differing agendas (for example, the agenda of a parent movement will never coincide with academic deadlines of bringing in research proposals and re-working papers); and (c) committing to "the dance" among partnerships (that is, maintaining open communication about such tensions and practicing equitable "give and take").

Working with a coalition, for us, means that participants share "spaces"/places. Our three network companions share offices with our academic staff. Sharing space opens up opportunities for informal contact and quick consultation moments. But beyond such exchanges, sharing space with our partners reminds us as faculty—who function daily in a very competitive academic world—to remain committed to a long-term focus on the wellbeing of families and children.

Building such a coalition has proven to be desirable and beneficial for all stakeholders. It has afforded everyone involved the experience of shifting positions of hierarchy and stratification, depending upon what a particular situation and moment requires. The coalition has provided DSE faculty with the critical partners needed to help us remain open to views outside of a traditional campus—a sort of parallel world. In a traditional university setting, "the laptop researcher" features heavily. This researcher concentrates on data stored in some data pool. His or her agenda is most often individualistic and guided by personal interests. Our comments about the laptop researcher are not meant to be judgmental, but rather reflective of the research demands that a typical university structure places upon faculty. As a point of contrast to the work of a laptop researcher, we instead value and rely upon lived insider perspectives of people with disabilities and their families. Lather (1986) defines the goal of insider research as the process of moving people "from articulating what they know to theorizing about what they know, a process the researchers term 'collaborative theorizing'" (p. 264). In other words, this (research) methodology is characterized by negotiation.

Ghent University provides us with a meeting place for the campus coalition to gather and try out the following:

- *Anti-essentialism*: We continually work toward creating a hybrid space in alignment with our definition of coalition. Together, we are building a space for cultural, social, and epistemological change where competing knowledges and discourses challenge and (hopefully) reshape both academic and everyday knowledge (Barton, Tan, & Rivet, 2008, citing Moje, Collazo, Carillo & Marx, 2001). Skrtic's notion of adhocracy (1995) plays an important role in how we share and prioritize an agenda that includes activism, university teaching, and research.
- *Retroduction*: In our research and activism, we make use of an inductive way of working (Biklen, 2005) as well as a social interpretation perspective that reveals insights in a more deductive way (Fereday & Muir-Cochrane, 2006). Using an open collection of conceptual tools (e.g., the social model of disability, an explicit human-rights perspective—through the United Nations Convention on the Rights of Persons with Disabilities, embodiment theory, the impact of disablism, the intersectionality of disability with other "social markers" such as race, class, and culture, disability culture), we try to make sense of the complex reality of our coalition partners and other excluded persons and groups with a label (Emerson, 2004, citing Becker, 1998; Bulmer, 1979; Katz, 1983, Lofland, 1976).

In light of the theoretical orientation just described, our campus coalition believes in the power of bringing the "real world" to campus—a move that has changed the atmosphere in our department from "silencio to agora" (according to the Head of Department). Our experiences with the coalition remind us of the "chaosmos" that Julie Allan (2008) describes:

> Deterritorialization creates 'chaosmos' (Deleuze & Guattari, 1994) …which Deleuze and Guattari considered an apt account of the effects of deterritorialization: 'composed chaos, neither forseen nor preconceived' (p. 204) and precipitating new ways of thinking and acting: 'once one ventures outside what's familiar and reassuring, once one has to invent new concepts for unknown lands, then methods and moral systems break down' (Deleuze, 1995, p. 322). The potential areas for deterritorialization cannot be specified; rather it is a case of being alert to opportunities to interrupt. (p. 63)

Having a DSE-oriented campus coalition as a basecamp heightens our chances of impacting the real lives of persons with labels and their families, the environment we share, and the perspectives of university students who learn understandings of disability other than the ones offered by "professional experts." Chinnery (2003) compares this kind of professional preparation of future teachers to the work of jazz players:

> Engage in rigorous study and practice in order to build up their memory of repertoires, then, at the moment of performance, they must suspend deliberation and abandon the known in order to embrace risk and vulnerability. It is about the capacity to vulnerability and exposure to the Other, to the pains and pleasures of human life. (p. 13)

In the sections to follow, we describe five aspects that are crucial to the life of our campus coalition: (1) co-teaching; (2) an educational philosophy; (3) a scientific strategy; (4) a political perspective; and (5) a dialogue among cultures.

Our Coalition and Co-Teaching

Within the DSE group at Ghent University, faculty members maximally involve the coalition partners in our training and teaching program. We strongly believe it is a win-win situation for all members of the coalition. Working with self-advocates and families raising children with disabilities makes it possible to integrate their specific talents within our program. For some of our partners, it is essential that their poetry or creative associative thinking or storytelling capacities become basic tools in the educational process of our students. A self-advocate explains: "We have to come out and show ourselves, before the students come to us. It is very important that they get to know that we are people with our own possibilities before they start to write our individual plans." For our teaching and research staff members, this involvement of talents creates instructional opportunities other than routine-like teaching (also known as the "PowerPoint presentation dogma") and eases the challenge of preparing, teaching, and carrying full responsibility for the education of students. Moreover, the contact between coalition partners and our students has opened windows of opportunities for students to volunteer to support and/or coach persons labelled with disabilities in complex situations (for example, political decision processes, inclusive education in the Flemish regular schools, individual desires and dreams of finding volunteer work, learning to cook).

We have also observed that our two most stable coalition partners have begun to work together more and more—an example of the table metaphor used by the parent quoted at the beginning of this chapter. We have seen how the organizations involve each other in their own ways of working, "steal" ideas and inspiration to bring into their own work, and ask one another for advice about how to organize things for themselves. The overflow of learning between the organizations is organic, which means that it varies in topic and intensity. It is very informal on one side (for example, exchanging ways to find grants and budgets, driving together to meetings, eating together in the café where one of the self-advocates works as a volunteer) and structurally embedded on the other side (for example, one of the leading members of the parent movement serves on the governmental board for the self-advocacy movement, a man with Down syndrome became an active member of Our New Future because he wanted to attend meetings just like his mother in the parent group).

We are seeing strong advantages of this way of working together with possibilities for all partners involved, but have not yet found the "philosopher's stone." A lot needs to be done to solve problems regarding pace, abstract language, English as "lingua academia," and paying our partners more than pocket money. We observe and learn each day that the co-teaching strategy with our coalition partners brings us different research questions and different[2] research strategies. "Nothing about us without us" is no longer merely a slogan but an integral part of our cooperative research agenda. We have also observed a transformation in our co-teaching relationship over time. We have moved from inviting partners to co-teach with us about our chosen topics to having our partners take ownership of the teaching process by highlighting their own priorities and favourite topics.

Our co-teaching is a continual work in progress. The following items represent a set of actions for the near future:

- We plan to involve our coalition partners in the preparation of the "quality evaluation process" that our department (and DSE coalition) will confront in 2015.
- During the follow-up phase of the quality evaluation process, we will need to re-organize some of our courses (standard procedure). This will offer a great opportunity to involve our coalition partners in setting up new course modules or in adapting already available courses.
- We would like to give a co-teaching symbol to our courses to signify that these modules are built on shared responsibilities among the DSE faculty and coalition partners—from the construction of the course to its final evaluation.

Our Coalition and an Educational Philosophy

The faculty of Psychology and Educational Sciences at Ghent University has chosen to build a program for the students in Educational Sciences to become "reflective practitioners." In our continuing efforts to (re)define the concept of coalition and campus, we introduce our students to the "perfect chaos" called life by having them partner with families in our coalition. It quickly becomes clear to our students—on small and large scales—that persons labelled with disabilities and their families have to survive within complex and threatening realities. For some students, it is an incredible adventure to experience how a mother and father of several children (including a child with extra support needs related to activities of daily living) manage to get all the kids together at the same moment to school in the morning. For other students, working with young women labelled with disabilities becomes a very intense experience upon learning how these women are dealing with issues of sexuality and the female body struggle under the care of clinicians who display what Allan (2007) shrewdly refers to as "professional thought disorder."[3]

Our coalition partners are real experts in taking students with them to situations where they can learn to doubt what seems obvious and not understand or know what to do. In these confrontations, students get the opportunity to appreciate uncertainty and ambiguity. We have observed fear in the eyes of some of our students upon realizing that their papers would be evaluated by co-teachers with the label of "cognitive impairment." Other students sweat when young children ask straight questions about the way someone with the label of Down syndrome learns to read. Such real-life scenarios encourage students to consider just how irrelevant the *Diagnostic and Statistical Manual* can be in the real lives of persons labelled with disabilities as well as for their advocates. Allan (2008, p. 156) shares a quote from Taylor and Saarinen (1994) in which she challenges us to "inter-stand" rather than "under-stand":

> "When depth gives way to surface, under-standing becomes inter-standing. To comprehend is no longer to grasp what lies beneath but to glimpse what lies between ... Understanding is no longer possible because nothing stands under ... Inter-standing has become unavoidable because everything stands between." (pp. 2–3)

The consequences of inter-standing are not easy and demand praxis in the Freirean sense. Allan (2008) further states,

> The pursuit of inter-standing involves risking the personal (Ware, 2002) because it requires individuals to tolerate the diminishment of the borders which define their identities and their sense of place and much of the knowledge which is used as warrants for action. (p. 156)

Our faculty has adopted the "reflective practitioner" as a signboard for the education and training of students. Schön (1983) describes reflective practitioners as displaying "a kind of artistry: ...so practice can never be reduced to a set of techniques that can be mastered and applied" (p. 243). By engaging students in the lives of our coalition partners, we hope that they will build their knowledge from parents and self-advocates in contrast to:

- Pathologizing and oppressing the perspectives of parents and self-advocates in tandem with the imposition of systems and meanings where only particular systems and meanings are granted legitimacy (Bourdieu, 1977)
- Establishing and reaffirming the image of crazed and destructive parents (Danforth & Gabel, 2006, citing Kliewer, 2006), an image that flourishes easily in the university context where reason and reflectiveness are associated with forms of knowing that originate from situations most distant from lived experiences (as in the metaphor of the ivory tower)

In practice, we introduce students within the first period of their studies to the foundations of DSE by giving them safe opportunities to learn. Beyond the experience of being in a class where co-teaching occurs, students also have multiple opportunities to dialogue with parents in small groups. Students are invited to volunteer on Parents for Inclusion meeting days (for example, helping to make coffee; taking care of a group of children). Other students are introduced into the practice of coaching self-advocates. Many of our students assist the self-advocacy movement or the Expertise Center for Students with Special Needs in Higher Education on conference days or during workshops. We continually strive to find the right balance between learning moments (elements that are given to the students) and the time and energy that our students give to the projects of our partners.

Our Coalition and a Scientific Strategy—From Je pense, donc je suis (I think, therefore I am) to We Learn/Work, so We Are

DSE is compatible with the "action turn" in the social sciences toward a kind of research/practice open in principle to anyone willing to commit to the integration of inquiry and practice in everyday personal and professional settings. In fact, we all inevitably integrate inquiry and practice implicitly into our everyday conduct. Nevertheless, the call to integrate inquiry and practice represents a demand that few persons in history have attempted to accept (Reason & Torbert 2001):

> ...the action turn is to bring scholarship to life, is to bring inquiry into more and more of our moments of action—not just as scientists if that happens to be our profession, but as organizational and family members, and in our spiritual, artistic, craft, exercise, conversational, sexual, and other activities. (pp. 6–7)

In this way, we rely upon our campus coalition to build "communities of practice" (Wenger, 1998) in which we:

- "negotiate meaning" as to how we experience the world and our engagement in it as meaningful
- actively participate in social processes
- co-ordinate perspectives and actions in order to direct energies toward a common purpose

In this sense, we try to follow a Freirean (1998) way of learning and working to make sure that knowing can be understood as a social process, whose individual dimension, however, is not forgotten or devalued. As Lather (1986) writes:

> Emancipatory knowledge increases awareness of the contradictions hidden or distorted by everyday understandings, and in doing so it directs attention to the possibilities for social transformation inherent in the present configuration of social processes. (p. 259)

The process of knowing, which involves the whole conscious self, feelings, emotions, memory, affects an epistemologically curious mind focused on the object and equally involves other thinking subjects; that is, others also capable of knowing and being curious. This simply means that the relationship called "thinking" is not enclosed in a "thinking subject–knowable object" relationship because thinking necessarily extends to other thinking subjects. Davies et al. (2013, p. 689) places this relationship in Deleuzian terms of singular *and* plural subjected beings:

> We are neither the singular subjected being nor the collective terms of our subjection ... but singular *and* plural, taking up our always emergent being with a "single and same voice for the whole thousand-voiced multiple, a single and unique Ocean for all the drops, a single clamor of Being for all beings." (Deleuze, 1994, p. 304)

In light of our collective understanding regarding the "process of knowing," we cannot underscore just how complex and confusing our campus coalition can sometimes be.

Our Coalition and a Political Perspective

Within our campus coalition, we strive to conscientize[4] together with our partners around the idea that "pedagogy is politics" and that persons labelled with disabilities and their families can be seen as companions in a political struggle (Danforth & Gabel, 2006, citing Kliewer, 2006, p. 101). When we think about political engagement, it is not dependent on an individual or several individuals. Rather, it is necessary to think in terms of connections and movements in order to take steps toward social change. It is our goal to develop a coalitional consciousness (Sandoval, 2000). As Naraian (2011) notes, "The nature of this work is difficult and complex, you feel threatened to the core" (quoted in paper presented DSE Conference 2011). We agree with Pisters (2007) that our aim is to resist, "to resist to power, to resist to the intolerable, resist to fear and resist to shame, resist to the injustice of the present" (p. 20). Such micropolitical acts of resistance give signs of hope in this majoritarian jungle and provide slightly different perceptions of the world. For example, we try to realize these ideas in everyday activism/activities like working in schools, participating in school-parent meetings, attending/ working for parent conferences, giving practical support for art exhibitions, coaching self-advocates, organizing practice places for students together, formulating research questions together, and having discussions with politicians.

These day-by-day actions are the basis for cooperative processes with families and persons labelled with disabilities to subvert labelling practices that put them into categories.

In short, all of the campus coalition's activities lead toward one overarching (political) goal: working together with families and persons labelled with disabilities to make the shift away from a charity model of disability towards a model of participation and human rights (Biklen, 2005, pp. 256–258, citing Rogoff, Paradise, Arauz, Correa-Chavez, Angelillo, 2003).

Our Coalition and a Dialogue Among Cultures

Given that 80% of the world's disabled population live in so-called developing countries, our campus coalition is committed to reaching out to NGOs in Uganda, the Down Syndrome Association in Cape Town, PhD students from Cameroon and Rwanda, and NGOs from the Flemish-speaking part of Belgium whose work is conducted outside the country (e.g., Bulgaria, South Africa, China). We begin from the idea that our work is enriched by engaging in explicit dialogue with diverse cultures in regard to human rights and emancipatory thinking. It is important to the campus coalition to take care not to exclude the global majority of disabled people from the dominant disability discourse (Meekosha & Shuttleworth, 2009, p. 54). We believe that dialogue is of absolute importance: "It is an idea of dialogue ... as a process of transformation where you lose absolutely the possibility of controlling the final result ... You can get lost" (Rinaldi, 2006, p. 184).

Why We Do What We (Think We) Do

Last year, our research group was fortunate to work for three months under the guidance of Professor Bronwyn Davies, who describes herself on her weblog (http://bronwyndavies.com.au/about-bronwyn) as follows:

> Bronwyn Davies is an independent scholar based in Sydney, Australia. She is also a Professorial Fellow at the University of Melbourne. The distinctive features of her work are her development of innovative social science research methodologies and their relation to the conceptual work of poststructuralist philosophies. Her research explores the ethico-onto-epistemological relations through which particular social worlds are constituted. She is best known for her work on gender, for her development of the methodology of collective biography, and her writing on feminism and poststructuralist theory.

Within our intensive period of collaboration with Professor Davies, "ethico-onto-epistemological" questions about our cooperation with families and persons with disabilities were brought to the table through her central and returning question: "Can you tell me (and find out for yourself) how it is that you recognize the human being when no one else can recognize him or her? What is involved in that act of recognition and that commitment to ongoing recognition no matter the difficulties?" In order to make a start in answering these questions, we reformulated the question to consider: "Why has this group (this department) chosen to follow families and persons with disabilities in their struggle for an inclusive society?"

In answering this question, we found it helpful to rely upon the metaphor of a rhizome to capture our way of working and thinking:

> Deleuze and Guattari propose the notion of a rhizome, which grows or moves in messy and unpredictable ways ... Rhizomes have multiple connections, lines and points of rupture, but no foundation or essence, and the connectivity of these lines make a rejection of binarism inevitable. (Allan, 2008, p. 60)

For us, it is a kind of a rhizomatic family journey—deduced from dozens of stories we have come to cherish as a result of working with people labelled with disabilities and their families. We learn every day that there are no simple and orderly lives. What follows can be conceptualized as a house with many entrances. We have marked the entrances with the symbol →→ to represent our rhizomatic, rather than linear, thinking. What follows is what we have come to know.

→→Before children are born, Flemish families live their dreams about the not-yet- born new citizen (De Belie &Van Hove, 2012)—dreams molded by cultural expectations and illusions as portrayed by the media: the happy family with the beautiful and smiling baby. It seems there is a powerful force field that sweeps up parents in a collective eagerness to take their place within the normative center. But what if the baby that comes is not healthy, lively, and perfect? What if the baby does not meet the norms required of newborns? There is tremendous emotion in the telling of stories about sharing the news with family that "something is wrong with the baby" or stories about first meetings with members of the professional community. These experiences could be compared with a kind of "working through" as introduced by Braidotti (2004, p. 29) who describes the process in which people take up a position where, on the one hand, they do what is expected of them, while on the other hand, they formulate their own assessment and look for new codes and opportunities. New fathers and mothers are transformed in the position as parent upon the birth of a less-than-perfect infant and an endless way of searching with their child starts for many families at this moment.

→→In some of our contacts, families live from the beginning with the tension between the WHAT? (for example, diagnoses, impairment, symptoms, syndromes, DSM, scales) and the WHO? (that little fellow/girl) (Isarin, 2004). We have learned from parents that people can only get past the WHAT through little moments/relations where real contact with the WHO can be built slowly (Goodley & Van Hove, 2005, citing Van Hove, 2005). Parents tell us that the relationship with the child is often dominated by what is wrong with the child: the disease, the deficit, and the developmental possibilities. The child, much more than all these labels, only becomes visible later on when the mothers and fathers are able to connect with him or her. They experience through contact that the child with his/her disability is a unique and irreplaceable creature and above all their own child (Isarin, 2005). This is confirmed in what we learn from social psychology (McManus, Feyes, & Saucier, 2010): greater quality of contact (sharing activities, enjoying things together) is more influential in engendering positive attitudes towards persons with intellectual disabilities than greater (technical) knowledge. The basic idea is that more connection and contact helps.

→→In a lot of the stories shared, we learn that some family members crack the binary way of thinking (e.g., autonomous/dependent; able/disabled; competent/incompetent) that is a powerful framework in our world. These soft and warm anarchists should be understood as pathfinders who resist and keep on resisting institutions and persons who—in their experience—try to "capture" the child in parallel (special) worlds. This resistance is "refusing to let those variations be assimilated to binary categories or their implicit tendencies blocked from unfolding new ways of living" (Lorraine, 2008, p. 68). It "is not and cannot be a state, a station, but must be a process that leaves nothing intact in its wake" (Bensmaia & Curtis Gage, 1993, p. 62). We learned more about "stigmergy" through our contacts with Lieven De Couvreur, one of the most influential designers within the framework of Design for All:

> Stigmergy is built on the principle that the trace left in the environment by an action stimulates the performance of a next action, by the same or different agent. In that way, subsequent actions tend to reinforce and build on each other, leading to the spontaneous emergence of coherent, apparently systematic activity. (http://ecco.vub.ac.be/?q=book/export/html/145; slide show: pp. 9, 11, 12)

→→Parents and family members simultaneously use and become trapped by "citational chains" (Davies et al., 2013):

> It is through … repeated acts of recognition, that we are subjected and subject ourselves to discourses that are, Butler argues, in some sense *prior* to us, and *external* to us. The citational chains enable the accomplishment of ourselves as recognizably human, autonomous beings with a viable sense of *individual* identity. (p. 682)

Citational chains are used to describe, to talk about, to situate children and adults with disabilities in various ways and through multiple lenses. How these stories are told, who tells them, when they are told, how much they are told depends upon relations of power. Because of the Catholic/Christian background in the Flemish-speaking part of Belgium, a lot of citational chains are built on or reference feelings of guilt, charity, dependency, and/or specialisms. We are fascinated by the ambiguous way families handle such citational chains. They produce them as oppositional strategies through repeating the extra-value and capacities of their child. Within "re-signification" processes, we learn from families that categories can be broken up—most of the time through precious stories or descriptions of key incidents. In this way, new images and stories help to re-cite other existing (with mostly negative connotations) chains. At the same time, families catch themselves in citational chains (or produced repetition) of the normative terms in society concerning disability (for example, weak, not-able, in need of pity). It seems that they need such moments of compliance from a very pragmatic perspective in order to secure (financial) support for their child and pass the "gaze" of experts (Foucault, 1973).

→→We consider desire (as streams of energy) to be a very productive force that allows movements, flows, and transformations for children with disabilities and their families. Desire is about experimenting with "dare to become all that you cannot be" (O'Shea 2002, p. 930, citing Massumi, 1992). Desire gives families endless opportunities to keep in movement and continuously become by crossing borders, dichotomies, and categories. "Productive desire is a power, a passion that moves one towards something new, the other. Desire does not lack anything; it does not lack its object. It is, rather, the subject that is missing in desire or desire that lacks a fixed subject; there is no fixed subject unless there is repression" (Deleuze & Guattari, 1972, p. 26). By acting along this set of ideas, families (and their companions) are opening up ways for the children to become someone we do not know yet—and with these actions they subvert the one iconic story about "the person with a handicap" we all learned to know. When we take desire seriously, it has consequences for the way we look, think, talk, and represent children with a disability. It comes very close to Rinaldi (2006), who describes a "competent child" as one

> who has the ability to learn, love, be moved and live, the child who has a wealth of potentials, the powerful child in relation to what (s)he is and can be right from birth … Competent because he/she has a body, a body that knows how to speak and listen, that gives him/her identity and with which he/she identifies things. A body equipped with senses that can perceive the surrounding environment. A body that risks being increasingly estranged from cognitive processes if its cognitive potential is not recognized and enhanced. (p. 92)

When we look at a child with a disability as a competent child, s/he becomes a fascinating child, a child who intrigues, a child we want to know.

Concluding Thoughts

Within our DSE group, we desire to continue learning from and listening to persons with disabilities and their advocates. In this way, we resist stagnant habits that can colonize our minds towards "collaborative affective inquiry" (Boler, 1997, pp. 422–425) as we learn to look at difference in an affirmative way. Difference, according to Deleuze (1994), is therefore mediated (p. 38) by being subjected to identity, opposition, analogy, and resemblance. Differences can open up space to look for potentialities (Goodley & Runswick-Cole, 2012, 2013) for conceptualizing disability as not (always) a lack but an opportunity to revise notions of normality, independence, and autonomy.

With this choice, we tap into a pedagogy of desire (Zembylas, 2007, p. 331) as a pedagogy that can be theorized in ways that mobilize creative, transgressive, and pleasurable forces within teaching, learning, and living to-gether. In this interpretation, "a pedagogy of desire" is situated in complete opposition to a "pedagogy of special needs." The latter starts from certain idea about expertise (we know what you need) and the different positions experts and "clients" have. The pedagogy of desire questions these assump-tions and tries to tap into the energy of families and persons with disabilities to escape dichotomies and to resist stratifications. It tries to cooperate—in a serving role—in processes of belonging/becoming part of something, in processes of connecting people, and in the productive moments of passion to move to the other and to something new.

We are taken by what Ann Turnbull (2010) calls a quest for an "envi-able life." Families want to have "a good life" for themselves and for their children. They are driven by the desire to live as a family, and within these processes desire is not an imaginary force based on lack, but a real, productive force that goes from chaos to moments of pride and belonging (Deleuze & Guattari, 1972) to honoring the vulnerability in all of us.

Notes

1. Self-advocacy movements are movements of people with special needs where they are encouraged to speak up for themselves, with the emphasis on actions that help to find how the human rights concept actually affects their lives.
2. By "different" we refer to "different than standard expectations in the closed campus."
3. Professional thought disorder (PTD): a person with PTD is unique; however it is use-ful to recognize the common symptoms. Sufferers have: a compulsion to analyze and compartmentalize the experiences of others, an inability to display empathy to others in distress, rigidly held beliefs, a tendency to ask strange questions that are unrelated to the context in which they are being asked, a confusion between their own wishes and those of the person they are supposed to be helping, and delusions of grandeur (Lowson, 1994). (Julie Allan, lesson to students, October 2007).
4. The process of developing a critical awareness of one's social reality through reflection and action. Action is fundamental because it is the process of changing the reality. Paulo Freire says that we all acquire social myths that have a dominant tendency, and so learn-ing is a critical process that depends upon uncovering real problems and actual needs.

References

Allan, J. (2008). *Rethinking inclusive education: The philosophers of difference in practice*. Dordrecht: Springer.

Barton, A., Tan, E., & Rivet, A. (2008). Creating hybrid spaces for engaging school science among urban middle school girls. *American Educational Research Journal*, *45*(1), 68–103.

Bensmaia, R., & Curtis Gage, J. (1993). The exiles of Nabile Fares: Or, how to become a minority. *Yale French Studies, 83*(2), 44–70.

Biklen, D. (2005). *Autism and the myth of the person alone.* New York University Press: New York.

Boler, M. (1997). Taming the labile other: Disciplined emotions in popular and academic discourses. *Philosophy of Education, 47*(2), 416–425.

Bourdieu, P. (1977). *Reproduction in education, society and culture.* Los Angeles, CA: Sage.

Braidotti, R. (2004). *Op doorreis. Nomandisch denken in de 21ste eeuw.* Amsterdam: Uitgeverij Boom.

Chinnery, A. (2003). Aesthetic of surrender: Levinas and the disruption of agency in moral education. *Studies in Philosophy and Education, 22*(1), 5–17.

Danforth, S., & Gabel, S. (eds.) (2006). *Vital questions facing disability studies in education.* New York: Peter Lang.

Davies, B., De Schauwer, E., Claes, L., De Munck, K., Van De Putte, I., & Verstichele, M. (2013). Recognition and difference: A collective biography. *International Journal of Qualitative Studies in Education, 26*(6), 680–691.

De Belie, E., & Van Hove, G. (eds.) (2012). *Wederzijdse emotionele beschikbaarheid (Mutual Emotional Availability).* Berchem: Uitgeverij Maklu.

Deleuze, G. (1994). *Difference and repetition.* London: Athlone Press.

Deleuze, G., & Guattari, F. (1972). *Anti-Œdipus* (Trans. R. Hurley, M. Seem, & H. R. Lane). London and New York: Continuum, 2004

Emerson, R. (2004). Working with 'key incidents.' In C. Seal, G, Gobo, J. F. Gubrium, & D. Silverman (Eds.), *Qualitative research practice.* London: Sage.

Fereday, J., & Muir-Cochrane, E. (2006). Demonstrating rigor using thematic analysis: A hybrid approach of inductive and deductive coding and theme development. *International Journal of Qualitative Methods, 5*(1). Retrieved from http://www.ualberta.ca/~iiqm/backissues/5_1/html/fereday.htm

Ford, M. (2007). Situating knowledges as coalition work. *Educational Theory, 57*(3), 307–324.

Foucault, M. (1973). *The birth of the clinic: An archeology of medical perception.* New York: Pantheon Books.

Freire, P. (1998). *Teachers as cultural workers: Letters to those who dare teach.* Boulder, CO: Westview Press.

Goodley, D., & Van Hove, G. (2005). *Another disability studies reader? People with learning difficulties and a disabling world.* Antwerp, Belgium: Uitgeverij Garant.

Goodley, D., & Runswick-Cole, K. (2012). Reading Rosie: The postmodern disabled child. *Educational and Child Psychology, 29*(2), 53–66.

Goodley, D., & Runswick-Cole, K. (2013). The body as disability and possibility: Theorizing the 'leaking, lacking and excessive' bodies of disabled children. *Scandinavian Journal of Disability Research, 15*(1), 1–19.

Isarin, J. (2004). *Kind als geen ander. Moeders van gehandicapte kinderen tussen wie en wat.* (Child as no other. Mothers of children with disabilities between who and what). Budel, Netherlands: Uitgeverij Damon.

Isarin, J. (2005, October 26). *Het onachterhaalbare eigen … Symposium geestelijke verzorgers in de verstandelijk gehandicaptenzorg.* Doorn.

Kliewer, C. (2006). Disability studies and young children: Finding relevance. In S. Danforth & S. L. Gabel (Eds.), *Vital questions facing disability studies in education* (pp. 91–102). New York: Peter Lang.

Lather, P. (1986). Research as praxis. *Harvard Educational Review, 56*(3), 257–278.

Lorraine, T. (2008). Feminist lines of flight from the majoritarian subject. *Deleuze Studies, 2,* 60–82.

Lowson, D. (1994) Understanding professional thought disorder: A guide for service users and a challenge for professionals. *Asylum, 8*(2): 29–30.

McManus, J., Feyes, K., & Saucier, D. (2010). Contact and knowledge as predictors of attitudes to persons with intellectual disabilities. *Journal of Social and Personal Relationships.* Advance online publication. DOI: 10.1177/0265407510385494.

Meekosha, H., & Shuttleworth, R. (2009). What's so "critical" about critical disability studies? *Australian Journal of Human Rights, 15*(1), 47–75.

Naraian, S. (2011, May). *Towards a mestiza consciousness in inclusive education: Lessons from a Southern context.* Paper presented at the 11th Annual Second City Conference on Disability Studies in Education, Chicago, IL.

O'Shea, A. (2002). Desiring desire: How desire makes us human, all too human. *Sociology, 36*(4), 925–940.

Pisters, P. (2011). The mosaic film: Nomadic style and politics in transnational media culture. In M. Bal and M. Hernandez-Navaro (Eds.), *Art and visibility in migration culture: Conflict, resistance and agency* (pp. 175–190). Amsterdam: Rodipo.

Reason, P., & Torbert, W. (2001). The action turn: Toward a transformational social science. *Concepts and Transformation, 6*(1), 1–37.

Rinaldi, C. (2006). *In dialogue with Reggio Emilia. Listening, researching and learning.* London: RoutledgeFalmer.

Rogoff, B., Paradise, R., Mejía Arauz, R., Correa-Chávez, M., & Angelillo, C. (2003). Firsthand learning by intent participation. *Annual Review of Psychology, 54,* 175–203.

Sandoval, C. (2000). *Methodology of the oppressed.* Minneapolis: University of Minnesota Press.

Schön, D. (1983). *The reflective practitioner: How professionals think in action.* New York: Basic Books.

Skrtic, T. (1995). *Disability and democracy. Reconstructing special education for postmodernity.* New York: Teachers College Press.

Turnbull, A. (2010). Transitioning to enviable lives for adults with autism. Lecture at the University of Texas at Austin. Retrieved from http://www.meadowscenter.org/library/resource/transitioning-to-enviable-lives-for-adults-with-autism

Van Hove, G., Roets, G., Mortier, K., De Schauwer, E., Leroy, M., & Broekaert, E. (2008). Research in inclusive education as a possible opening to disability studies in Education. In S. L. Gabel & S. Danforth. (Eds.), *Disability and the politics of education: An international reader.* (pp. 121–140). New York: Peter Lang.

Wenger, E. (1998), *Communities of practice: Learning, meaning, and identity*, Cambridge: Cambridge University Press.

Zembylas, M. (2007). Emotional ecology: The interaction of emotional knowledge and pedagogical content knowledge in teaching, *Teaching and Teacher Education, 23,* 355–367.

9. *Madness and (Higher Education) Administration: Ethical Implications of Pedagogy Using Disability Studies Scholarship*

NIRMALA EREVELLES

In the past year, a spate of shootings in university settings attributed to pre-sumed "mad"[1] men/women has resulted in an increased surveillance of those individuals who are either suspected of or have a diagnosis of mental illness. Since several of these shootings were done by individuals associated with the university, there has been a corresponding heightened policing of faculty/students/staff presumed to manifest symptoms of mental illness. In this con-text, university administrators have embraced proactive measures such as de-signing complex evacuation and public safety procedures in case of an actual shooting on campus. But these proactive measures do not just end there. Instead, university administrators have encouraged their constituents to be increasingly vigilant in identifying faculty/students/staff they suspect have a mental disability; in referring them to "appropriate" professionals; in expel-ling them from campus; and in ensuring, if necessary, the administration of involuntary medication and/or involuntary commitment to a mental insti-tution of those individuals deemed to be potentially dangerous to the cam-pus (Price, 2011; Stuart, 2012). Therefore in a context where mental illness has become synonymous with danger, the very presence of students/faculty/staff with psychiatric disabilities places them in extreme jeopardy on college/university campuses.

In a context where such drastic actions against "mad" colleagues are con-ceived of as common sense, an intervention from a critical disability studies standpoint is both necessary and urgent. Critical disability studies explores the discursive, cultural, material, and relational politics of the body/mind that constitute contested notions of normativity/disability (Goodley, 2011). Actively challenging a medical model of disability that locates the problem of difference in the individual rather than in social/cultural representations and/or political and economic practices, a critical disability studies perspective argues that disability offers a unique, transgressive, and desirable standpoint from which to engage the social world. Located in this generative tradition, Margaret Price's (2011) book, *Mad at School: Rhetorics of Mental Disability and Academic Life*, addresses the complex challenges faced by people with psychiatric disabilities in U.S. universities by offering a counter-perspective to reading "madness" as "naturally" violent in the first place, and then proposing concrete ways to intervene in academic contexts that will honor both the humanity and the civil rights of those perceived/diagnosed with mental illness. I have used Price's book in a doctoral-level course I teach for higher educational administrators (BEF 681: Ethics and Education). Many of the administrators taking this course are caught between their ethical "duty" to keep the campus safe and their ethical "responsibility" to respect the rights of their students/faculty/staff with psychiatric disabilities. I argue here that a critical disability studies perspective nuances a discussion on ethical administrative practice when mental disability is interpreted and understood within social, political, and economic contexts, rather than relying solely on a simple medical diagnosis.

To contextualize this argument, I begin this chapter with a brief and rather general discussion of the social/political climate in which madness and violence are constructed as synonymous, and the implications such rhetoric has on administrative policies in higher education. Next, I engage Margaret Price's book *Mad at School* as an example of disability studies scholarship, where her critical analysis of the rhetoric of madness radically expands this scholarship to explore its implications for people with psychiatric disabilities in the hallowed halls of academe. In the third section of the chapter, I offer a brief description of the course I teach to higher education administrators who engage with Price's book in a writing assignment for the course. Using short excerpts of student writing, I will next discuss how engaging with ethical theories informed by a critical disability studies perspective enabled students to construct alternative interventions and challenge commonsensical understandings of madness. Finally, I discuss the implications these interventions can have for ethical administrative policy attuned to a critical disability studies perspective.

Terror at the University: Reasoned Responses to Madness?

The recent spate of shootings by college students/faculty in higher educational institutions and elsewhere has placed administrators, faculty, staff, students, and parents on edge. On January 21, 2014, Cody Cousins, a teaching assistant in the engineering department at Purdue University, shot and killed a fellow teaching assistant, Andrew Boldt, in a classroom before being arrested. In a movie theater in Aurora, Colorado, James Holmes, a doctoral student in the neuroscience program at the University of Colorado, Denver, shot 70 people on July 20, 2012. A year and a half earlier, Jared Loughner, a student who had recently withdrawn from Pima Community College, shot 16 people including U.S. Representative Gabrielle Giffords, in Tucson, Arizona, on January 8, 2011. At the University of Alabama, Huntsville, a biology professor, Amy Bishop, shot and killed three colleagues and wounded three others at a departmental meeting on February 12, 2010. But perhaps the deadliest of all was the shooting rampage by Seung-Hui Cho, a student at Virginia Tech University who shot and killed 32 people and wounded 17 others before turning the gun on himself on April 16, 2007.

Along with the horrific murders, the one other significant commonality that reportedly bound these individuals together was their alleged diagnosis of mental illness that was generally assumed to have triggered this impulse to commit mass murder (Coverdale, Coverdale & Nairn, 2013; McGinty, Webster, & Barry, 2013; Mossman, 2009; Price, 2011; Reiss, 2010). Put simply, you had to be "mad" to commit this crime. Such assertions came with irritable queries as to how so many people could have missed the obvious "signs" of madness that preceded each of these killings. Thus, after every one of these mass shootings, communities have huddled in front of television sets, have hunched over computer screens, and have strategized in board rooms in an effort to generate effective measures to prevent these violence acts of "mad" men/women from reoccurring with such regularity. Questions abounded. Did the killer give us any clues as to his/her intent to kill? Were there patterns of behavior that were indicative of emotional/mental stress? What measures could have been taken to separate this individual from the campus community? What kinds of medical/social/administrative interventions would have been successful to interrupt this deadly trajectory towards mass violence? How pervasive is mental illness in higher education such that it can be perceived as a tangible risk to "normal" academic life as we know it?

Contrary to public perception, however, students/faculty/staff/administrators with psychiatric disabilities are not uncommon on college campuses. In fact, administrators of counseling services across the nation have pointed out that the number of students with mental disabilities is on the rise (Quinn, Wilson, MacIntyre, & Tinkin, 2009; Stuart, 2012; Watkins, Hunt, & Eisenberg, 2011). According to a 2008 National College Health Assessment sponsored by the American College Health Association

(ACHA-NCHA), more than one in three undergraduate students reported feeling so depressed that they found it difficult to function, and nearly one in ten reported seriously considering attempting suicide (Watkins et al., 2011, p. 320). Stuart (2012) reports that severe depression affects 49% of college students and 14.9% of them meet the criteria for clinical depression (p. 328). In interviews with more than 2,000 college students, researchers found that 45.79% had a psychiatric disorder that included 20.3% with alcohol-use disorders, 17.6% with personality disorders, 10.62% with mood disorders, and 11.94% with anxiety disorders (Stuart, 2012; p. 328). A study at a large Midwestern public university reported that 7% of respondents were taking medication for psychiatric purposes (Stuart, 2012; p. 326), an estimated 1,100 college and university students will commit suicide in a year, and another 1,400 will die of alcohol-related causes (p. 329). These statistics indicate that, rather than being the exception, people with psychiatric disabilities are no strangers to college campuses and that more of them are susceptible to self-harm than of taking the lives of those around them.

What is evident is that the prevailing research situates mental disability solely within the individual—as the sum total of his/her individual negative experiences and his/her inability to cope with these stressors—and therefore advocates personal responsibility for improving one's mental health. Thus, one of the key arguments of university/college administrators is that even though universities provide comprehensive mental health services that students can voluntarily access, very few students actually do so (Knis-Matthews, Bokara, DeMeo, Lepore, & Mavus, 2007; Quinn et al., 2009; Stuart, 2012). Quinn et al. (2009) report that the perception of stigma enables only a relatively small number of students with psychiatric disabilities to seek help. As a result, on U.S. campuses, the proportion of students who did not receive any services ranged from 37% to 84% depending on the nature of their diagnosis of mental illness (Quinn et al., 2009, p. 406). In another study, 69% of students were more likely to seek help from friends and family or other trusted adults before actually accessing formal services (p. 406).

However, after Seung-Hui Cho killed 33 people including himself at Virginia Tech, college campuses across the U.S. have been forced to create and enact directives that are included with other "disaster management" plans (such as natural disasters, terrorist attacks, etc.) to build the key components of a "disaster-resilient university" (Kapucu & Khosa, 2012, p. 5). Such neoliberal policies require administrators to develop an efficient system that delves into the medical histories of students/faculty/staff with psychiatric disabilities to enhance their capacity to predict risk. Often the onus of these predictions is based on the dubious observational powers of untrained professionals steeped in subjective and oppressive ideologies of madness like "the inability to express joy; being a misfit; expressing disproportionate anger or humor; and the use of alcohol or drugs" (Mossman, 2009, p. 112). And yet, at any given time, any number of students could demonstrate many of these "warning" signs and yet not be at any risk of committing these random acts of extreme violence.

Mad at School: A Critical Disability Studies Perspective

One of the reasons that I chose *Mad at School* as one of the required books in Ethics and Education is because Price's argument exists in sharp contrast to the administrative decision-making tradition that is steeped in a utilitarian ethic of the greatest benefit for the greatest number of people. Price (2011) draws on the theoretical and activist perspective of disability as "a mode of human difference, one that becomes a problem only when an environment or context treats it as such" (Price, 2011, p. 3). Thus, a disability studies' perspective shifts the discussion from individuals towards institutional structures that deploy disciplinary practices to contain and colonize difference. *Mad at School*, however, not only engages disability studies, it also expands its scope by foregrounding its own unconsciously defined boundaries that sometimes locates mental disability outside its purview by privileging bodily difference over the mind. For example, in order to argue for inclusion within academic spaces, disabled scholars have felt pressured to prove that their "different" embodiment has little or no impact on their "sound" minds. In *Mad at School*, Price engages this troubling predicament.

In the hallowed halls of academe, the rational mind is prized over all else in the pursuit and dissemination of knowledge. Therefore, even a remote challenge to the hegemony of rationality in higher education is tantamount to sacrilege. A rhetorician by training, Price draws on the rhetorical construct of *topos* or "lines of thought that bear on a person's credibility in this or that rhetorical situation" (p. 5). Topoi (plural of *topos*) are invoked when a rhetoric reinforces dominant values and/or challenges the beliefs of outsiders to punish/exclude/marginalize certain groups. Price argues that the elite status of higher educational institutions as repositories of advanced knowledges deploys certain topoi that justify their propensity for favoring only a chosen few as its valued members. She provides us this list of topoi that intersect rather uncomfortably with mental disabilities in exclusionary ways: rationality, presence, participation, productivity, collegiality, security, coherence, truth, and independence, among others (p. 5). Price troubles the easy embrace of these topoi via the following questions:

[W]hat does "participation" in a class mean for a student who is undergoing deep depression and cannot get out of bed? Or a student who experiences such severe anxiety, or obsession, that he can barely leave his dorm room or home? What about the student on the autism spectrum who has difficulty apprehending the subtle social cues that govern classroom participation, the difference between "showing engagement" and "dominating conversation," the sorts of spontaneous oral performances that are considered "smart"? What does "collegiality" mean for a faculty member who has the same difficulties? What happens to the "productivity" of the academic writer who struggles to achieve the linear coherence that most academic writing demands? ... [D]oes the demonstration of coherence indicate a stronger mind? How do new requirements of "security" in U.S. academic environments resonate with (or against) our cherished values of free speech and independence? (Price, 2011, pp. 5–6)

I quote from *Mad at School* at length to highlight the range of questions that challenge the foundational tenets that serve as the bulwark of traditional academic practices. Price insightfully points out that ensuring that these tenets manifest themselves in everyday academic practice appeals to a medicalized logic that has unsuspectingly become central to our pedagogies. For example, in the aftermath of the spate of shootings listed earlier, faculty are urged to carefully observe student behavior and student writing to establish whether they meet education standards of rationality, independence, collegiality, and coherence, and if they do not, then they face the risk of being deemed unfit for the classroom and consequently unfit for life.

One of the most useful concepts that Price deploys in her book is *kairotic space*—"the less formal, often unnoticed area of academe, where knowledge is produced and power is exchanged" (p. 60). Examples of kairotic space in higher education include open classroom discussions, academic conferences, peer-response workshops, study groups, departmental parties and gatherings, and student-professor conferences, to name a few. The informal organization of kairotic space is replete with challenges like the real-time unfolding of events; impromptu communication that is required or encouraged; in-person contact; a strong social element; and high-stakes social situations (Price, 2011, p. 61). Because the bulk of higher educational research has focused predominantly on structured pedagogical contexts, kairotic spaces are understudied in pedagogical research as are those participants with psychiatric disabilities who find themselves in stressful situations when engaging in these spaces. Price offers examples of instances in job interviews or teacher-student conferences where the individual with a psychiatric disability is riddled with anxiety about breaking social rules of communication and interaction that seem almost natural/invisible to those who move in these spaces with ease. Classroom space, in particular, is another example of kairotic space that is crisscrossed by stringent time constraints that expect students "to arrive on time, absorb information at a particular speed, and perform spontaneously in restricted time frames" (p. 63).

Understanding how one moves through kairotic space is critical because such maneuverings determine how one's "presence" is constituted as (ir)rational. Price rejects the normative notion of "presence" as a set of stable and rational practices of a coherent body existing in a coherent moment. In pedagogical research, this notion of presence is exemplified by the actual physical presence of students in the classroom who are able to navigate the demands of the classroom kairos to participate in normative and rational communication. On the other hand, Price argues that students with mental disabilities reflect a more Derridean notion of "presence" as "a series of repetitions whose imaginary original referent is endlessly deferred" (p. 64). Here, Price is referring to how "presence" is contextual and shifting as students with psychiatric disabilities struggle to conform to normative classroom codes that have little patience for non-linear thought, conversational outbursts, and overwhelming anxiety among other behaviors that erupt unpredictably in the classroom. Thus, a critical focus on kairotic space could offer unconventional readings of "presence" that alter normative expectations of appropriate social behavior. As Price thoughtfully asks:

> What sort of academic culture are we creating if the job candidates we accept are *only* those who successfully avoid outbursts, memory lapses, or "outlandish coif[s]? Can we imagine a collegiality that embraces mistakes and grows stronger through the ways we address those mistakes? (p. 120)

In raising these questions, Price shifts the pedagogical/academic focus from pathologizing individual behaviors to foregrounding the normative features of kairotic space that are disruptive and exclusionary to "mad" students/faculty/staff. This conceptual shift does not ignore the reality of mental illness, nor does it strive to render invisible its "presence" in academic space (e.g., race and "color blindness"). Rather, this shift engages the dialectical relationship between "kairotic space" and "presence" with the ultimate goal being to enable the "mad" subject to negotiate the space on terms that are mutually beneficial and inclusive to all concerned.

It is this conceptualization of kairotic space that enables us to revisit the issue of mass murder with which I began this chapter. In *Mad at School*, Price offers a critique of the "public myths about mental disability, race, class, nationality, and gender, as well as myths about the proper functioning of higher education itself" (p. 142). She describes several rhetorical strategies that were deployed by popular media that functioned problematically as (medical) case studies of the killers in an attempt to demonstrate that the pathology of mental illness ultimately escalates towards violence. It is here then, that the concepts of topos and kairotic space as deployed by Price shift the discussion from individual pathology (medical model) to enquire into the ways social structures/practices (social model) serve to construct "madness" in academia in the first place. A critical disability perspective, Price suggests, will raise questions about the violent practices in education that harm students who are different, or social practices like war that actually cause many of the symptoms that may contribute to mental disabilities. Critical of higher education policies that require "mad" students/faculty to be amenable to practices of containment and control and that result in the elimination of civil rights of people with psychiatric disabilities, Price suggests that the focus should be on alternative/inclusive pedagogical practices, adequate support services, and effective policies against hate speech, bullying, and other forms of discrimination on the basis of difference. In light of this discussion, I found *Mad at School* especially useful as a pedagogical tool because it offers a cogent critique of higher education administrative policies that seem hell-bent on practices of search and destroy, or at least, remove and segregate, rather than to reconfigure academic space so that it is accessible to all people including those with mental disabilities.

Enabling Ethical Discussions of Administrative Praxis

I have taught the course Ethics and Education to four consecutive cohorts of higher educational administrators enrolled in an executive doctoral program at the university over four weekends in the summer term. I also teach this course to doctoral students across the College of Education who are teacher/administrators in local K–12 schools. The course provides an introduction to ethical theory that explores the following questions: What is the meaning of "good" and "right"? How does one justify an action as "good"? What role does "social justice" play in the enactment of ethical behavior? What are appropriate ethical responses to social difference (that is, race, gender, class, sexuality, and disability)? To answer these questions, I utilize case studies and design course assignments so that students can apply the ethical theories in the course to professional praxis in their respective fields. The readings for this course include major ethical theories of the Western intellectual tradition (idealism, realism, deontology, existentialism, pragmatism, utilitarianism) together with more recent theoretical developments drawn from the theoretical frameworks of Marxism, feminism, postcoloniality, and postmodernism (Gregory & Giancola, 2003). Additionally, I utilized articles that included voices both inside and outside the field of education so that students could make connections across genres and disciplines and learn to integrate the practice of ethical decision making in both their professional and personal lives.

For the case studies, I utilized books on a variety of interesting ethical questions such as the politics of patriotism, the implications of high-stakes tests in public education, the hiring of adjunct faculty in colleges and universities, the economic and academic interests of college sports, the inclusion of LGBTQ students in K-12 settings, and the politics of being "mad" in higher educational settings. *Mad at School* was one of the books of choice for the last section of the course where students grappled with utilitarianism (Mills); ethics of justice and community (Marx/Fanon/Freire), an ethics of care (Gilligan/Noddings), and an ethics of self/other (Levinas/Buber/Nietzsche). In addition to these authors, the students in my fall 2013 course were also assigned readings by Harry Brighouse (2001), *Can Justice as Fairness Accommodate the Disabled*, and Anita Silvers (1995), *Reconciling Equality to Difference*, that were useful in nuancing the discussion on disability in ethical discourse.

While looking over student papers in the three years I had taught this book, students offered interesting insights on how *Mad at School* enabled them to think critically about mental disability and enabled them to nuance their ethical perspectives. To preserve the students' confidentiality, I use no names or any identifying information when sharing excerpts from their papers. Except for two doctoral students in my fall 2013 course who had taken an earlier course with me in disability studies, none of the other students had any background in disability studies. Many of these students also had very little knowledge of social/philosophical theory. I foreground their limited knowledge in both disability studies and ethical theory to emphasize that their understandings prior to this course were rooted in normative common sense. Many viewed ethics as a deeply religious practice and almost all of them conceived of disability via the medical model. Thus, engaging with ethical theories from a secular standpoint and reconceptualizing disability as a political construct were initially challenging for many of the students. That is why, I argue, that their thoughtful engagement with the issues raised in *Mad at School* at the juncture of secular ethics and disability studies scholarship was both remarkable and transformative.

Enabling Ethical Possibilities

For this writing assignment, I had required students to summarize the key issues in *Mad at School,* and to deploy what they considered the most appropriate ethical principles/theories to reflect on ethical praxis. In this section,

I focus on how both ethical theory and a critical disability perspective nuanced/transformed their understanding of mental disability in the academy. Looking across the different papers, I first coded segments according to themes and then collapsed these segments into broader themes based on the commonalities in content and came up with the following: (a) Deconstructing the Rhetoric of Normal/Rational in the Academy; (b) Alienation and Colonialism in the Academy: Against the Medical Model; (c) Caring for (Mental) Difference in Ethical Contexts; (d) Student Reflections of Pedagogical Possibilities in *Mad at School*. I now turn to the discussion of these themes.

Deconstructing the rhetoric of normal/rational in the academy

The stereotypical notions of academia being mostly rational spaces that function primarily to exclude those who are non-rational was an argument that prior to reading *Mad at School* was accepted without question by students. In fact, for many of them, to "fit" in academia required that they suppress all forms of irrationality in themselves. Thus, in the following quote a student offers an interesting riff on the term "fit" in order to begin to deconstruct the rhetoric of madness in academia:

> People with mental disabilities do not actually "run screaming" from the academy, they do frequently have to leave the halls of ivy due to a bad fit—in both senses of the word: their mental disabilities do not "fit" well with the physical demands of presence and the capacity for consistent rational exchange expected of them. Also, the ways their bodies and minds at times respond to these stressful demands is experienced as a frightening "fit of madness" to the non-disabled, and these "disorderly minds" are thus removed to make others feel safer.

Drawing on the rhetoric of "fit" also brought into play unquestioned notions of what "normal" meant in academia. Price's argument inspired one student to ask:

> What is normal? Are behaviors valued in academic discourse the norm because they are more productive in academia? Did they come to be valued because that is how the majority of people in academia acted? ... How do we measure or identify normal behavior? Is it what the majority of people would do in a given situation? What if the action most people would take is not considered normal? Does it suddenly become normal because majority rules?

Significant in the previous quote is that following Price's cue, the student implicitly began to question the medical model of mental disability and began to foreground the social construction of normativity in the questions posed in his/her own text. However, this shift often ran into problems such as the ways in which "rationality" is deified in academia. For example, one student described his/her struggle as follows:

With the truth of her claim acknowledged, I have to say that of all the norm-busting books I have read, Price's *Mad at School* was the most uncomfortable for me ... [I] will have to begin with a confession that, at the start of her book, I thought she was taking inclusiveness to the point of irrationality. Price would say, "Precisely!" ... Though endeavoring to be an open-minded person, I feared when I started reading *Mad at School* that Margaret Price was taking me somewhere I finally just could not go—a classroom where neither the students, nor the faculty should be expected to be present or participate in discussions or even always be coherent in their writing ... Higher education is where one goes to learn how to do that. If I did not want to strengthen that particular aspect of myself, I would not be in school ... So, while I consider myself to be a person with an open mind, ready to hear and validate the experiences of people marginalized by discriminatory practices, I apparently have my limits. Thus, as I walk the reader through the ethical arguments to be made for and against Margaret Price's challenge to reconsider long-held values regarding rationality and autonomy that tacitly privilege an "able" mind in the academy, I am going to be walking myself through it as well, and sometimes dragging myself against "all reason."

I quoted this student at length in this section to illustrate the radical pressure from a disability studies perspective to re-think deeply entrenched commitments to rationality, autonomy, and coherence—all characteristics that locate students/faculty with mental disabilities outside the hallowed hall of academia. To even begin to imagine inclusive spaces for those who do not "fit" the norm required that one first begin with the questions Price posed earlier in this chapter.

Alienation and colonialism in the academy: against the medical model
In order to shift from a medical model of mental illness/disability to examining its location in its social/political/economic context, the students drew on the historical materialist analysis of Karl Marx and Frederick Engels (Gregory & Giancola, 2003). Based on the Marxist notion that ideologies have their roots in political economy, students used historical materialism to explain why issues of rationality, autonomy, and coherence and their links to academic productivity were valued in the academy and how this implicated "mad" students/faculty. One student wrote:

The ethical perspectives of Karl Marx ...[and Frederick Engels] inform an understanding of justice within Price's text. Marx's critique of capitalism and philosophy of dialectical materialism (Gregory & Giancola, 2003) challenge the notion of production in higher education. When students and faculty members receive promotion based only on their means to produce a satisfactory financial return, members of society who have mental disabilities get pushed out of the mainstream.

In the above quote, the student begins to deconstruct the "naturalness" of characteristics deemed essential for success in academia by drawing on social constructivism via a historical materialist critique of capitalism. Thus, Price's critique of the medical model opened up an intellectual space for students to inquire into the actual processes of creating this dichotomy of rational/irrational students/faculty and the implications this dichotomy had for those who were devalued in this process. Take for example, this student's perspective:

> The expectations of professors often include people who are energetic, think in linear and rational organization, and who are able to be present in class and at conferences. This often becomes a struggle for people who have mental disabilities. Part of the issue is as Karl Marx describes as our worth being tied to our production and our social value being tied to modes of reproduction. Faculty members with mental disabilities might try to pass in order to not be hypervisible due to their struggle. The desire to pass can also lead to further exhaustion and alienation.

This student interpreted Price's description of "containment and control" as a condition of alienation that could then be linked to the experience of colonialism described by Algerian postcolonialist theorist Frantz Fanon. As another student wrote:

> Fanon explains that moral psyche is formed in the context of social relations and we become incapable of blending in societies, in this case schools, continue to look inward. In many ways by calling the academy an ivory tower, we are rejecting that "madness" has always been present, even before we began to look at the situations of school shootings. By projecting that we lock up or contain all people with mental disability we once again seek to colonize a group of people based on their differences or perceived differences. By using scare tactics this will be easier to do in a society that places competition over care.

In an interesting move inspired again by Price's argument that troubles society's instinctive reaction to lock up those perceived as mentally ill, another student wrote:

> Fanon stresses the normalization of one culture over another as a form of and a method of colonizing cultures and individuals into the more dominant group. The concept of normality and illness are delineated ideas that society, culture, and medicine support through language and treatment of those whose mental capabilities may function differently than others. The habit portrayed by Price that expresses this ability to separate those with mental illness is the need to diagnose and heal. There is power established in the ability of one individual or group of individuals to describe the abilities or limits of another group of people through their own discourse. In addition, the power is fully achieved in the ability to dictate the need to change from their state of abnormality to meet the accepted normality of the group in power.

Further exploring the implications of these practices of "diagnose and heal," another student wrote:

Fanon indicates that this normalization of one group over another creates a hierarchy. Price indicates her support for this idea in her descriptions of mental illness and violence in chapter 4 as she expresses the separation between the "them" and "us" the media creates through its desire to diagnose those causing such violent crimes with some mental illness, thus defining them as not normal. Fanon describes the use of exploitation, tortures, raids, etc. to assert control over another group. For individuals with mental illness, the history is indicative of these very actions using medical backing to justify the need for lobotomies, electroshock therapy, and institutionalization of those who do not meet the standard of "normal" mental capacity.

The above quote demonstrates how a disability studies perspective enabled students to understand the unethical implications of supporting a medical model of mental illness that necessitated the oppressive binary of "us" versus "them." Interestingly enough, this argument, I argue, offers an extension of Price's rhetorical analysis by situating it within a historical materialist critique that offers critical nuance to theorizing mental illness (Erevelles, 2002).

Caring for (mental) difference in ethical contexts
The recognition of interdependent disabled and non-disabled subjectivities as ethical praxis also enabled students to offer a critique of ethics that foreground autonomy. Whereas, prior to reading *Mad at School*, students would have opted for a utilitarian perspective (greatest good for the greatest number of people) to respond to mental disability in academia, students now were willing to explore a feminist ethic of care. As one student explained:

> [When] ethical responsibility shifts from the individual ... we become accountable to each other and reject exclusion of those deemed different or "Other." Nel Noddings explains that relationships are built on receptivity, relatedness, and responsiveness. Ethics should be based in reciprocity that is not based in positions of power. The one who claims the disability must maintain a voice in how they are treated and how the classrooms are designed to be more inclusive. Negotiation should begin with conversations instead of silencing the person and resist individualistic solutions.

But the ethics of care as articulated by feminists and disability studies scholars also enables oppressive practices that may actually complicate the relationship between carer and cared for. Utilizing assigned readings from several different perspectives, students reflected on these complexities, as apparent in the following quote:

> In his article entitled "Can Justice as Fairness Accommodate the Disabled," ... [Harry] Brighouse argues for the pity-deficit model with Rawlsian foundations. He essentially argues that society must take care of the disabled, because they cannot take care of themselves (Brighouse, 2001). [On the other hand] in her article entitled "Reconciling Equality to Difference: Caring for Justice for People

with Disabilities," Silvers argues for an equality model in which there is value in being both the caregiver and the patient [sic] in a mutually-respectable and reciprocating relationship.

Explaining this further, another student describes reciprocity and mutual respectability in the following way:

> Noddings views feminist care ethics as contextual and relational ... She states ... "Taking relations as ontologically basic simply means that we recognize human encounter and affective response as a basic fact of human existence. As we examine what it means to care and to be cared for, we shall see that both parties contribute to the relation; my caring must somehow be completed in the other if the relation is to be described as caring." (Gregory & Giancola, 2003, p. 340)

Once again foregrounding the centrality of interdependence while at the same time respecting Price's analysis of how people diagnosed with mental illness/disabilities are subject to "containment and control," feminist ethics of care as articulated via an emancipatory notion of reciprocity would nurture ethical relationships with people with mental disabilities.

Student reflections of pedagogical possibilities in mad at school

While much of the earlier discussion is very abstract, it was encouraging to recognize that students had learned very practical things regarding pedagogy and access for students/faculty with mental disabilities. Thus for example, one student wrote:

> Price's text has raised my awareness of the way I use the kairotic space of my classroom and office. As a faculty member I recognize my tendency to classify any student behavior that does not ascribe to the established norm as deviant; "mad." When I consider the ways higher education personnel discuss mental illness I agree with Price that we have an obligation to these students, faculty members, and staff. I plan to become more aware of the design and layout of my classrooms and courses as I progress in my career. I agree that a universal [design] perspective as described by Price can help meet all of our stakeholders' needs.

In the context of responding to the threat of violence in higher educational institutions and its problematic association with mental illness, another student had this to say:

> Price (2011) documents the report from the Virginia Tech review panel that calls for the elimination of the civil rights for persons with disabilities in the interest of "public safety." ... The call for background checks may be first, then a national registry for persons with mental illness. While a utility view may sound like the best ethical decision for the greater good and safety of society, but what happens when one is determined to be mentally ill just because they do not conform to what the majority deems is "normal." Mental illness has a long history of abuses and persons with mental disabilities often lack a voice in society.

Students were also delighted that Price offered concrete ideas for being more inclusive. One student wrote:

> The text we read by Dr. Margaret Price showed me ways to not only improve my syllabus but also to improve my teaching techniques ... Specifically, Price offers ways to be more transparent and discuss specific issues of "presence" and how people learn in diverse ways ... By addressing this and allowing vulnerability without judgment, students might feel more at ease and less dehumanized or "Othered" in the classroom.

At a broader level, students also learned about more general ideas about their own ethical relationships to social difference via *Mad at School*. Thus for example, a student wrote:

> Ethically speaking, we have learned that while we live relationally in our society and our communities, it is important to be able to choose our own way of living ... In choosing our own reality, we must also reject the desire for domination over "Others." Buber tells us that we should seek to form I/Thou relationships rather than I/It relationships. We must reject using people as a means to an end and instead realize that interdependence is what often forms community. We should accept and respect people regardless of their ability and offer agency for all people over their own destinies. Respect becomes critical in changing the academy. Respecting each person's stance will add depth to positive changes for a more accessible academy. As Price concludes her text, "If we wish to change the educational system, we will need all our minds." (Price, 234)

Conclusion: Towards a Pedagogy of Vulnerability

The much-vaunted ivory towers of academia populated by autonomous, rational, and coherent humanist subjects have been idolized as spaces where "minds" always triumph over "matter." In these spaces where the intellect is valued over all else (universities are for smart folks only), there is little tolerance for anyone who fails to measure up to these ideals. As such, it is very difficult in academia to disclose one's vulnerabilities, let alone celebrate them. It is in this context that I argue that disability studies can radically intervene in higher educational contexts.

In the examples I provided in this chapter, I foreground how disability studies scholarship enabled higher educational administrators (and students in general) to re-think their allegiances to these ideals of rationality, autonomy, and coherence in order to imagine a different, more vulnerable context in which to do their work. Disability studies scholarship celebrates vulnerability as pervasive and enabling. Thus, for me the most significant transformation in my students was their reluctant realization that vulnerability is something that is necessary and pervasive in their everyday lives, and that interdependence was preferable over autonomy. Without vulnerability, there would be no ethical imperative. Without disability, there would be no human-ness.

To me, most poignant of all was the moment when one of my most resistant students, a university administrator, disclosed his own vulnerabilities regarding mental disability in the very last paragraph of his review of *Mad at School*. He wrote:

> I too have a son who is now age 19 who is considered "mad" by many and who has been institutionalized since age eleven. My son's mental disabilities were highlighted by his non-normative and disruptive behavior in a public school setting. Price noted that the exclusion of students in "normal" classrooms begins by the requirement to manage emotions in the classroom. As a realist, I must agree that when my son becomes frustrated, he also becomes loud and violent. I also agree that this type of behavior and the potential for harming others must draw the ethical actions of faculty and administrators to protect the others in the classroom. In this case, I would agree with the ethical stance of Mill's and protect the majority; however, Price's concept of Universal Design has the potential to address the ethics of inclusion and of care. Her Universal Design has a great spirit and I agree that the framework is needed, but I am overwhelmed by how it will ever get addressed. I can only imagine how difficult attending "normal" school was for my son and how extraordinary school would have been if the "spaces" that allowed educators to working with his abilities not his disabilities actually existed … Not every "mad" person is "MAD" simply because they do not fit into a normalized world. Everyone fits somewhere; we simply need to remain diligent in recognizing the need for additional "spaces."

Since teaching this course, I have thought a lot about this administrator's somber reflection about an alternative future for his son. The power of a disability studies' perspective in educational contexts emphasizes an urgency of advocating for pedagogies of vulnerability that create more accessible spaces for all those who are mad at school.

Notes

1. Throughout the essay, I have used different term to describe mental illness/disability. I have used "mad," "mental illness," "mental disabilities," and "psychiatric disabilities." I do this to foreground that there is no consensus on any one descriptor or self-identifier. Many of my colleagues and friends who claim several of these identities have shared their preferences of the terms and explained how the choice of different terms/identities have implications and meanings for them. Language is important. So my usage of different terminology honors this diversity even while noting the complications that may arise as a result of my usage.

References

Brighouse, H. (2001). Can justice as fairness accommodate the disabled? *Social Theory and Practice*, *27*(4), 537–560.

Coverdale, J. H., Coverdale, S., & Nairn, R. (2013). "Behind the mug shot grin": Uses of madness-talk in reports of Loughner's mass killing. *Journal of Communication Inquiry*, *37*(3), 200–216.

Erevelles, N. (2002). Voices of silence: Foucault, disability, and the question of self-determination. *Studies in Philosophy and Education*, *21*(1), 17–35.

Goodley, D. (2011). *Disability studies: An interdisciplinary introduction*. Washington, DC: Sage.

Gregory, W. T., & Giancola, D. (2003). *World ethics*. Belmont, CA: Wadsworth/Thomson Learning.

Kapucu, N., & Khosa, S. (2012). Disaster resiliency and culture of preparedness for university and college campuses. *Administration & Society*, *45*(3), 3–37.

Knis-Matthews, L., Bokara, J., DeMeo, L., Lepore, N., & Mavus, L. (2007). The meaning of higher education for people diagnosed with a mental illness: Four students share their experiences. *Psychiatric Rehabilitation Journal*, *31*(2), 107–114.

McGinty, E. E., Webster, D., & Barry, C. L. (2013). Effects of news media messages about mass shootings on attitudes towards persons with serious mental illness and public support for gun control policies. *American Journal of Psychiatry*, *170*(5), 494–501.

Mossman, D. (2009). The imperfection of protection through detection and intervention. *Journal of Legal Medicine*, *30*(1), 109–140.

Price, M. (2011). *Mad at school: Rhetorics of mental disability and academic life*. Ann Arbor: University of Michigan Press.

Quinn, N., Wilson, A., MacIntyre, G., & Tinklin, T. (2009). "People look at you differently": Students experience of mental health support within higher education. *British Journal of Guidance and Counseling*, *37*(4), 405–418.

Reiss, B. (2010). Madness after Virginia Tech: From psychiatric risk to institutional vulnerability. *Social Text*, *28*(4), 25–44.

Silvers, A. (1995). Reconciling equality to difference: Caring (f)or justice for people with disabilities. *Hypatia*, *10*(1), 30–55.

Stuart, S. P. (2012). "Hope and despondence": Emerging adulthood and higher education's relationship with its nonviolent mentally ill students. *Journal of College and University Law*, *38*(2), 319–380.

Watkins, D. C., Hunt, J. B., & Eisenberg, D. (2011). Increased demand for mental health services on college campuses: Perspectives from administrators. *Qualitative Social Work*, *11*(3), 319–337.

Section IV

Policy

10. Critiquing Policy: Limitations and Possibilities

JULIE ALLAN

"There are times in life when the question of knowing if one can think differently than one thinks, and perceive differently than one sees, is absolutely necessary if one is to go on looking and reflecting at all."
—Foucault, (1985, p. 8)

Introduction

Bruno Latour (2004) suggests that our critical spirit has "run out of steam" (p. 225), and we have become like mechanical toys, endlessly repeating the same gesture, trying to conquer territories that no longer exist whilst being unprepared for the "new threats, new dangers, new tasks, new targets" (ibid.) that we face. This chapter will examine the limited success of critique of educational policy and will consider the specific contexts of Sweden, the United Kingdom, and the United States, each with different educational traditions and trajectories but with some convergences in patterns of critique. Latour calls urgently for progress towards "a fair position" and for the development of "new critical tools" to work positively and constructively towards social change. The potential of analytical resources, derived from within disability studies in education and through its orientation to the humanities, to deliver acceptable and appropriate critique and to mobilise political action will be explored.

Critical Limitations

The exercise of critique involves time and effort and thinking, but Lyotard (1992) reminds us that, in a world in which success is equated with saving time, thinking reveals its "single but irredeemable fault: it's a waste of time" (p. 47). Value has replaced values (Peters, Lankshear & Olsson, 2003) within spaces of educational policymaking, and both thinking and critique struggle to prove their "worth." A more significant problem might be a resistance to criticality because of the disturbance it potentially creates for what Nicholas Kristof (2009) calls "the daily me," whereby information is gathered merely to support pre-existing views and what potentially clashes with them is ignored:

> There's pretty good evidence that we generally don't truly want good infor-mation—but rather information that confirms our prejudices. We may believe intellectually in the clash of opinions, but in practice we like to embed ourselves in the reassuring womb of an echo chamber.

Torrance (2008) suggests that a reticence about criticality comes from both educational policymakers and educational researchers:

> Governments, and some within the scholarly community itself, seem to be seek-ing to turn educational research into a technology that can be applied to solving short-term educational problems, rather than a system of enquiry that might help practitioners and policymakers think more productively about the nature of the problem and how it might be addressed. (p. 522)

The disability and inclusion policy arenas appear to invite adherence rath-er than criticality and create a sense that any engagement in the latter risks counter-critiques that the very notion of inclusion is being challenged. Policy guidance on inclusion consists largely of help in finding or discovering it, to-gether with an abundance of metaphors that involve either journeys or roads. For example, the European Union offers "Pathways to Inclusion" (p. 2i), with its training course promising a "moving towards an inclusive education," while the Training and Development Agency's (2012) "Pillars of Inclusion" provides building exercises. Even the name *Index to Inclusion* (Booth & Ainscow, 2011), translated into languages and in widespread use by schools (EASPO, 2012) suggests that it is pointing or guiding towards something. The abundance of "what works" materials that exist in relation to inclusive education convey a promise of a destination that can be reached, providing that certain simple measures are followed. These measures, however, repre-sent inclusive education as a technical problem, provide "clarity bordering on stupidity" (MacLure, 2005, p. 393) and ensure sight of "what matters" is lost (Ferri, Gallagher, & Connor, 2011, p. 222).

Stephen Ball (2013) suggests that a further restriction on critical possibil-ities within disability and inclusion policy comes from the positioning of these elements as always in (inferior) relation to the mainstream. This othering of difference is not helped, Ball argues, by mainstream policy critics' work, which further distances it through a process of commatizing of disability (Troyna, 1994) alongside other markers of difference such as race, class, and gender. The act of commatizing gives the appearance of having addressed the issue, whilst leaving it among the "dangling ... 'other' inequalities and oppressions" (Ball, 2013, p. 84; original emphasis).

Becoming Critical?

It is not surprising that researchers do not engage extensively in critique, given the lack of support and guidance on becoming critical. Texts on educational research, especially those aimed at doctoral students and with such alluring titles as *How to get a PhD* (Phillips & Pugh, 1987), or books on the foundations of social or educational research (e.g., Crotty, 1998) deny both the intensely political aspect of educational research and the interwoven nature of theory, philosophy, practices, and material realities (Kuhn, 1970; Shostak, 2002; Punch, 2005). The failure to acknowledge and engage with these interactions means that students part with their cash in the hope of gaining meaningful advice and instead find themselves unable to cope with the series of "derailments" (Shostak, 2002, p. 5) that their research presents and enter the "logical graveyard where sense and nonsense fuse and meanings are loosened from their anchorage in master narratives" (ibid.). The foundational texts, such as that by Crotty, provide frameworks which align methods, methodologies, theoretical perspectives, and epistemologies in, by his definition, a "reasonably clear-cut way" (p. 1), but in a manner that fails to connect with students' sense of the social world and leaves them trying to squeeze their research, and their theory, into the framework and not giving up until it fits, however uncomfortably. By the time students hit a passing but unexplained reference to paradigms, as they do in the Crotty text, followed by a dismissive assertion that "ontology and epistemology tend to merge together" (ibid, p. 10), they have usually lost the plot.

The prolific "lensification" in educational research suggests a further ambivalence in relation to criticality. A lens is given either by particular concepts, for example "provided by Foucault's concept of knowledge and power" (Rodriguez & Craig, 2007, p. 739), used as a means of "complicating power relations" (Fenech & Sumeson, 2007, p. 109), or in order to seek alternative educational possibilities (Butin, 2002). Curiously, there is such a material thing as a Foucault lens, an optical device (a microscope), that bears the name of Foucault, its optician inventor, but which was developed to counteract the aberrations caused by imaging by lenses at high power. He also developed a "Foucault Test" for evaluating astronomical mirrors, described as "cheap and easy to do" (Java Optical Design and Analysis Software, 1990). It may be unfair to suggest that those adopting lenses have been enticed by a similar apparent simplicity, but the limited use made of the theories themselves, with lenses in many cases serving as little more than a gloss, may warrant such a suggestion.

The Consequences of Doing Without Critique

Arendt (2006) warns of the dangers of silence as signaling a descent into depoliticized ground and recognizes that this silence may stem from a loss of authority, making it difficult for us to think for ourselves in the "gap that separates the 'no longer' from the 'not yet'" (Kohn, 2006, p. xxi). Arendt urges us to avoid leaping to the assumption of a concomitant "loss of the human capacity for building, preserving, and caring for a world that can survive us and remain a place fit to live in for those who come after us" (Arendt, 2006, p. 95), but also acknowledges and laments the inevitability of such a move.

The loss of criticality from within teacher education, through the removal of educational studies and the general reduction of theoretical content from courses, has been acknowledged as a global phenomenon, but Dennis Beach (2012) draws on Basil Bernstein to illustrate the negative impact this has had on beginning teachers' thinking. Bernstein (1999, p. 161) distinguishes between a horizontal, the everyday, discourse, linked to commonsense understandings and often tacit, oral, and context specific, and a vertical discourse, produced within universities and which offers "specialised symbolic structures of explicit knowledge." The erosion or the removal of the vertical discourse (through a move away from an emphasis on scientific praxis or the removal of philosophy of education) could, Bernstein suggests, be part of a move to undermine the knowledge interests of a professional discourse and open them up to influences. But as others have argued (Apple, 2001; Beach, 2012; Lauder, Brown, & Halsey, 2009; Oancea & Bridges, 2009; Sleeter, 2008), the erosion of the vertical discourse removes the capacity of beginning teachers to think critically and to understand the global influences on their profession and their selves precisely at a time when the effects are considerable. Furthermore, the absence of this discourse, and the criticality that comes with it, may leave teachers less able to recognize the competing demands of equity and choice and therefore find a balance between them (Alexandersson, 2011), and make them in turn at greater risk of political manipulation and economic exploitation (Sleeter, 2008).

Missing or Making the Critical Point?

Two of the examples given here illustrate a limited capacity on the part of educational researchers to engage critically with matters of concern directly affecting them and even suggest some complicity on their part. The first example, from the U.K., relates to educational research and concerns a group of researchers, charged with establishing standards for qualitative research, succeeding in reducing the scope for criticality through a process of resolving theory by reducing it to a set of categorical positions. The example from Sweden concerns a lack of resistance, particularly from academics, to the demise of the powerful discipline of education science. A third example, however, from the U.S. and relating to disability, illustrates an exceptional level of critical engagement by individual scholars. Although each of the examples is different, the comparisons from the three contexts are of particular interest because of the rather different political contexts and contrasting educational histories that appear currently to be both converging and diverging. The U.K. education system has had recent experience of the effects of neo-liberal ideas such as competitiveness, freedom of choice, and performativity in a context of devolved responsibility for education; Sweden's traditions of comprehensive schooling, resting upon national independence and with democratic values and social welfare as cornerstones, are increasingly being challenged by these ideas; the United States' system of early and high-stakes testing threatens to undermine its own promise of "No Child Left Behind" by precipitating the segregation of particular groups. The governments of these countries, whilst appearing to offer continued support for inclusive education, at least at a rhetorical level, are also contributing, through their legislation and policies, to the "irresistible rise of the SEN [Special Education Needs] industry" (Tomlinson, 2012, p. 267).

U.K. research: Resolving theory
Within the U.K., a group of academics was commissioned by the Strategy Unit of the government Cabinet Office (Spencer, Richie, Lewis, & Dillon, 2003) to produce "guidelines" for assessing the quality of qualitative approaches and methods. It was in the process of succumbing to the imposition of "standards" on qualitative research—troubling enough in itself—that the researchers addressed theory, and resolved it, according to Harry Torrance (2008), "in a bloodless, technical and strangely old-fashioned counsel of perfection" (p. 515). The academics, in developing their framework for making judgments about qualitative research, tried to understand theory, or in their words, the "various philosophical assumptions which underpin different approaches to qualitative research" (Spencer et al., 2003, p. 8). In so doing, they sought to pin down qualitative research as no more than a series of oppositions between quantitative and qualitative and between scientific and naturalistic paradigms; they then tried to "position" researchers, claiming to

have found among its interviewees a "realist," a "subtle realist," an "interaction constructionist," and an eclectic who referred to him or herself as "a bit of a whore" (p. 49). Such positioning of researchers as fixed in theory is, of course, unhelpful; but after declaring the diversity of ontological and epistemological positions and the impossibility of encompassing these within its framework, the researchers then set about "specifying the range of philosophical and methodological assumptions with which we believe our framework is compatible and those which lie outside its scope" (p. 49). Astonishingly, they then produced a table, which ruled assumptions, relating to the nature of reality, relationships between research and researched, the relationship between facts and values, the nature of knowledge and appropriate methods, either in or out of their framework. They also removed from the discussion of research any acknowledgement of the Other, in the shape of "contingencies, political pressures and decisions that have to be made" (Torrance, p. 2008, p. 516).

Education science silence in Sweden
The introduction, and then subsequent erosion, in Sweden, of education science illustrates an attempt to establish a stronger theoretical component within teacher education, or establish a vertical discourse to enable critical thinking, which was then pushed back out in favour of a re-traditionalisation (Beach & Bagley, 2012, p. 297) of teacher education and a retreat. Education science has only been in existence in Sweden as a university subject since 1999 (Beach, 2011), introduced in order to establish a research area concerned with the science of teaching, learning and their outcomes, deemed necessary because of the new competence required of teachers in response to such reforms as decentralisation, criterion-referenced grading, and independent schools (Beach 2011; Fransson & Lundgren, 2003). This occurred even though earlier commissions (Teacher Education Expert Committee, in 1960; the Teacher Education Investigation, 1974) had already argued for training in research as a means of making teachers not just competent but critical (Beach, 2011). The committee from which education science had emerged, Lärarutbildningskommittén (LUK 97), argued that pedagogical research had not served teacher education sufficiently well and had called for a better integration rather than a separate discipline. However the Swedish government, instead of accepting the committee's proposals, set up a special science-education committee, then charged it with developing (separately) education science explicitly for teacher education. What has ensued over the last 12 years, cemented by a government commission green paper (SOU, 2008) and a government white paper based on the recommendations of the commission (Swedish Government Bill 2009/10), has been a

competence-oriented knowledge relating to teacher behaviour, with an emphasis on a functionary knowledge base rather than critical thinking (Beach, 2011; Sjöberg, 2011). Specialised content relating to the sociological, political, philosophical, economic, and ideological dimensions of professional knowledge has been stripped (leaving only psychology and brain-based theorization), plus subject knowledge, in Beach's words, "blown away and replaced by something less profound" (2011, p. 218).

According to Inge-Bert Täljedal (2011), a former vice-chancellor of Umeå, academics themselves have also led to the constraining and limiting of education science as "practitioner focused and practice based." He notes that it was left to the universities to direct some of their research funding towards education science and they could only manage marginal redistributions of their existing institutional grants. Thus the intended strengthening of teacher education was "effectively limited to a half measure" (Täljedal, 2011, p. 326). This vice-chancellor also noted a "power struggle" (p. 327) between the traditional professors of pedagogiks, wanting to hold onto this discipline, and the teacher educationists, wanting something that was more practice oriented. As a former medical professor forced to adjudicate between these two "camps," Täljedal found the established education academics' (pedagoger) arguments "academic and theoretical" (p. 327), and those of the teacher educators "more valid and convincing" (p. 327), but suggested that in the end the conservatives (the pedagoger) won out. Lindström and Beach (2013) endorse the argument that conservatism prevailed, evidencing it in the official representation to the various government teacher education committees for greater practical relevance. They also note that the proposition for education science provoked "a heated response from the discipline's old guard" (p. 13). In the case of Sweden, government actions have limited the extent to which strong educational theory has been allowed to function, but academics may have let some of the opportunities to influence the direction pass them by.

An Exceptional (U.S.) Response: To Intervention
Critiques of the U.S. reform Response to Intervention (RTI), undertaken by Beth Ferri (2012), Alfredo Artiles (Artiles, Bal, & King Thorius, 2010; Artiles, 2011), and others (Gallagher, 2010; Gresham, 2007), have been particularly exceptional. These critiques have drawn attention to an intervention that is explicitly maintaining segregated provision, "reinvigorating" many of the foundational assumptions of special education practices and contributing to the "irresistible rise in the SEN industry" (Tomlinson, 2012, p. 267). RTI is an intensive intervention approach to students identified as being at risk of failure as a result of learning or behavioral difficulties. It also involves a system

of systematic monitoring performance and, most controversially, provides an alternative basis for the eligibility for a diagnosis of learning disability from the pre-existing IQ/achievement discrepancy model. A key feature of RTI is its early and intensive screening, aimed at discovering students "at risk" even before the teacher notices them having problems in the classroom (Ferri, 2012). As Ferri and others have noted (e.g., Gallagher, 2010), there is a fuzziness behind RTI which arises from a discourse that "speaks of fidelity, universal protocols and standardization on the one hand and [has] a glaring lack of consensus or research behind the model on the other" (Ferri, 2012, p. 867). Alongside this fuzziness, however, observes Artiles (2011), "tiers of increasing intensity and individualization" (p. 437) are built into educational processes.

Claims that RTI will reduce the overrepresentation of minority ethnic students in special education (Gresham, 2007) are not so far supported with research evidence. Indeed the social justice premises of RTI and the claims that it includes all learners is questioned by Artiles (Artiles et al., 2010; Artiles, 2011), who suggests that it does not take into account the institutional and social structures that give rise to inequalities in education. Thus, the framing of RTI as a technical intervention that neither acknowledges, nor promises to address, "misrecognition injustices through more precise identification procedures" (Artiles et al., 2010, p. 252) introduces its own restrictions. Artiles prevails on the government to revisit the vision on which RTI is based and to take up a revised notion of social justice that includes the "elimination of institutionalized domination and oppression" (Young, 1990, p. 15).

This critique of RTI from within disability studies in education and from the field of critical special education that Artiles has tended to be located within, whilst exceptional, is not the only example of effective critique of U.S. policy; and strong critiques have been offered from within critical special education, Critical Race Theory, and the intersections of race and disability (Connor & Ferri, 2013). Nevertheless, it is the offer of guidance towards alternative ways of thinking and acting that distinguish this critique from other forms and render it *respons-able*. In spite of the weight of these critiques of RTI, the discourse is so powerful and has such strong backing from educational textbook publishers that individual directors have ties to (Paley, 2007), that, as Ferri (2012) notes, trying to interrupt its contribution to the expansion of the SEN industry would be "like stopping a moving train" (p. 877).

Latour's (2004) calls for progress towards "a fair position" (p. 225) and for the development of "new critical tools" is a challenge to return to "the matters of concern that we cherish" (p. 248) and an invitation to engage in "mediating, assembling, [and] gathering" (p. 248). It is posed as an alternative to settling into quiescence "like a piano no longer struck" (p. 248). The critical tools potentially afforded and accessed from within disability studies in education, through its engagement with the humanities, are discussed below.

Assembling Critique

> The critic is not the one who debunks, but the one who assembles. The critic is not the one who lifts the rugs from under the feet of the naïve believers, but the one who offers the participants arenas in which to gather. The critic is not the one who alternates haphazardly between antifetishism and positivism like the drunk iconoclast drawn by Goya, but the one for whom, if something is constructed, then it means it is fragile and thus in great need of care and caution. (Latour, 2004, p. 246)

The purpose of critique is to understand the political ends intended by specific practices and to make these explicit, serving "as public memory to recall what is forgotten or ignored" (Said, 1995). It is not, Foucault (1988, p. 154) contends, "a matter of saying that things are not right as they are" but rather "of pointing out on what kinds of assumptions, what kinds of familiar, unchallenged and unconsidered modes of thought the practices that we accept rest" (p. 155). Critique also seeks out the under-represented, the disenfranchised, and misrecognized other, and names and privileges their voices and identities, making a discourse of that which has formerly been a noise (Rancière, 2008) and engaging in a process of rupture:

> For me a political subject is a subject who employs the competence of the so-called incompetents or the part of those who have no part, and not an additional group to be recognised as part of society. 'Visible minorities' means exceeding the system of represented groups, of constituted identities … It's a rupture that opens out into the recognition of the competence of anyone, not the addition of a unit. (p. 3)

The critic wades into the "conflict between truth and politics" (Arendt, 2006, p. 227) and attempts to "find out, stand guard over, and interpret factual truth" (pp. 256–257). However, the critical work invoked here amounts to far more than truth-telling, and is positive and constructive, pointing to new ways of conceptualizing and critiquing disability and new forms of political action arising from this critique. These are discussed below.

Contrapuntal Critique

Undertaking critique involves engaging in exercises in political thought, which as Arendt (2006) points out, requires practice. Critique, thus, is a form of training that does not prescribe what we should think but helps us to learn *how* to think. This accomplishment represents a fighting experience gained from standing one's ground between "the clashing waves of past and future" (Arendt, 2006, p. 13) and is exemplified in Kafka's parable:

> He has two antagonists: the first presses him from behind, from the origin. The second blocks the road ahead. He gives battle to both. To be sure, the first supports him in his fight with the second, for he wants to push him forward, and in the same way the second supports him in his fight with the first, since he drives him back. But it is only theoretically so. For it is not only the two antagonists who are there, but he himself as well, and who really knows his intentions? His dream, though, is that some time in an unguarded moment ... he will jump out of the fighting line and be promoted, on account of his experience of fighting, to the position of umpire over his antagonists in their fight with each other. (Cited in Arendt, 2006, p. 7)

A methodology for critique, which enables the identification of erasures, closures, and silences, has been developed by Edward Said (1993, 1999) through an elaboration of the concepts of contrapuntality and fugue, taken directly from Western classical music. This methodology aspires not merely to represent identity and voice, but allows "the telling of alternative stories by those that are currently marginalized and exiled" (Chowdry, 2007, p. 103). It seeks to speak of both oppression and resistance to it, achieved by "extending our reading of the texts to include what was once forcibly excluded" (Said, 1993, p. 67), but recovering these voices and dissonances. The great merit of contrapuntals is the way various themes are allowed to play off one another without privilege being accorded to any one. The wholeness of the piece of music comes from that interplay of the themes, which can be as many as 14, as in Bach's *Art of Fugue*, but with each of them distinct (Symes, 2006): "History is a giant fugue of interweaving themes and voices, of subject and reply. A contrapuntal reading of culture entails the entire constellation of its 'voices'" (Symes, 2006, p. 324). As Chowdry (2007, p. 105) notes, contrapuntal analysis amounts to more than a simple appeal for a plurality of voices, but is a call for "'worlding' the texts, institutions and practices, for historicizing them, for interrogating their sociality and materiality, for paying attention to the hierarchies and the power-knowledge nexus embedded in them. It is also a plea for the recovery of 'non-coercive and non-dominating knowledge' (Said, 2000, p. 444)." A contrapuntal analysis, characterized by "counterpoint, intertwining and integration" (Chowdry, 2007, p. 107), destabilizes conventional readings and "reveals the hidden interests, the embedded power relations and the political alignments" (ibid.).

Contrapuntal critique of disability involves a reading of disability as culture and of attending to its practices of description, communication, and representation through which certain narratives succeed in blocking others and whereby particular "philological tricks" (Said, cited in Chowdry, 2007, p. 110) allow disability culture to be rendered distinct from the rest of the world and inferior. Crucially, contrapuntal analysis also seeks out those voices of disability culture "which flow across cultures, that defy space and time, that start local, become global" (Symes, 2006, p. 314). Furthermore, contrapuntal analysis has a particularly exciting potential for intersectional analysis and the interrogation of disability in its counterpoint with race, class, gender, and other forms of oppression. It takes us beyond analyses of oppression, however, by taking us away from the positioning of antagonisms, of "absurd opposition" (Said, quoted in Salusinszky, 1987, p. 147), and of disadvantage always being presented as caused by another's advantage. It offers instead a "mollifying (though note not solving)" (Symes, 2006, p. 320) by allowing different elements to sit in relation to one another in a kind of "fugal resolution" (p. 321).

Demos-stration

The contrapuntal critique advocated above involves detailed work on the cultural practices—and specifically the language games that are used—that goes beyond being merely representative, moving "head over heels and away" (Deleuze, 1986, p. 26). They have the potential for generating an impetus by "setting fire to the unjust state of things instead of burning the things themselves, and restoring life to primary life" (Deleuze, 1986, p. 108). Whilst this has clearly enormous potential, there is a need for some form of political action to breathe life into the critique. Critchley (2007, p. 130) advocates a form of demonstration which takes up the "demos," meaning the people, and materializes them through a process of "*demos*-stration, 'manifesting the presence of those who do not count'" (ibid.). Critchley suggests that the scope for political action has been reduced by the disarticulation of names that are inherently political, such as the "proletariat" or the "peasant," but cites the examples of "indigenous" achieving the status of a force for change in Mexico and Australia.

Arendt (1958) advocates seeking out spaces for public action, suggesting that these may be anywhere and invoking the *polis* as meaning the "space of appearance" and a space for political action:

> The *polis*, properly speaking, is not the city-state in its physical location; it is the organization of the people as it arises out of acting and speaking together, and its true space lies between people living together for this purpose, no matter where they happen to be. (p. 198)

Arendt extends an invitation to the academic to undertake such political work, but recognizes that academe has never succeeded in achieving Plato's vision of being a "counter-society" (2006, p. 256). Nevertheless, she does articulate some investment in education and wills some action from educators:

Education is the point at which we decide whether we love the world enough to
assume responsibility for it and by the same token to save it from that ruin which,
except for renewal, except for the coming of the new and the young, would be
inevitable. And education, too, is where we decide whether we love our children
enough not to expel them from our world and leave them to their own devices...
(Arendt, 2006, p. 193)

Scholars of disability studies in education have clearly taken up this responsibility, through education and critique, and are already "rewriting ... discourses
of disability" (Ferri, 2008, p. 420) and are managing to "'talk back' to forces
in education that undermine inclusive values" (Connor, Gabel, Gallagher, &
Morton, 2008, p. 455). But the responsibility for critical work remains and is
a collective one, thus we must all walk the "path paved by thinking [and] ...
must discover and ploddingly pave it anew" (Arendt, 2006, p. 13).

Conclusion: Disability Studies in Education at Work on Policy

It is perhaps fitting, in conclusion, to reflect on the standard set by Ellen
Brantlinger for disability studies in education, even before it became known
as such, and to consider its capacity for work upon policy and for a "coun-
termovement to oppose stratifying measures and ... overcome hierarchical
and excluding relations in school and society" (Brantlinger, 2006, p. 224).
Brantlinger took on the giants of special education, the very people who dismiss disability studies in education as "purely ideological" (Brantlinger, 1997)
and unraveled their own arguments; she challenged the producers and the
advocates of the "big glossies" (Brantlinger, p. 2006, p. 45), the textbooks
on special education for giving beginning teachers fake confidence based on
a drilling of deficits, and demanded some answers to the question of "who
benefits from special education?" (Brantlinger, 2006). She also delighted in
securing significant policy changes, such as the abandonment of the zoning of
children to particular schools on the basis of social class (Brantlinger, 2003)
and the ending of a policy on teacher transfer, made all the sweeter for her
when she caused major annoyance among the policymakers (Allan & Slee,
2008). But these achievements are salutary in reminding us of the potential
costs of undertaking critical work of this kind. Ellen Brantlinger, Deborah
Gallagher, and Scot Danforth have all received personalized vilifications and
denunciations as a direct result of their work in disability studies in education
(Mostert, Kavale, & Kauffman, 2007; Kavale & Mostert, 2004; Kauffman &
Sasso, 2006). They were sufficiently well established—and tenured—to with-
stand such attacks and to even subject them to counter-critique. A concern
remains, however, that more novice scholars embarking on disability studies

in education face some substantial career-threatening risks. A volume such as this, which attests to the quality and worth of disability studies in education, should go some way to inspire confidence, as will the active support and endorsement from senior scholars within the academy.

Disability studies in education is a powerful force, enabling us, in Foucault's (1985) words, to think and perceive differently and to do so "better" than we have hitherto done. It allows us to see policy for what it is and what it does to people, and to ask questions about the consequences for individuals. Scholars of disability studies in education are emboldened to undertake "fearless critiques of special education" (Connor, 2013, p. 1229) that are defensible on account of their rigour and which are purposeful with their regard—always—for the disenfranchised and disadvantaged Other. Finally, disability studies in education does not stop at critique, but rather urges its proponents to progress towards a fair position and to specify the means and the mechanisms for social change.

References

Alexandersson, M. (2011). Equivalence and choice in combination: The Swedish dilemma. *Oxford Review of Education, 37*, 195–214.

Allan, J., & Slee, R. (2008). *Doing inclusive education research*. Rotterdam, Netherlands: Sense.

Apple, M. W. (2001). Markets, standards, teaching, and teacher education. *Journal of Teacher Education, 52*(3), 182–196.

Arendt, H. (1958). *The human condition*. Chicago: University of Chicago Press.

Arendt, H. (2006). *Between past and future: Eight exercises in political thought*. New York: Penguin Books.

Artiles, A. J. (2011). Toward an interdisciplinary understanding of educational equity and difference: The case of the racialization of ability. *Educational Researcher, 40*(9), 431–445.

Artiles, A. J., Bal, A., & King Thorius, K. A. (2010). Back to the future: A critique of response to intervention's social justice views. *Theory into Practice, 49*(4), 250–257.

Ball, S. J. (2013). *Foucault, power, and education*. London, U.K.: Routledge.

Beach, D. (2011). Education science in Sweden: Promoting research for teacher education or weakening its scientific foundations? *Education Inquiry, 2*(2), 207–220.

Beach, D. (2012, April 26–27). Sixty years of policy development in teacher education in Sweden: Changing professional discourses in teacher education policy. Keynote address at the International Conference on the Transformation of School and Teacher Professionalism, Gothenburg.

Beach, D., & Bagley, C. (2012). The weakening role of education studies and the retraditionalisation of Swedish teacher education, *Oxford Review of Education, 38*(3), 287–303.

Bernstein, B. (1999). Vertical and horizontal discourse: An essay. *British Journal of Sociology of Education, 20*(2), 157–173.

Booth, T., & Ainscow, M. (2011). *The index for inclusion: Developing learning and participation in schools.* Bristol, U.K.: Centre for Studies in Inclusive Education.

Brantlinger, E. (1997). Using ideology: Cases of nonrecognition of the politics of research and practice in special education. *Review of Educational Research, 67*(4), 425–59.

Brantlinger, E. (2003). *Dividing classes: How the middle class negotiates and justifies school advantage.* New York: Routledge.

Brantlinger, E. (2006). The big glossies: How textbooks structure (special) education. In E. Brantlinger (Ed.), *Who benefits from special education? Remediating (fixing) other people's children* (pp. 45–75). Mahwah, NJ: Lawrence Erlbaum.

Butin, D. (2002). This ain't talk therapy: Problematizing and extending anti-oppressive education. *Educational Researcher, 31*(3), 14–16.

Chowdry, G. (2007). Edward Said and contrapuntal reading: Implications for critical interventions in international relations. *Millennium: Journal of International Studies, 36*(1), 101–116.

Connor, D. J. (2013). Risk-taker, role model, muse, and 'charlatan': Stories of Ellen—An atypical giant. *International Journal of Inclusive Education, 17*(12), 1229–1240.

Connor, D. J., & Ferri, B. (2013). Historicizing disability: Creating normalcy, containing difference. In M. Wappett & K. Arndt (Eds.), *Foundations of disability studies* (pp. 29–67). New York: Palgrave Macmillan.

Connor, D. J., Gabel, S., Gallagher, D., & Morton, M. (2008). Disability studies and inclusive education: Implications for theory, research, and practice. *International Journal of Inclusive Education, 12*(5–6), 441–457.

Critchley, J. (2007). *Infinitely demanding: Ethics of commitment, politics of resistance.* London/New York: Verso.

Crotty, M. (1998). *The foundations of social research: Meanings and perspective in the research process.* Sydney, Australia: Allen & Unwin.

Deleuze, G. (1986). *Cinema I.* London/New York: Continuum.

European Association of Service Providers for Persons with Disabilities (EASPD). (2012). Retrieved from http://www.includ-ed.eu/good-practice/pathways-inclusion-p2i

Fenech, M., & Sumeson, J. (2007). Early childhood teachers and regulation: Complicating power relations using a Foucauldian lens. *Contemporary Issues in Early Childhood, 8*(2), 109–122.

Ferri, B. (2008). Doing a (dis)service: Reimagining special education from a disability studies perspective. In W. Ayers, T. Quinn, & D. Stovall (eds.), *The handbook of social justice in education.* New York: Lawrence Erlbaum.

Ferri, B. (2012). Undermining inclusion? A critical reading of response to intervention (RTI). *International Journal of Inclusive Education, 16*(8), 863–880.

Ferri, B., Gallagher, D., & Connor, D. J. (2011). Pluralizing methodologies in the field of LD: From what works to what matters. *Learning Disability Quarterly,*

34(3), 222–231. Retrieved from http://www.academia.edu/1124709/Pluralizing_Methodologies_in_the_Field_of_LD_From_What_Works_to_What_Matters

Foucault, M. (1985). *The history of sexuality: The use of pleasure.* New York: Pantheon.

Foucault, M. (1988). *Politics, philosophy, culture: Interviews and other writings 1972–1977.* London: Routledge.

Fransson, K., & Lundgren, U. P. (2003). *Utbildningsvetenskap—Ett begrepp och dess sammanhang* [*Education—A concept and its context*]. Vetenskapsrådets rapportserie, rapport 1/2003.

Gallagher, D. (2010). Educational researchers and the making of normal people. In C. Dudley-Marling & A. Gurn (eds.), *The myth of the normal curve* (pp. 25–38). New York: Peter Lang.

Gresham, F. M. (2007). Evolution of the response-to-intervention concept: Empirical foundations and recent developments. In S. R. Jimerson, M. K. Burns, & A. M. VanDerHeyden (Eds.), *Handbook of response to intervention: The science and practice of assessment and intervention* (pp. 10–24). New York: Springer.

Java Optical Design and Analysis Software (1990). Foucault simulation. Retrieved from www.myoptics.at/jodas/foucault.html

Kauffman, J., & Sasso, G. (2006). Toward ending cultural and cognitive relativism in special education. *Exceptionality, 14*(2), 65–90.

Kavale, K., & Mostert, M. (2004). *The positive side of special education: Minimizing its fads, fancies and follies.* Lanham, MD: Scarecrow Education.

Kohn, J. (2006). Introduction. In H. Arendt (Ed.), *Between past and future: Eight exercises in political thought* (pp. vii–xxiv). New York: Penguin.

Kristof, N. (2009, March 18). The daily me. *New York Times.* Retrieved from http://www.nytimes.com/2009/03/19/opinion/19kristof.html

Kuhn, T. (1970). *The structure of scientific revolutions.* Chicago: Chicago University Press.

Latour, B. (2004). Why has critique run out of steam? From matters of fact to matters of concern. *Critical Inquiry, 30,* 225–248.

Lauder, H., Brown, P., & Halsey, A. H. (2009). Sociology of education: A critical history and prospects for the future. *Oxford Review of Education, 35*(5), 569–585.

Lindström, M., & Beach, D. (2013). The professionalization of the field of education in Sweden: A historical analysis. *Professions and Professionalism, 3*(2).

Lyotard, J. (1992). *The postmodern explained to children: Correspondence 1982–1985.* Sydney, Australia: Power.

MacLure, M. (2005). Clarity bordering on stupidity: Where's the quality in systematic review? *Journal of Education Policy, 20*(4), 393–416.

Mostert, M., Kavale, K., & Kauffman, M. (2007). *Challenging the refusal of reasoning in special education.* Denver, CO: Love.

Oancea, A., & Bridges, D. (2009). Philosophy of education in the UK: The historical and contemporary tradition, *Oxford Review of Education, 35*(5), 553–568.

Paley, A. R. (2007, April 21). Key initiative of 'No Child' under federal investigation: Officials profited from Reading First program. *Washington Post*, A01. Retrieved from   http://www.washingtonpost.com/wp-dyn/content/article/2007/04/20/ AR2007042002284.html

Peters, M., Lankshear, C., & Olsson, M. (2003). *Critical theory: Founders and praxis.* New York: Peter Lang.

Phillips, E., & Pugh, D. (1987). *How to get a PhD.* Milton Keynes/Philadelphia: Open University Press.

Punch, K. (2005). *Introduction to social research: Quantitative and qualitative approaches.* London: Sage.

Rancière, J. (2008). Jacques Rancière and indisciplinarity: An interview. *Art and Research, 2*(1), 1–10.

Rodriguez, L., & Craig, R. (2007). Assessing international accounting harmonization using Hegelian dialectic, isomorphism and Foucault. *Critical Perspectives in Accounting, 18*(6), 739–767.

Said, E. (1993). *Culture and imperialism.* New York: Alfred Knopf.

Said, E. (1995). On defiance and taking positions, *American Council of Learned Societies. Occasional Paper No. 31.* Retrieved from http://archives.acls.org/op/op31said.htm#said.

Said, E. (1999). *Out of place: A memoir.* New York: Alfred Knopf.

Said, E. (2000). An interview with Edward Said. In M. Bayami & A. Rubin (Eds.), *The Edward Said reader* (pp. 419–444). New York: Vintage Books.

Salusinszky, I. (1987). *Critiques in society.* New York: Methuen.

Shostak, J. (2002). *Understanding, designing and conducting qualitative research in education.* Buckingham/Philadelphia: Open University Press.

Sjöberg, L. (2011). *Bäst i klassen? Lärare och elever i Svenska och Europeiska policydokument.* Göteborg: Acta Universitatis Gothenburgensis.

Sleeter, C. (2008). Equity, democracy, and neo–liberal assaults on teacher education. *Teaching and Teacher Education, 24*(8), 1947–1957.

SOU. (2008). *En hållbar lärarutbildning. Betänkande av utredningen om en ny lärarutbildning* [*A sustainable teacher education*] (HUT 07). Stockholm: Fritzes.

Spencer, L., Richie, J., Lewis, J., & Dillon, L. (2003). *Quality in quality evaluation: A framework for assessing research evidence.* London: Cabinet Office.

Swedish Government Bill (2009/10) *Bäst i klassen* [*Top of the class*]. Stockholm: Regeringskansliet.

Symes, C. (2006). The paradox of the canon: Edward W. Said and musical transgression. *Discourse: Studies in the Cultural Politics of Education, 27*(3), 309–324.

Täljedal, I. (2011). Reform and reaction in teacher education at Umeå university. *Education Inquiry, 2*(2), 319–329.

Tomlinson, S. (2012). The irresistible rise of the SEN industry, *Oxford Review of Education, 38*(3), 267–286.

Torrance, H. (2008). Building confidence in qualitative research: Engaging the demands of policy. *Qualitative Inquiry, 14*(4), 507–527.

Training and Development Agency. (2012). *ITT trainees: The pillars of inclusion. Inclusive teaching and learning for pupils with special educational needs (SEN) and/or disabilities. Training toolkit.* Retrieved from https://www.european-agency. org/agency-projects/Teacher-Education-for-Inclusion/country-study-visits-2011/ london-uk-england/ITT-trainees-the-pillars-of-inclusion.pdf

Troyna, B. (1994). The 'everyday world' of teachers? Deracialised discourses in the sociology of teachers and the teaching profession. *British Journal of Sociology of Education, 15*(3), 325–339.

Young, I. M. (1990). *Justice and the politics of difference.* Princeton, NJ: Princeton University Press.

11. Using Disability Studies in Education to Recognize, Resist, and Reshape Policy and Practices in Aotearoa New Zealand

MISSY MORTON

Introduction

In this chapter, I begin by describing the wider policy context in which we are working to develop inclusive education in Aotearoa New Zealand—arguably one of the countries with the fewest students (approximately 0.4%) attending separate special education services. We are still some way from achieving the Ministry of Education's aim of a "world-class inclusive education system" or all schools being inclusive schools by 2014 (Ministry of Education, 2010). Aotearoa New Zealand, like many countries in the Organization for Economic Cooperation and Development (OECD), has had a series of governments that draw on neoliberal ideologies to develop policy and practices in education and more widely. At the same time, there is a history of developments and practices that have presented opportunities to advance policies and practices that are more inclusive of all learners. My rationale for presenting this context is twofold. First, I think this shows that work towards inclusive settings and practices can continue even in a less-than-ideal environment. The second aspect is that readers from other countries may recognize similar opportunities in their own contexts, making possible new connections and ways of working. Disability studies in education (DSE) is a valuable framework for both recognizing and resisting exclusion as well as for developing policies and resources that make inclusive practices more likely and more sustainable.

Connor, Gabel, Gallagher, and Morton (2008) argue, "DSE itself may be seen as a counter-narrative to the prevailing and intertwined hegemonic discourses of normalcy, deficiency, and efficiency operating in (special) education" (p. 455). In the second half of this chapter, I describe the development of three resources to support inclusive practices in schools in Aotearoa New Zealand: the *New Zealand Curriculum Exemplars for Learners with Special Education Needs* and *Narrative Assessment: A Guide for Teachers* (Ministry of Education, 2009a), *Collaboration for Success: Individual Education Plans* (Ministry of Education, 2011), and the *Teachers and Teachers' Aides Working Together* (Ministry of Education, 2014). I highlight three principles that underpin the development of the resources. These principles are recognizing and resisting deficit discourses; recognizing, celebrating, and building on competence; and collaborative learning. I want to suggest that these three principles have served us well in providing a counter-narrative. Further, these three principles may be helpful in other policy contexts where neoliberal discourses of (special) education continue to prevail.

The Aotearoa New Zealand Policy Context

Aotearoa New Zealand, as elsewhere, has a complex policy context. Legislation, policy guidelines, implementation, monitoring, consequences, and press releases about all of these often send mixed signals to practitioners, researchers, and policymakers alike. Reforms in one sector can support or impede the work in another sector, or even the work stream of another part of the *same* sector. In this section on the Aotearoa New Zealand policy context, I describe some of the aspects of policy that have been most evident in supporting and impeding the opportunities for all children in Aotearoa New Zealand to attend school, to enjoy school, and to feel they are welcomed, valued, learning, and achieving while they are at school.

Aims, Implementation and Impacts of Neoliberal Reforms

The election of a Labor Government in 1984 saw the rapid introduction of neoliberal reforms to policies and practices in a number of sectors. Key ideas included reducing the size of state involvement in areas such as health, education, and welfare; dramatically reducing costs to the state (at the same time reducing state income through taxation); and expecting that "the market" would achieve all this while at the same time improving both quality and efficiency. Through the twin forces of competition and individual consumer choice, bad services would be weeded out, good services would flourish, and all consumers would be able to then choose amongst these surviving better services.

The same government brought in the 1989 Education Act, with significantly altered expectations for schools' performance, school management and governance, as well as school support. A number of aspects of the Act have shaped opportunities for participation in education for disabled children and their families. Aspects of the reforms that are particularly relevant to this paper include changes in schools' governance and management, teacher professional learning and development, and review and accountability. Before going on to explore these aspects, it's important to acknowledge the impact the Act had on the potential participation for disabled children: For the first time, the Act required *all* public schools to enroll *all* children.

Before this Act, most disabled children, if they went to school at all, went to a special school. However, even special schools were not required to accept all disabled children. A number of children attended "preschools" run by voluntary organizations initially established by parent groups. Many children stayed at these preschools until they were 18 or older, at which point they moved into sheltered workshops, also run by the voluntary organizations, usually within the same grounds as the preschool (along with group homes or hostels). Other children were admitted to *psychopaedic* (literally, "the mind of a child") institutions, or psychopaedic wards within psychiatric institutions. Some of these children left the institution during the day to attend special schools in the nearest town. Other children left their wards and attended the "psychopaedic training unit" within the institution, graduating from this unit to attend the sheltered workshop also located on the institution campus. The focus of the training in these facilities was on self-help skills (such as eating, dressing, toileting, bed making, food preparation) and behavior—thereby laying the groundwork for smooth transition to the sheltered workshop, which typically included both further training for self-help skills and behavior, along with simple work skills that enabled the workshops to take up contracts and generate a small income (e.g., packaging clothes pegs and other small items, making craft work, woodworking and simple carpentry). Finally, in every psychopaedic institution and/or ward there were disabled children (and adults) who spent all day in the ward, considered too "handicapped" to be able to participate in, or benefit from, any form of training let alone education (Millar & Morton, 2007; Morton, 2012). Dever, Gladstone, and Quick (2013) note that these low expectations are little changed for many disabled students leaving special schools or special classes today.

Prior to the change in the 1989 Act, there were, of course, schools (primary and secondary) and kindergartens (state-provided early childhood education for 3- to 5-year-olds) that were already including almost all "local" children, even disabled children who otherwise would be at home all day, or moved into a distant town that was able to "provide services." It was the example of these schools that were *already* "mainstreaming" disabled students that provided both impetus for, and confidence in, the moral, educational, and practical possibilities for what eventually came to be known as inclusive education in Aotearoa New Zealand (Ballard & Morton, 1987). In the almost 25 years since the implementation of the 1989 Education Act, Aotearoa New Zealand has been described by some as the most inclusive education system, with only 0.4% of children with special educational needs enrolled in separate special schools.

The majority of the reforms ushered in by the 1989 Education Act were based on a belief that education leads to

> ...personal gain (rather than a public good). Education is thus a commodity in the market place, to be bought and sold. The education system is seen as but one form of delivery of this product. There is a concomitant focus on inputs (including direct and indirect costs), outputs (such as student achievement data and qualifications) and accountability. (Gordon & Morton, 2008, p. 238)

The State took a very large step away from the direct administration and governance of schools, and schools became "self-managing." Governance of schools became the responsibility of locally elected boards of trustees for each school. In theory, this shift would enable schools to be more flexible and responsive to the needs of their local communities.

The actual effects are, at best, uneven (Wylie, 2012). Gordon and Morton (2008) have noted that those schools with the least resources before the reforms often did worse following the reforms. Only those families with financial and cultural capital were able to "shop around in the education marketplace" and exercise their "rights to individual choice." For most families with disabled children, the only choice being exercised was that of schools choosing to not enroll those children. Despite it being illegal to refuse to enroll a child who lived within the neighborhood or enrolment zone of a school, many families describe being turned away (Macartney & Morton, 2013; Morton & McMenamin, 2011).

Following these reforms, the Education Review Office (ERO) was created to audit and review schools to ensure that schools met their new legal requirements for planning, reporting, and evaluating procedures—with the focus on reporting to the Ministry of Education rather than to local communities of interest. Thrupp and Smith (1999) describe this new regime of compliance as based on a particular form of managerialist philosophy.

This philosophy focused on "ensuring that schools delivered the curriculum properly, met their contractual obligations to the state, had good financial systems in place and developed and implemented school policies as required" (Gordon & Morton, 2008, p. 240). The ERO monitored schools for their compliance for planning and reporting, but paid no attention to whether or not schools did in fact enroll all who were now legally entitled to enroll.

The previous system of regional and national support for the professional development of teachers and principals was dismantled. Schools would determine their own needs and individually contract for the professional development that they identified. Professional development services became available for competitive tender by the most efficient "deliverer." The effectiveness of professional development contracts was to be measured by gains in student achievement. Such a narrow focus on student achievement as an outcome measure has been critiqued locally in Aotearoa New Zealand (Ballard, 2013; Thrupp & Smith, 1999; Wylie, 2012) and internationally (e.g., Berliner, 2013; Lather, 2009). Lather (2009) calls the current culture of audit in an era of accountability "technicist policy-making that is over-rationalized and out of touch" (p. 48) with the complexity of the real world's messiness, uncertainty, and complexities. She suggests the effect has been to reduce accountability to auditability and "rituals of verification" with resources "funneled into monitoring compliance" (p. 47).

For some schools, students with special education needs were seen as an additional burden. If individual students did not arrive at a school with extra resources, they were either turned away or their experiences and participation at school were so narrowly prescribed that their families eventually removed them (Macartney & Morton, 2013; Morton & Gordon, 2006; Morton & McMenamin, 2009). Professional learning and development in schools often did not include learning about how to support *all* learners. When teachers or schools identified a need for support around students with "special education needs," they turned to services and support focused on the needs of the individual student, rather than professional development in areas of curriculum and assessment for diverse learners (Millar & Morton, 2007; Morton & Gordon, 2006). Not surprisingly, many schools noted that they did not feel competent or confident about how the *New Zealand Curriculum* (including pedagogy and assessment) applied to disabled students in their classrooms (Morton & McMenamin, 2011).

Lather (2009) calls on educators to "push back" in this current audit culture. In the next section, I describe some of the ways Aotearoa New Zealand educators have long pushed back. Our history of resistances and innovations in Aotearoa New Zealand creates spaces for re-thinking inclusive education.

Pushing Back and Moving Forward

Connor, Valle, and Hale (2012) argue that when DSE (indeed any) scholars ask different questions, then different possibilities for research and action emerge. The crucial question these authors ask is "How can we better connect knowledge, beliefs and values to practice?" (p. 5). This question requires us to attend to the *ethics* of our actions in any sphere: research, scholarship, practice, advocacy, and the different ways we combine these actions. Many researchers have argued that any research that purports to be value-free or somehow neutral or apolitical has been, and continues to be, a form of violence to marginalized groups (Harrison, MacGibbon, & Morton, 2001; Lather, 2009).

In Aotearoa New Zealand, I would characterize one quality that has guided much work as that of challenging the notion that there is such a thing as a decontextualized individual that comprises a useful unit of analysis. Within DSE, Paugh and Dudley-Marling (2011) have eloquently described how the "unrelenting focus" on the individual continually re-invokes and reinscribes deficit views of individual students, at the same time pathologizing both students and their families. Similarly, work by Russell Bishop and colleagues in Aotearoa New Zealand has documented how Māori (indigenous peoples of Aotearoa New Zealand) students and their *whānau* (families) have been framed as deficient (see, for example, Berryman & Woller, 2013; Bishop, Berryman, Tiakiwai & Richardson, 2003; Bishop & Glynn, 1999) and blamed for their perceived failure within the education system. These authors argue for a reconnection of culture, identity, values and beliefs to our educational practices (Berryman & Woller, 2013; Bishop, Berryman, Tiakiwai & Richardson, 2003; Bishop & Glynn, 1999; Macfarlane, Macfarlane & Glynn, 2012). They argue that *relationships* are central to all students being able to participate and flourish in classrooms and schools. Relationships between teachers, students, and students' whānau and families are only possible when teachers work at knowing their students. A question then arises: how do our current beliefs and practices in curriculum, pedagogy, and assessment support or get in the way of forming meaningful relationships with students?

The groundbreaking work in early childhood curriculum by Margaret Carr and colleagues also directly challenges traditional psychological and developmental ways of framing individual learning (Carr & Lee, 2012; Cowie, 2009; Cowie & Carr, 2009; Cowie & Carr, in press). Turning to sociocultural perspectives on learning moves the focus from the individual to the individual in context, to learning as a social activity. Understanding early childhood centers as learning communities frames all members as learners, including the adults in the settings.

The Aotearoa New Zealand education system is also able to draw on the occasional practice of teachers, policymakers, and researchers working together on some significant developments. Wylie (2012) notes that where this approach has been followed, teachers and schools have been supported to make significant changes. Noteworthy examples have been the development of the *New Zealand Curriculum* (Ministry of Education, 1996; 2007) and *New Zealand Curriculum Exemplars* (Ministry of Education, 2003; 2009a; 2009b; 2009c).

The key ideas that come from this work in Aotearoa New Zealand are that curriculum, pedagogy, and assessment have to support the development of learning communities. Curriculum, pedagogy, and assessment should be framed to support the development of positive relationships between students and teachers, between schools and families, amongst students, and amongst teachers (Carter & MacArthur, forthcoming; Cowie & Carr, forthcoming; Guerin, forthcoming; Hipkins, forthcoming; McIlroy, forthcoming; Morton, forthcoming). These understandings are available to us precisely because of the work done in and through DSE. The next section describes three projects where these understandings have been put to work.

Putting DSE to Work in Aotearoa New Zealand

I have been fortunate to be able to work with educators throughout Aotearoa New Zealand to design and build resources for educators in primary (elementary) and secondary (high) schools. In various teams, we brought questions and insights from disability studies in education (DSE) to our projects, in particular the curriculum and assessment projects begun in 2006 under contract to the Ministry of Education. Julie Allan has noted, the "introduction of a DSE perspective on difference frames new questions that yield different answers" (Allan, 2012, p. 8). Understanding disability as socially constructed made us vigilant to the ways we understood and constructed disability and identities, both in the ways we worked with students, educators, and whānau (families), as well as in the resources we created. The projects are described in detail in other places (Ministry of Education, 2009a, 2009b, 2011, 2014; Morton, 2012; Morton, forthcoming; Morton, McMenamin, Moore, & Molloy, 2012). In this section, I want to focus more on the issues we grappled with, the tensions these issues created, and how we attempted to work within those tensions. I want to stress here that these are my reflections on and analysis of our work at this time; not all of the participants will necessarily share my view of this work. In this section, I explore how three principles emerged from and shaped our work. These principles are recognizing and resisting deficit discourses; recognizing, celebrating, and building on competence; and collaborative learning.

Recognizing and Resisting Deficit Discourses

Traditional approaches to special education have located problems of learning and participation within the individual diagnosed or otherwise labeled as disabled. Deficit discourses are increasingly seen as problematic, even while difficult to resist. Various individuals, or groups, have had their turn under the microscope, being examined and blamed for failures at the individual, classroom, school, and/or system level.

Deficit discourses are easiest to recognize in the language we apply to differences amongst and between groups of people. This language reveals assumptions about lack of ability, based on membership of a group or assigned category, rather than knowledge of a person. When the Aotearoa New Zealand Ministry of Education established the process for assigning individualized funding for disabled students, they decided not to go down a route of using diagnostic categories to allocate funding. The approach chosen was to ask teachers, associated educational professionals, and families to work together to describe a child's needs for support in order to access the curriculum and participate in school.

On the face of it, this approach challenged the traditional expert and professional knowledge of a few to label and predict the learning and life outcomes of disabled children. Within a relatively short space of time, this approach to applying for funding revealed its flaws. From families' perspectives, the lengthy application process was both painful and frustrating. A successful funding application required painting a grim picture of their child, in particular describing a set of problems that were long term, possibly intractable. From the perspectives of educators and schools, they needed to show that without individualized funding and support, they and the student would really struggle to engage in the curriculum and support learning and achievement. Unsuccessful funding applications often resulted in students (and their families) being discouraged from enrolling in, or attending, their local schools (Kearney, 2011; Macartney & Morton, 2013).

Successful individualized funding applications sometimes had paradoxical effects. The funding was ostensibly used to access additional teacher expertise to support the classroom teacher and/or employ a teacher's aide to work alongside the student. However, for some students, if the funding did not extend to providing teacher aide support in the lunch break and on the playground, that student did not participate in lunch-time activities. If the funding did not cover the whole of the school day, the student's family might be asked to take the student home, fund additional hours to employ a teacher's aide to "provide cover," or even to become the teacher's aide in their child's classroom. (Kearney, 2011; Macartney & Morton, 2013; Rutherford, 2012). Those children whose support had been funded also needed to demonstrate that they continued to need this individualized funded support. The student's IEP was required to demonstrate ongoing need for support. Consequently, the preparation for and participation in the IEP meeting perpetuated the deficit focus. There was little incentive to focus on achievement if this could result in a loss of funding. Thus, IEPs tended to largely repeat the same goals from year to year, showing minimal progress, and often were not explicitly related to the *New Zealand Curriculum*.

A rather gloomy picture emerged. Aotearoa New Zealand had avoided the competition for the most "favorable" diagnosis tied to funding experienced in other countries (Mitchell, Morton, & Hornby, 2011). However, children could still be turned away from their local school (illegally) if their need was not sufficiently great to generate individualized funding. Those children with individualized funding were forever not learning or at least not enough and not participating in the *New Zealand Curriculum*. Their teachers believed that the curriculum was not relevant to this group of students and that they were not competent to teach this group of students (Kearney, 2011; Macartney & Morton, 2013; McMenamin et al., 2004; Rutherford, 2012).

In 2006, the Ministry of Education commissioned a project with five aims. The first aim was to develop a set of curriculum exemplars that showed authentic student learning annotated to the *New Zealand Curriculum*. The second aim was to work with teachers and teacher educators within a culture of professional learning and development. The third aim was to support inclusive teaching practice through a focus on learners accessing the *New Zealand Curriculum*. The fourth aim was to focus on assessment of the "Key Competencies" within the context of the "Learning Areas" (described in more detail below). The final aim of the project was to illustrate an approach to assessment that could capture the complexity of learning that happens in the context of relationships. These final two aims were grounded within a sociocultural perspective of teaching and learning (Morton, McMenamin, Moore & Molloy, 2012). Thus, the explicit intent of the subsequent three resources (the *Curriculum Exemplars*, the *Narrative Assessment Guide*, and the online resource *Through Different Eyes*) was to support all teachers to recognize all students as learners and to promote understanding of the *New Zealand Curriculum* for *all* students (Ministry of Education, 2009a, 2009b).

The introduction of the *New Zealand Curriculum* (Ministry of Education, 2007) included both traditional individualistic *and* sociocultural understandings of curriculum and pedagogy. The subject or "Learning Areas" were slightly expanded, but continued to be framed and presented in a matrix of (presumably) increasing levels of difficulty. Each curriculum area is presented as a relatively standalone subject. This new curriculum also introduced the "Key Competencies." The five competencies are thinking, managing self, participating and contributing, using language symbols and texts, and relating to others. The key competencies draw on knowledge, attitudes, and values. They are both "a means to an end and a valued educational outcome." The *New Zealand Curriculum* (Ministry of Education, 2007, p. 12) describes how key competencies involve the learner in engaging personal goals, other people, community knowledge and values, cultural tools, and the knowledge and skills found in learning areas. "People use these competencies to live, learn, work, and contribute as active members of their communities" (p. 12).

Many of the project team also brought a commitment to a social model of disability as expressed in the *New Zealand Disability Strategy* (NZDS) (Ministry of Health, 2001). The NZDS argues that we need to pay attention to how our institutional practices may unintentionally exclude disabled people. An important implication for teaching and learning is that we cannot use a student's disability as an explanation for why we might not have met their learning needs (Morton & McMenamin, 2011, p. 212).

Relatively early in the project, an issue that emerged was how to describe the students whose work and achievements appeared in the exemplars. On the one hand, teachers writing the exemplars (the teacher-writers) were able to see and document learning that had not previously been obvious to the teachers (see the two following sections). On the other hand, some of the teacher-writers wanted those teachers who might read the exemplars to "know just how hard it was to work with these students." The teacher-writers' rationale was that teachers reading the exemplars might assume that the students featured in the exemplars were not like the students in their own classrooms and dismiss the exemplars as not relevant, not useful. The teacher-writers wanted other teachers to be able to "buy into" the exemplars. The teacher-writers wanted to be able to share their excitement about what they had learned about their students, and what they had learned about themselves by learning to use the approach of narrative assessment adopted in developing the exemplars.

The publishers of the exemplars also believed that teachers reading the exemplars would be better "able to identify with the teachers and their students" if each exemplar contained a description of the child that included a diagnostic label or some details of the student's needs. I am, at best, ambivalent about this decision on how to present the exemplars. Each exemplar celebrates learning and student achievement; each exemplar identifies and celebrates the learning of the teachers working with those students. The exemplars, individually and collectively, illustrate the importance of getting to know a student, along with some of the best ways to do so. Each exemplar also begins with a description of the student that includes a label or list of needs. My lingering doubt is that some of the exemplars read as if the student's learning has occurred *in spite* of the label. I wish we had persisted in our efforts of coming up with a way to more clearly make the point that a label or list of needs is not a means to predict student learning (or lack of learning).

On the other hand, those of us working on the exemplars project gradually recognized what we were missing when we focused only on the individual (disabled) student when looking for (evidence of) learning. The understandings of learning embedded in the Key Competencies in the context of the Learning Areas of the *New Zealand Curriculum* challenged us, and provided us with the space to rethink whose learning we were noticing, together with how we might assess, describe, and report on learning.

How Do We Recognize, Celebrate and Build on Competence?

The *Curriculum Exemplars* and the *Narrative Assessment* projects (Ministry of Education, 2009a, 2009b) were developed within an explicitly sociocultural understanding of curriculum, pedagogy, and assessment. The Key Competencies of the *New Zealand Curriculum* are grounded within a sociocultural perspective of teaching and learning, similar to that used by Margaret Carr and colleagues in their work on the Aotearoa New Zealand early childhood education curriculum. A shift in curriculum and pedagogy also requires a shift in assessment (Broadfoot, 2007; Hipkins, 2007; Morton, 2012). In these two projects, the shift in assessment was a shift away from the focus on the individual to a shift to the individual in context. It was a shift away from a predefined list of required outcomes to an emergent, co-constructed understanding of competence. In these projects, we adopted the "notice, recognize, and respond to learning" approach initially developed by Carr and colleagues in Learning Stories, the assessment approach used in early childhood, and by Cowie and colleagues in secondary science classrooms (Carr & Lee, 2012; Cowie, 2009; Cowie & Carr, 2009; Cowie & Carr, forthcoming). An important impact of this approach is a focus on competence, building on students' strengths and interests. The eight subject areas of the *New Zealand Curriculum* (science, social sciences, the arts, learning languages, health and physical education, English, mathematics and statistics, and technology), however, continue to follow a traditional approach of presumable increasing levels of complexity and sophistication. Assessment in these subject areas, particularly in the senior years of secondary education, is very much focused on the performance of the individual student, suitably organized to prevent any collaboration that might be construed as cheating.

Writing about the U.K., Swann, Peacock, Hart and Drummond (2012) describe the impact of limited views of learning, and learners, on both students and educators. They describe the current climate as one

> in which teachers are required to use the certainty of prediction as a reliable tool in their planning and organization of opportunities for learning. Targets, levels, objectives, outcomes—all these ways of conceptualizing learning require teachers to behave as if all children's potential is predictable and their futures knowable far in advance, as if their power as educators can have only a limited impact on the lives of many children and young people. Furthermore, closely associated with this view of learning (as linear, measurable and quantifiable) is an equally damaging view of the children who do the learning, who can themselves be known, measured and quantified in terms of so-called ability, a fixed, internal capacity, which can be readily determined." (p. 1)

We have observed the effects of a very similar climate at work in Aotearoa New Zealand. One effect of this climate is that teachers may come to hold very limited views of the potential of some children and young people to learn. Teachers may question how some children and young people can possibly participate in a curriculum that sets out a sequence of levels of learning objectives—a sequence that makes it look as if it is only possible to participate in the "upper levels" having demonstrated competence in previous levels. Teachers may doubt their ability to be teachers in relation to children and young people who are not recognized as learners (Morton & McMenamin, 2011).

The *Curriculum Exemplars* and the *Narrative Assessment* projects (Ministry of Education, 2009a, 2009b) attempted to navigate the tensions between these two aspects of the *New Zealand Curriculum*: the sociocultural views of learning within the Key Competencies, and the traditional views of curriculum, pedagogy, and assessment associated with the eight subject areas of the curriculum. The approach we took was to focus on learning in the Key Competencies within the context of the Learning Areas. We asked the teachers in the project to begin by writing a story about students' learning (a learning story, or narrative assessment). This could be a photograph or series of photographs, a couple of lines. We stressed that there were no right or wrong answers. As a project team, we together constructed a format that would work for all of us. A series of principles emerged that we iteratively examined and amended as necessary as we developed the narrative assessment. Our first agreed-upon criterion was that teachers would begin with what we called an "Aha!" moment, something they noticed that surprised them. We asked the teachers to also pay attention to the context of their "Aha!" moment. The context included the learning focus or intentions they had set up, what the class as a whole was doing, what they were doing in the moment, what the particular student was doing that surprised them.

When we came together as a project group to share these early stories of students' learning, the teachers were also attending to what they had learned. They noticed what surprised them and why it surprised them. They talked about "seeing their students through different eyes" (Morton & McMenamin, 2011, p. 112); they were seeing learning that they had not previously recognized. The teachers talked about how their previous focus on IEP goals possibly led them to miss seeing students' competencies, their learning. "Have our students *always* had these competencies—perhaps we simply hadn't noticed before?" (Morton & McMenamin, 2011, p. 213).

Recognizing their students' competencies had four consequences. The first consequence was that the teachers could see that their students were indeed learning within the Key Competencies and the Learning Areas of the *New Zealand Curriculum*. The teachers understood that some contexts were more conducive to allowing students to demonstrate competence, to share their strengths and interests. The teachers understood that they were learning about new ways to create accessible contexts and that *they* were pivotal to creating these contexts. In the right contexts, students were exceeding teachers' expectations.

This led to the second consequence. Students' individualized funding was linked to not achieving in the *New Zealand Curriculum*, in particular to achieving below Level 1. Some of the special schools in Aotearoa New Zealand had begun developing a separate curriculum, based on the U.K. P Scales (performance scales). The P Scales were designed in response to the U.K. Level 1 of the National Curriculum (NC) being perceived as starting "at too high a level for their children, so, as an afterthought, the P-scales were invented to sit below Level 1 of the NC" (Stobbs, n.d.). Using an assessment approach that only measures learning purportedly below Level 1 potentially meant that access to funding would be guaranteed. What the teachers in the *Curriculum Exemplars* and the *Narrative Assessment* projects were finding was that the students were achieving within Level 1, and sometimes beyond Level 1 of the *New Zealand Curriculum*. The projects demonstrated that there has not been a need to develop a new "lower-level" curriculum in Aotearoa New Zealand.

The third consequence is likewise related to funding. IEPs had previously been used to review students' individualized funding. Thus, IEPs tended not to celebrate learning, but rather demonstrated that students still needed the funding to access the curriculum. A subsequent project on reviewing and revising the IEP process in Aotearoa New Zealand determined that IEPs would no longer be tied to student funding, making it possible for IEPs to focus on student success. The new resource is titled *Collaboration for Success: The Individual Education Plan* (Ministry of Education, 2011).

The fourth consequence is the focus on *all* participants' learning in the new IEP process. What do teachers, teachers' aides, and related resource people need to learn in order to provide the best contexts for learning for all students in their classrooms?

Collaborative Learning: Learning Together to Support Learning and Being Together

Our most recent project has been the development of a resource to support *Teachers and Teachers' Aides Working Together* (TTAWT) (Ministry of Education, 2014). The TTAWT project draws on the learning from the previous projects and on the work of Rutherford (2012). Rutherford looked at the experiences of disabled students and their teachers' aides in schools in Aotearoa New Zealand. The TTAWT team consisted of participants from the previous projects as well as teachers from around New Zealand. The project team worked collaboratively and iteratively to develop key principles to underpin the resources. Some of these principles included:

- Teachers have full responsibility for the learning and behavior of all the students in their class. It is the same for students with special education needs as for any other student.
- The *New Zealand Curriculum* is for *all* students.
- The teacher-student relationship is paramount.
- Teacher's aide time in a classroom should enhance relationships between the teacher and students, and peer-to-peer relationships and learning.

The resource consists of nine modules grouped into three key themes: "The ways we work together"; "Understanding our students"; and "The work we do together." Each module begins with a statement of a main idea, followed by key principles. For example, Module Four is part of the second theme, "Understanding our students." Module Four is titled "Getting to know students in respectful and positive ways." The main idea in this module is: "When teachers and teachers' aides have positive relationships with their students, they recognize and respond to students' strengths and view all students as capable learners. Teachers and teachers' aides play a critical role in providing students with opportunities and support to actively participate in school and community life."

The key principles in Module Four are:

- People's own beliefs and values determine how they see and work with others.
- All learners are active, capable, and competent.
- Teachers and teachers' aides have a responsibility to provide opportunities for students to reveal their strengths, prior knowledge, and what they bring from their culture.
- In inclusive communities, everyone is a teacher and a learner, and people learn from each other. (Ministry of Education, 2014).

Each module follows an inquiry cycle approach, where teachers and teachers' aides engage with information about the topic, reflect on an aspect of their work in relation to the topic, plan a new strategy or an approach to try in their work, implement the strategy, and then evaluate the outcome.

In this module, we are building understandings that identities—for example, as a learner, or not a learner—are constructed, and these identities can be reconstructed, and co-constructed. The language we use to talk about learners and learning is important, especially recognizing and resisting deficit thinking when we talk about learners and learning. In this newest national resource, we support teachers and teachers' aides to use an inquiry cycle, working together to learn new things (and modeling pedagogy as an inquiry cycle), illustrating that shared learning is an important part of building relationships. Drawing on the tenets of DSE in this work made us vigilant to the ways we understood and constructed disability and identities. Thus, we developed resources that would help the users to likewise pay attention to their own assumptions and understandings about disability.

Finally, a Relatively Simple Message

Sociocultural views of learning also require (and create opportunities for) new ways of thinking about assessment (Carr & Lee, 2012; Cowie, 2009; Cowie & Carr, 2009; Cowie & Carr, forthcoming; Hipkins, 2007). Cowie and Carr (2009) remind us that learning always occurs in social-political-cultural contexts. Changing, and contested, understandings of assessment, curriculum, and pedagogy highlight the inter-relatedness of these concepts. Broadfoot (2007) argues that assessment models "work to shape the way people think about and practice education" (p. 24). Hatherly and

Richardson (2007) claim, "We can only transform curriculum and pedagogy by also transforming the way we assess learning" (p. 151). Educational transformation will not come about by focusing only on the learning of individual children. Our assessment practices need to also reflect these wider social-political-cultural contexts.

I want to suggest that a possible counter-narrative to the technicist approaches to special and inclusive education may be as much about the quality of the relationships we have (with students, with their families, with other educators) as it is about the quality of data or evidence. Much of our more recent history of special education has been grounded in assumptions about the very limited potential of some students for learning in traditionally valued curriculum areas. We have become very adept at operationalizing precise goals that we, as professionals, determine to be potentially achievable. We have become very adept at micro-teaching micro-goals in environments that we control. We believe that *our* control is central to producing quality evidence of *our* effective teaching (and perhaps we are less concerned with evidence of quality learning). What seems to matter is the perceived capacity of an "objective" teacher (carefully choosing only evidence-based teaching strategies, carefully choosing "next-step" goals defined by those evidence-based teaching strategies) controlling "variables" within an instructional context in order to "effectively" teach a student.

The projects described in this chapter illustrate the centrality of contexts to creating or closing down opportunities for people (students *and* educators) to demonstrate competence. As educators, we have responsibility for those contexts we create and to make room for students to co-create together and with us. We can choose to create contexts with more or less control over what and whose learning is valued, what is learned, and who gets to be seen as a learner. As we create contexts, we make possible particular constructed identities and relationships. When we construct children and young people as learners, we are also constructing our identities as educators, working with whānau and families to form relationships with students, getting to know our students' strengths and interests (making educators also learners), recognizing, celebrating, and building on their competencies. I'd like to return to a question I posed earlier: how do our current beliefs and practices in curriculum, pedagogy, and assessment support or get in the way of forming meaningful relationships with students? This is one of those "different questions" that we might ask from a DSE perspective to provoke different conversations and provide new opportunities to influence practices.

References

Allan, J. (2012). Differences in policy and politics: Dialogues in confidence. *Review of Disability Studies: An International Journal, 8*(3), 14–24.

Ballard, K. (2013). Thinking in another way: Ideas for sustainable change. *International Journal of Inclusive Education, 17*(8), 762–775.

Ballard, K., & Morton, M. (1987). *Mainstreaming* [Video]. Produced by the Higher Education Development Centre, University of Otago, Dunedin, New Zealand.

Berliner, D. (2013). Inequality, poverty and the socialization of America's youth for the responsibility of citizenship. *Theory into Practice, 52*(3), 203–209.

Berryman, M., & Woller, P. (2013). Learning about inclusion by listening to Māori, *International Journal of Inclusive Education, 17*(8), 827–838.

Bishop, R., Berryman, M., Tiakiwai, S., & Richardson, C. (2003). *Te Kotahitanga: Experiences of year 9 and 10 Māori students in mainstream classrooms, Final Report to the Ministry of Education.* Wellington: Ministry of Education.

Bishop, R., & Glynn, T. (1999). *Culture counts: Changing power relations in education.* Palmerston North: Dunmore Press.

Broadfoot, P. (2007). *An introduction to assessment.* New York: Continuum.

Carr, M. (2009). Kei tua o te pae: Assessing learning that reaches beyond the self and beyond the horizon. *Assessment Matters, 1*(1), 20–46.

Carr, M., & Lee, W. (2012). *Learning Stories: Constructing learning identities in early education.* Sage: London.

Carter, B., & Macarthur, J. (forthcoming). In M. Morton (Ed.), *Supporting inclusive education: Learning from narrative assessment.* Rotterdam: Sense.

Connor, D. J., Gabel, S. L., Gallagher, D. J., & Morton, M. (2008) Disability studies and inclusive education: Implications for theory, research and practice. *International Journal of Inclusive Education, 12*(5–6), 441–457.

Connor, D. J., Valle, J. W., & Hale, C. (2012). Forum guest editors' introduction. Using and infusing disability studies in education: Where and how? *Review of Disability Studies: An International Journal, 8*(3), 5–13.

Cowie, B. (2009). Teacher formative assessment and decision making: A consideration of principles and consequences. *Assessment Matters, 1*, 47–63.

Cowie, B., & Carr, M. (2009). The consequences of socio-cultural assessment. In A. Anning, J. Cullen, & M. Fleer (Eds.), *Early Childhood Education: Society and culture* (2nd ed.) (pp. 105–116). London: Sage.

Cowie, B., & Carr, M. (forthcoming). Assessing a connected person-plus learner: Considerations of agency, responsibility and happiness. In M. Morton (Ed.), *Supporting inclusive education: Learning from narrative assessment.* Rotterdam: Sense.

Dever, A., Gladstone, C., & Quick, C. (2013, June 7–9). *The "personal and the professional": The relational dimension and intellectual disability research.* Paper presented at the Disability Studies in Education annual conference, (Re)Imagining and (Re)Building Education for All, Christchurch, New Zealand, University of Canterbury.

Gordon, L., & Morton, M. (2008). Inclusive education and school choice: Democratic rights in a devolved system. In S. Gabel & S. Danforth (Eds.), *Disability and the politics of education: An international reader* (pp. 237–250). New York: Peter Lang.

Guerin, A. (forthcoming). Promoting partnership through assessment. In M. Morton (Ed.), *Supporting inclusive education: Learning from narrative assessment*. Rotterdam: Sense.

Harrison, J., MacGibbon, L., & Morton, M. (2001). Regimes of trustworthiness in qualitative research: The rigors of reciprocity. *Qualitative Inquiry, 7*(3), 323–345.

Hatherly, A., & Richardson, C. (2007). Building connections: Assessment and evaluation revisited. In L. Keesing-Styles & H. Hedges (Eds.), *Theorising early childhood practice: Emerging dialogues* (pp. 51–70). Castle Hill, NSW: Pademelon Press.

Hipkins, R. (2007). *Assessing the key competencies: Why would we? How could we?* Wellington: Learning Media.

Hipkins, R. (forthcoming). Key competencies: A promising curriculum direction. In M. Morton (Ed.), *Supporting inclusive education: Learning from narrative assessment*. Rotterdam: Sense.

Kearney, A. (2011). *Exclusion from and within school: Issues and solutions*. Rotterdam: Sense.

Lather, P. (2009). *Engaging science policy: From the side of the messy*. New York: Peter Lang.

Macartney, B., & Morton, M. (2013). Kinds of participation: Teacher and special education perceptions and practices of 'inclusion' in early childhood and primary school settings. *International Journal of Inclusive Education, 17*(8), 776–792. http://dx.doi.org/10.1080/13603116.2011.602529

Macfarlane, A., Macfarlane, S., & Glynn, T. (2012). In S. Carrington & J. MacArthur (Eds.), *Teaching in Inclusive School Communities* (pp. 163–188). Brisbane: John Wiley & Sons.

McIlroy, A. (forthcoming). Belonging in the curriculum. In M. Morton (Ed.), *Supporting inclusive education: Learning from narrative assessment*. Rotterdam: Sense.

McMenamin, T., Millar, R., Morton, M., Mutch, C., Nuttall, J. & Tyler-Merrick, G. (2004). *Curriculum Policy and Special Education Support*. Final report to the Ministry of Education. Wellington: Ministry of Education. Retrieved from http://www.educationcounts.govt.nz/publications/special_education/curriculum_policy_and_special_education_report

Millar, R., & Morton, M. (2007). Bridging two worlds: Special education and curriculum policy. *International Journal of Inclusive Education, 11*(2), 163–176.

Ministry of Education (1996). *Te Whariki: He Whariki Matauranga mo nga Mokopuna o Aotearoa/Early Childhood Curriculum*. Wellington: Learning Media.

Ministry of Education. (2003). *The New Zealand curriculum exemplars*. Wellington: Learning Media. Retrieved from http://assessment.tki.org.nz/Assessment-tools-resources/The-New-Zealand-Curriculum-Exemplars

Ministry of Education. (2007). *The New Zealand Curriculum*. Wellington: Learning Media.

Ministry of Education. (2009a). *The New Zealand curriculum exemplars for learners with special education needs*. Wellington: Learning Media.

Ministry of Education. (2009b). *Narrative assessment: A guide for teachers*. Wellington: Learning Media.

Ministry of Education. (2009c). *Kei Tua o te Pae/Assessment for Learning: Early Childhood Exemplars*. Wellington: Learning Media.

Ministry of Education. (2010). *Fact sheet: Success for all—every school, every child*. Wellington: Ministry of Education.

Ministry of Education. (2011). *Collaboration for success: Individual education plans*. Wellington: Learning Media.

Ministry of Education. (2014). *Teachers and teachers' aides working together*. Wellington: Learning Media. Retrieved from http://teachersandteachersaides.tki.org.nz

Ministry of Health (2001). *The New Zealand Disability Strategy: Making a world of difference*. Wellington: Ministry of Health.

Mitchell, D., Morton, M., & Hornby, G. (2011). *Review of the literature on individual education plans: Report to the New Zealand Ministry of Education*. Wellington: Ministry of Education. Retrieved from http://www.educationcounts.govt.nz/publications/literacy/literature-review

Morton, M. (2012). Using DSE to "notice, recognize and respond" to tools of exclusion and opportunities for inclusion in New Zealand. *Review of Disability Studies: An International Journal, 8*(3), 25–34.

Morton, M. (Ed.) (forthcoming). *Supporting inclusive education: Learning from narrative assessment*. Rotterdam: Sense.

Morton, M., & Gordon, L. (2006, April 7–11). *In the public good? Preparing teachers to be inclusive educators. Report of a New Zealand research project*. Paper presented to the American Educational Research Association Conference, San Francisco, CA.

Morton, M., & McMenamin, T. (2009). *Families' choices: Choosing school(s). Part 1: Literature review, interviews and design of the questionnaire*. Final Report to NZCCS Disability Action.

Morton, M., & McMenamin, T. (2011). Learning together: Collaboration to develop curriculum assessment that promotes belonging. *Support for Learning, 26*(3), 109–114.

Morton, M., McMenamin, T., Moore, G. & Molloy, S. (2012). Assessment that matters: The transformative potential of narrative assessment for students with special education needs. *Assessment Matters, 4*, 110–128.

Paugh, P. C., & Dudley-Marling, C. (2011). "Speaking" deficit into (or out of) existence: How language constrains classroom teachers' knowledge about instructing diverse learners. *International Journal of Inclusive Education, 15*(8), 819–834.

Rutherford, G. (2012). In, out, or somewhere in between? Disabled students' and teacher aides' experiences of school. *International Journal of Inclusive Education, 16*(8), 757–774.

Stobbs, P. (n.d.). What are P scales and do we need them? *SEN Magazine*. Retrieved from https://www.senmagazine.co.uk/articles/articles/senarticles/what-are-p-scales-and-do-we-need-them-philippa-stobbs-investigates

Swann, M., Peacock, A., Hart, S., & Drummond, M. J. (2012). *Creating learning without limits*. London: McGraw-Hill, Open University Press.

Thrupp, M., & Smith, R. (1999). A decade of ERO. *New Zealand Journal of Educational Studies*, *34*(1), 186–198.

Wylie, C. (2012). *Vital connections: Why we need more than self-managing schools*. Wellington: NZCER Press.

12. A Disability Studies in Education Analysis of Corporate-Based Educational Reform: Lessons From New Orleans

KATHLEEN COLLINS

The city of New Orleans was ravaged by Hurricane Katrina in August 2005. Before the initial flood waters had receded, the city was hit by a second flood of privatized school reform that dismantled the existing public school system. As a result, New Orleans currently has the largest percentage of students enrolled in charter schools of any district in the United States, a "market share" of 84% as of the 2012–2013 academic year (Cowen Institute, 2013, p. 7).

Media reports have upheld New Orleans as an example of the success of privatized school reform, citing improvements in student measures on test scores and college acceptance rates as evidence (Anderson, 2010; Cowen Institute, 2013; Gabor, 2013; *New York Times*, 2011). However, little attention has been paid to understanding the constellation of effects that the discourses and policies of corporate school reform in New Orleans have had on students with complex support needs. In this chapter, I take up this issue from the perspective of disability studies in education (DSE), an orientation that argues for an examination of the institutional and cultural practices of schooling that shape the appearance, manifestation, and consequences of dis/ability (Collins, 2013; Connor & Gabel, 2013). Drawing on DSE, I examine the discourses and policies of school reform in post-Katrina New Orleans to identify the dominant narrative and how it positions students with complex support needs. I then make visible the profound effects of these policies and practices with examples from a selection of (counter)narratives of students with complex support needs and their families drawn from a pending class-action lawsuit, *P. B. et al. v. Pastorek* (2010).

Disability Studies in Education (DSE)

Disability studies (DS) is an interdisciplinary orientation to educational theory, research, and practice that works from a social and cultural model of disability and challenges the medical (or deficit) model to "normalize difference" (Baglieri & Knopf, 2004). Embodied, cognitive, psychological, and emotional variations in human experience are seen as natural (rather than as "deviant" or "deficient"). This perspective is expressed succinctly in the words of 10-year-old Lief O'Niell, a boy who identifies as autistic. Lief types to communicate, and he recently posted this description of autism on thisis-autismflashblog.blogspot.com:

> Autism is actual many different ways of being. Some people think it is a disease but it is a way of being … See me as smart. (O'Neill, 2013)

Lief's statement eloquently summarizes the tension between the traditional medical model of dis/ability and the social model that informs disability studies. Whereas a medical model locates dis/ability *within* individuals and proceeds to "diagnose" and "treat" the "problem," disability studies examines the cultural affordances and constraints as well as the sociopolitical interests that contribute to shaping a *difference* into a *disability*. A foundational concept of disability studies is the understanding that "disability" is a socially and politically constructed response to perceived difference. When Lief writes "See me as smart," he is asking for his way of being to be interpreted through a lens of possibility rather than one of deficiency, for those who interact with him to "presume competence" (Biklen & Burke, 2006).

Disability studies asserts that differences are made into "problems" or "gifts" by the interpretive and positioning effects of the responses to them—interpersonal, institutional, social, cultural, and political—and by the constraints and affordances of physical and discursive environments. Disability studies in education (DSE) applies this understanding to the exploration of dis/ability in educational contexts (Connor, Gabel, Gallagher, & Morton, 2008; Danforth & Gabel, 2006; Ferri, 2008; Ferguson & Nusbaum, 2012; Gabel, 2005; Valle & Connor, 2011). For example, when considering achievement and participation in classroom learning environments, DSE asserts the need to consider "ability" and "disability" as distributed across people, forms of literacy, discourses, and symbolic and physical tools privileged in an environment (Collins, 2013; Kliewer & Biklen, 2007; McDermott, 1993).

An important aspect of DSE scholarship is the attention that is given to documenting and learning from the voices and stories of people whose lives and ways of knowing have been pathologized by the dominant disability-as-medical-deficit model. Rather than privileging clinical or expert knowledge, DSE scholarship makes an effort to recognize, include, and learn from the experiences of people who have been positioned in special education categories or labeled as having a disability. DSE scholarship also makes an effort to include the voices of parents who have had to navigate "special" educational and medical systems on behalf of their child(ren). The centering of personal experience offers people who have been marginalized a way to "talk back" or "counter" the stories of deficit and/or deprivation told about them (Delgado, 1989; Ferri, 2011).

DSE Influences on Questions, Design, and Method

This inquiry into the policies and discourses that describe and shape schooling in post-Katrina New Orleans is influenced by DSE in two important ways. First, working from a DSE perspective to understand schooling in post-Katrina New Orleans means asking questions that relate to the policies, practices, and discourses that shape the appearance of dis/ability. When analyzing textual artifacts, such as transcripts of speeches and written policies, I specifically wanted to explore the narratives (and attendant ideologies) embedded in the text(s). Data for this portion of my analysis included publicly available speeches and policy documents related to the reform efforts in post-Katrina New Orleans.

A second influence of DSE is that the design of this study attends to the perspectives of those who are excluded by the dominant narratives. To this end the design of this study includes the experiences of a representative sample of students with complex support needs and their families who have attempted to navigate entrance and inclusion into the school system of post-Katrina New Orleans. The experiences of the children and families were collected and documented as part of a pending class-action lawsuit, *P. B. et al. v. Pastorek* (2010), filed by the Southern Poverty Law Center.[1]

Public Education in Post-Katrina New Orleans

Hurricane Katrina made landfall in Louisiana on August 29, 2005, a 29-foot-high wall of water that burst the area's levees and flooded more than 80% of the city of New Orleans. Delayed and mismanaged rescue and relief efforts compounded the initial damage from Katrina, and when the waters receded, the storm had claimed 1,836 lives, displaced hundreds of thousands of others, and wrought over a $100 billion in damage. Images of the people of New Orleans trapped, frightened, and fighting for their lives provoked shock, horror, grief, and anger around the world.[2]

A few, however, considered the storm-ravaged city of New Orleans not as a tragedy but as a strategic business opportunity. Naomi Klein (2007) describes this impulse to profit from collective trauma as "disaster capitalism," which she defines as "orchestrated raids on the public sphere in the wake of catastrophic events, combined with the treatment of disasters as exciting market opportunities" (p. 6). This drive to respond to public trauma as an opportunity for both personal profit and social engineering gained a strong foothold in New Orleans in the days following Katrina (Carr, 2013; Dingerson, 2008; Klein, 2007; Saltman, 2007).[3]

The New Orleans school system was a primary target of those who viewed the destruction of the city as "an historic opportunity to start anew" (Blanco, 2005). Two weeks after the storm hit, on September 14, 2005, U.S. Education Secretary Margaret Spellings announced that she was waiving federal guidelines that would have restricted charter schools in New Orleans. During the two weeks between Katrina's landfall and Spellings' lifting of federal restrictions on charter schools, lobbying groups representing corporate interests in public education had been working towards that goal (Dingerson, 2006, 2008).

On September 30, 2005, Secretary of Education Spellings announced the first of two large United States Department of Education grants. The first, $20.9 million, would be granted to Louisiana for the purpose of supporting the development of charter schools. The second grant, $24 million, was announced by Spellings on June 12, 2006. As reported by the *New York Times*, these monies served to establish New Orleans as the "nation's pre-eminent laboratory for the widespread use of charter schools" (Saulny, 2006).

Following Spellings' September 14 announcement, on November 9, 2005, Governor Kathleen Babineaux Blanco suspended portions of Louisiana's state law governing the establishment of charter schools, including restrictions that required garnering the support of communities before approving new charter schools, through the introduction of the Recovery School District (RSD) bill. In introducing the RSD bill, Blanco described the devastation wrought by Katrina as having created "the opportunity of a lifetime" for education reformers:

> It took the storm of a lifetime, to create the opportunity of a lifetime; an opportunity to start anew in a thoughtful, organized and measured way that serves every single child in New Orleans. (Blanco, 2005)

The RSD bill required the state of Louisiana to "take control and re-create" schools in New Orleans (schools formerly run by the Orleans Parish School Board) whose performance was identified as "below the state average" and place them in the state-run Recovery School District (Blanco, 2005). Once in the RSD, the schools would be run directly by the State Department of Education or handed over to a "provider with a proven record of success" (Blanco, 2005). As a result of the RSD Bill, 107 New Orleans public schools were placed under the control of the Recovery School District; only four remained controlled by the Orleans Parish School Board.

This lifting of restrictions on the establishment of charter schools, in addition to the devastation created by the storm itself, created an opportunity for private enterprise to move quickly into the sphere of public education in New Orleans. Just three weeks after Katrina made landfall, Paul Hill, a founding member of the Center on Reinventing Public Education, argued in *Education Week*:

> In the case of post-hurricane New Orleans, American school planners will be as close as they have ever come to a "green field" opportunity: A large public education system will need to be built from scratch. (Hill, 2005)

A "green field" opportunity or investment, in business discourse, is one that is unhindered by previous structures or practices. Hill viewed the damaged schools, scattered families, and 7,500 displaced employees of the New Orleans school district as having created an opening for a new education system to be built, a system informed by neoliberal principles of the open market, choice, and competition.

Hill was certainly not alone in perceiving New Orleans schools as a business opportunity. The language and values of neoliberal approaches to business and economics quickly gained momentum and began to dominate discussions of "rebuilding" public schools in New Orleans. Perhaps nowhere were these neoliberal values stated more clearly than in the words of Milton Friedman, influential economist and proponent of limited government and unfettered capitalistic growth. On December 5, 2005, Friedman, long an advocate of school vouchers, published an op-ed in the *Wall Street Journal* describing the devastation wrought by Katrina as "an opportunity to radically reform the educational system" (Friedman, 2005). Friedman described students as "consumers" and advocated for a "bottom-up" system of education in New Orleans where "parents would then be free to choose" the school best for their child (Friedman, 2005). He argued that school driven by the "competitive free market would lead to improvements in quality and reductions in cost" and that therefore the state of Louisiana should "encourage private enterprise to provide schooling" (Friedman, 2005). Friedman's words became a blueprint of sorts, and influenced the changes that would occur as lobbying groups took up his ideas and pursued school reconstruction in the "green field" of New Orleans.

Six months after Katrina hit New Orleans, in February 2006, all 7,500 unionized employees of RSD—from teachers to cafeteria workers—were fired by the state's Board of Elementary and Secondary Education (Dingerson, 2008).[4] These teachers were replaced largely with minimally prepared Teach for America recruits.[5] Within one year of Hurricane Katrina, 114 of the "public" schools in New Orleans were operating as charter schools as part of the state-run RSD and fewer than 20 remained under the control of the Orleans Parish School Board (OPSB) (Cowen Institute, 2013). There are currently three main groupings of public schools in New Orleans: (1) schools that were deemed failing and that are run directly by RSD; (2) charter schools managed by one of 42 different organizations but chartered by either the state or local school boards; and (3) schools that are operated by the OPSB. As stated previously, New Orleans has the largest percentage of students enrolled in charter schools of any district in the United States, a "market share" of 84% as of the 2012–2013 academic year (Cowen Institute, 2013, p. 7). Each charter school runs as its own "business" and sets its own admissions policies and expulsion policies.

As of the 2012–2013 school year, RSD directly runs 12 public schools, and the OPSB directly operates six schools. The non-charter direct-run OPSB schools are historically high-performing schools (including two magnet schools). The non-charter direct-run RSD schools are considered "schools of last resort" (Institute on Race and Poverty, 2010, p. 32) and "the dumping ground" because "they essentially have to take all-comers" (Garda, 2011, p. 20). Perhaps not surprisingly, the RSD direct-run, non-charter schools have the highest number of students with complex learning support needs, the highest percentage of students who identify as Black (97%), and the second highest percentage of students receiving free and reduced lunch (88%) (Cowen Institute, 2013; Garda, 2011).

The public and political discourse surrounding and shaping post-Katrina school-reform efforts in New Orleans clearly emphasized "competition" and "choice," explicitly drawing on business discourse to construct a narrative whereby the former school system was positioned as "failing" and the new corporate-model of education was introduced as a savior. In this story, Katrina was a strategic opportunity for private business interests to take over and save the "failing" school system. This dominant narrative and its reliance on business rhetoric positioned children and their families as "consumers" and promised that "school choice" would give parents and children the opportunity to find a school that would best fit their needs.

Notably, this dominant narrative of corporate reform did not include any mention or discussion of students with identified disabilities. Further, the ideologies embedded in the business model normalized a system where each charter school set its own enrollment and expulsion policies. No central authority took responsibility for ensuring access to "free and appropriate public education" (Individuals With Disabilities Education Act, 2004) for all children. As discussed in the following section, the intricate, decentralized system made it difficult for parents and caregivers to advocate for their children.

Learning From the Experiences of the "Leftover" Children" and Their Families

"We wanted charter schools to open and take the majority of the students. That didn't happen, and now we have the responsibility of educating the 'leftover' children."
—Louisiana state school board member (Quigley, 2007, p. 1)

The experiences of the "leftover children" and families featured here were documented by the Southern Poverty Law Center (SPLC) in preparation for filing *P. B. et al. v. Pastorek et al.* (2010), a class-action lawsuit filed on behalf of students with disabilities against Paul Pastorek, former superintendent of education in the state of Louisiana, the Louisiana Department of Education, and the Louisiana Board of Elementary and Secondary Education.[6] The lawsuit addresses a broad range of violations of the Individuals With Disabilities Education Act (IDEA), including failure to identify and evaluate children in need of support services ("child find"), failure to provide services to children with Individual Education Plans (IEPs), failure to provide students with disabilities with equal access to educational opportunities, and failure to provide children with disabilities a free and appropriate education.

The lawsuit is still pending; however, the related court filings and hearing transcripts are a matter of public record. This class-action lawsuit establishes the ten named students, ranging in age at the time of filing from 7 to 16, as representative of the estimated 4,500 students with disabilities who should be served by schools in New Orleans. The experiences of the ten students named as representative plaintiffs are documented throughout both the original filing (*P. B. et al. v. Pastorek et al.*, 2010), the transcript of state's motion to dismiss the case (*Cassandra Berry et al. v. Paul Pastorek et al.*, 2011), and the Renewed Motion for Class Certification (*P. B. et al. v. Paul Pastorek et al.*, 2013). First-person narratives from a subset of the ten children and their parents were also collected and published in *Access Denied: New Orleans Students and Parents Identify Barriers to Public Education* (Southern Poverty Law Center, 2010). I treated the legal documents as discursive data and used them to create a narrative profile for each of the ten named plaintiffs, documenting the students' words and experiences as well as the related testimony of family members. I then triangulated these narrative profiles with the first-person essays in *Access Denied*.[7] Finally, I conducted a paradigmatic analysis of the narrative profiles (Polkinghorne, 1995) to identify themes and patterns across them.

In this chapter I focus on explicating the broadest theme present in the narrative profiles: *exclusion*. Across the charter schools in New Orleans, approximately 7.8% of the students are identified as having a disability. In the Recovery School District, approximately 12.6% of the students are identified as having a disability. This disproportional representation in the non-charter RSD schools is a direct result of the charter schools' discriminatory enrollment, support, and disciplinary practices. The experiences of the children and families participating in the class-action suit bear witness to the different forms of exclusion normalized by the decentralized, market-driven charter school system in post-Katrina New Orleans.

The most prevalent form of exclusion reported by the families was being turned away at the schoolhouse door. Plaintiff P. B.'s mother, Cassandra Berry, testified that she and an advocate worked together and attempted to enroll P. B. in more than 30 different schools in a one-month period. She was told repeatedly that the school either could not accommodate P. B. or had reached its enrollment cap. As a result, P. B., who is diagnosed as having bipolar disorder and attention-deficit hyperactivity disorder (ADHD), was not enrolled in a school at the time of the filing of the initial lawsuit. A similar story was shared by Jeanette Johnson, mother of plaintiff T. J, who was 13 and in the fifth grade at the time of the original SPLC lawsuit. At that time T. J., who identifies as having dyslexia and ADHD, had been out of school for six months. His mother, relying solely on public transportation and walking, went to five different schools. She reported that school personnel at each school were quite direct in denying T.J. enrollment *because* of his learning support needs.

In addition to being turned away and denied enrollment of their children, parents reported being "counseled out" of applying for admission by office staff who advised that the school could not meet the needs of their children. Kelly Fischer, the mother of plaintiff N.F., a 9-year-old boy who has autism, developmental delays, and is blind, reported:

> Most charters said they don't have the staffing, training or materials. One woman literally said, "I don't think we're hurting kids with special needs but I know we're not helping them. You don't want your son to go here." (SPLC, 2010, p. 12)

The dominant narrative describing a system that provides parents and children with the opportunity to choose the school that's right for them (Freidman, 2005) and that serves all of the children of New Orleans (Blanco, 2005) is clearly at odds with the system experienced by parents like Kelly Fischer and Jeanette Johnson whose children have been systematically prevented from enrolling in school because of their learning support needs.

During the hearing of the state's motion to dismiss the case on April 26, 2011, United States District Court Judge Jay C. Zainey directly questioned the lawyer for the state, Ms. Marie Sneed, about the enrollment experiences of children and families:

> The Court: Now, you're telling me it's the obligation of the family of this person [T.J.'s mother] to go from school to school, public school to public school until a school finally accepts this child; is that what you are telling me the law requires?
>
> Ms. Sneed: Well, I'm saying that's a part of how choice works that parents make [an] application, parents choose to go, schools may be full. (*Cassandra Berry et al. v Paul Pastorek et al.*, 2011, p. 57)

The state, as represented by their legal counsel, does not see a problem with the difficulties faced by these families seeking to enroll their children in public school in New Orleans. Systematic and pervasive exclusion of children with complex support needs is simply "a part of how choice works."

For children with complex support needs in New Orleans the struggle to be included does not end with enrollment in a school. A primary form of after-enrollment exclusion reported by the plaintiffs and their families was the schools' withholding of assessment and support services. Nine-year-old N.F., described above, secured enrollment in Lafayette Academy Charter School but the school refused to meet the support needs detailed in his Individual Education Plan (IEP), claiming they were understaffed. His mother, Kelly, reported that she took up the role of assisting her son in school, and witnessed how the withholding of academic supports (such as audio recordings of texts) maintained her son's continued exclusion from the curriculum:

> He is in the 3rd grade and I had to attend school with him every day for the entire day for several weeks. The teacher just taught the regular curriculum. When a worksheet was handed out to the class, they would give one to my son, too, even though he's completely blind ... [He] has had to wait months to receive books on tape so he can learn what the other 3rd grade kids learn, but he has to wait so long he is always behind. (SPLC, 2010, p. 12)

Other parents shared similar stories where the denial of needed materials and of legally required assessment and support services contributed to their child's continued exclusion from the academic life of school and impacted them socially and emotionally. One mother described the school's repeated refusal, over a two-year period, to provide assessment and support services as required by her daughter's IEP. Instead, the school required her to repeat the eighth grade, again without academic supports:

> My daughter has been really down. This is a rough year for her, with peers that are so much younger than her in the elementary school setting. She's 16 now in the 8th grade. The first day of school she just cried. She feels stupid and wants to give up and drop out. (SPLC, 2010, p. 11)

After-enrollment exclusion also took the form of disciplinary actions designed to remove students with complex support needs from their classrooms. Statistics for the 2008–2009 school year document a 30% suspension rate within RDS for students with identified disabilities; this is 63% higher than the average suspension rate for the state of Louisiana (SPLC, 2010). Suspension rates for students with disabilities by the charter school are even more disproportionate, with several posting rates greater than 50% and as much as 200% higher than the state average (SPLC, 2010). At these same charter schools, suspension rates for students without identified disabilities are much lower, ranging from 12% to 23% (SPLC, 2010).

Several of the plaintiffs reported enduring disciplinary exclusions coupled with physical abuse and/or psychological abuse. Consider the experience of 7-year-old D. T., who began his second-grade year at Langston Hughes Charter School. D. T. demonstrates learning and behavioral differences that qualify him for evaluation under the IDEA's child-find mandate. The charter school refused both evaluation and accommodation for D. T., instead implementing a "behavioral intervention plan." The plan required D. T. to be isolated via in-school suspension (ISS) for 80% of the school day. This purposeful exclusion of D. T. did not address his needs and contributed to his increased lack of academic and social progress. School staff responded by using increasingly violent measures to restrain D. T.

> In December 2009, a teacher removed D. T. from the classroom and shoved him into a brick wall with such force that he sustained a head injury that required medical attention … On three separate occasions, D. T. was physically removed from the classroom and dragged down the hallway to the band room where he was locked in a dark closet for approximately an hour on each occasion. (*P. B. et al. v. Pastorek et al.*, 2010, p. 44)

The school-sanctioned abuse of D. T. led him to develop symptoms of post-traumatic stress, including a severe fear of school, frequent bed wetting, and nightmares.

Similarly, the experience of plaintiff D. B., a 9-year-old boy identified with an emotional disability, illustrates a two-year-long (2008–2010) downward spiral resulting from a repeated withholding of therapeutic and behavioral supports as called for in his IEP. As D. B.'s manifestations of his disability increased, his charter school continued to withhold therapy and instead increased its enforcement of disciplinary exclusions through in-school and out-of-school suspensions.

D. B. endured two incidents of abuse detailed in *P. B. et al. v. Paul Pastorek et al.* (2010). The first occurred on April 8, 2010, when D. B., described as "distressed" and "crying and mumbling unintelligibly," was approached by the behavior interventionist at Langston Hughes Charter School. D. B. calmed down until the behavior interventionist began to lead him to the in-school suspension (ISS) room, at which point he began to "panic":

> When [D. B.] fell to the floor sobbing, the behavior interventionist grabbed him by his arms and dragged him six feet into the ISS room. This was done with such force that D. B.'s face and mouth slammed into the ground, chipping his tooth. (pp. 49–50)

Instead of receiving medical attention, D. B was physically restrained for 15 minutes by the behavior interventionist who then carried him "to a small, soundproof closet, where he was held for another 30 minutes" (p. 50).

The second incident occurred less than a month later. D. B. was again carried to the ISS room after he allegedly refused to follow directions. At this point D. B. "panicked" and was "physically restrained" by the paraprofessional who told D. B. he would be "handcuffed and tasered." D. B.'s attempts to resist the dehumanizing abuse he suffered were thus criminalized, and the abuse and humiliation continued:

> The paraprofessional then sat on top of D. B.—constricting his breathing and eventually causing him to urinate on himself. (p. 50)

As a result of the school-sanctioned physical and psychological abuse that he endured at Langston Hughes Charter School, D. B. developed a fear of school.

Given these reported experiences of discrimination, exclusion, and abuse, it is no surprise that several of the plaintiffs reported a desire to drop out of school. This cycle is described by one father who relates how his son, who was 17 at the time and has autism, was beaten by a security guard and then chose to leave school:

> They said they would call the police on our son for anything he does wrong. And they actually did call. And, it just went downhill after that … One day my

son came home from school and said, "Dad, my back is hurting." And I said, "Son, well, why is your back hurting?" He said the security guard threw him on the ground and put his foot in his chest … He's gotten to the point where he doesn't want to stay and we don't want him to be there, so we'll just let him transition out … They've broken us down. What really upset me was when we had the meeting at the school and the special education chairperson told me … "[A]ll we can do is cage your son." He is autistic. (SPLC, 2010, p. 13)

Physical and psychological abuse perpetuated by the charter schools and their agents against children with disabilities is thus a form of *reproductive exclusion*. Not only does it exclude targeted children in the moment it occurs, it sets them up for further exclusion by criminalizing their behaviors and by encouraging them to exclude themselves permanently by dropping out.

There is currently no accurate count of the numbers of children and families who do respond to the forms of exclusion documented in *P. B. et al. v. Pastorek et al.* (2010) by absenting themselves from the school system. A 2010 estimate placed the number of school-age children not enrolled in school at approximately 4,000; however, there is no central oversight of this issue (Gabor, 2013). The state's attorney responded to questions about this lack of oversight by positioning the children themselves as at fault:

The court: […] Is it not the State's responsibility under the law to find the kids who are not in the school system […]?

Ms. Sneed: [Like in every other district there's some truant kids or kids who aren't enrolled and aren't in compliance with mandatory enrollment. (*Cassandra Berry et al. v Paul Pastorek et al.*, 2010, p. 39)

The state thus asserts that the onus is on the children to comply with the demands of a system that actively excludes and abuses them. Dropping out, a behavior that could be seen as self-protective, is criminalized. In this narrative, it is not the state that is non-compliant with mandatory federal law (IDEA); the problem lies within the "truant kids."

The experiences of the plaintiffs illustrate how children with complex learning and support needs in New Orleans are not only "left over" but *left out*, and, in some cases, *pushed out*. "School choice" here means that the school has the choice whether or not to educate certain children, and schools are choosing to say "no" to children and families with complex support needs. Exclusion of students with identified disabilities begins with the enrollment process. For those who make it through the schoolhouse door, exclusion continues through withholding needed assessment, support, and instructional materials as well as facilitating physical and social isolation, and physical and psychological abuse. Through words and actions, the plaintiffs and their families have been told that they *don't belong*; that their minds, bodies, and needs are *too different to be included*. Reproductive exclusion is being used as a strategy to construct, manage, limit, and contain dis/ability.

The New Orleans Charter School Experiment: Legislating Educational Inequity

The dominant media narrative holds that the charter school educational experiment in New Orleans has been nothing but a success (Anderson, 2010; Cowen Institute, 2013; Gabor, 2013; *New York Times*, 2011). Secretary of Education Arne Duncan reinforced this narrative with the assertion, "I think the best thing that happened to the education system in New Orleans was Hurricane Katrina" (Anderson, 2010). Nowhere in this narrative have politicians and policy makers addressed the unmet learning and support needs of the "leftover" children and their families.

Even after learning about the difficulties "school choice" has created for the children and families represented in *P. B. et al. v. Paul Pastorek et al.* (2010), the state's response has been to defend the privatization of the public schools. Being turned away because you are perceived as too different is simply "a part of how choice works." Falling further behind because you are denied instructional support and materials is an indicator that you need to repeat a grade. Defending yourself from further psychological and physical abuse by leaving the system means you are truant and noncompliant.

Attributions of disability have long been used to control access to education, citizenship and other social goods, services, and civil rights (Baynton, 2001; Schweik, 2009). Ferri and Connor (2005, 2006) document the intersecting histories of *Brown v. Board of Education* and the IDEA. As schools became desegregated, special education classrooms, tracking, and gifted and talented programs became a way to maintain separation by categorizing children by perceived ethnicity and dis/ability (Ferri & Connor, 2005, 2006). Similarly, school choice and voucher plans have also played an historical role in maintaining educational segregation. After *Brown v. Board of Education*, school choice plans were used as means of avoiding desegregation (Frankenberg & Siegel-Hawley, 2009), and the recent rapid rise in charter schools nationally has facilitated increased school segregation at an alarming rate (Frankenberg, Siegel-Hawley, & Wang, 2010).

Corporate school reform and the privatization movement are thus the most recent instantiations of resistance to integration and educational equity. The creation of a tiered school system in New Orleans demonstrates the effects of the neoliberal movement to privatize public schools and more deeply entrench separation and inequity by race, socioeconomic class, and dis/ability labels. Unfortunately, educational exclusion, segregation, and legislated inequity as a result of the privatization of public schools is a story that is being repeated in cities across the country (Ravitch, 2013). Turning this around will require a renewed commitment to ensuring equitable educational opportunities on the part of policymakers and legislators as well as a desire to interrupt the dominant narrative of neoliberal reform. Responding to the experiences of the children and families who have been left over, left out, and pushed out of schools in New Orleans is an important first step in countering this dominant narrative.

Notes

1. The lawsuit was filed in conjunction with the Lawyers' Committee for Civil Rights Under Law, the Community Justice section of the Loyola Law Clinic, and the Southern Disability Law Center.
2. Data compiled from *New York Times* archives: http://www.nola.com/katrina/ http://topics.nytimes.com/top/reference/timestopics/subjects/h/hurricane_katrina/index.html?inline=nyt-classifier
3. The impact of disaster capitalism is also depicted in *Tremé*, a fictional HBO series about life in post-Katrina New Orleans that that ran for 36 episodes.
4. On January 15, 2014, the court ruled that the teachers had been wrongfully terminated; an appeal is in progress.
5. Full discussion of the role of Teach for America in the corporatization of school reform in New Orleans is beyond the scope of this chapter. See discussion in Davis, 2013.
6. I did not personally have contact with any of the children and families. I am seeking funding to pursue research with the "leftover children." (Collins, in progress).
7. The families of named plaintiffs Lawrence Melrose (L.M.) and Noah Fischer (N.F) have decided to take their stories public in various media outlets. I drew on their public statements as informal sources of triangulation but did not include them in the data set because they were collected under different circumstances and for different purposes.

References

Anderson, N. (2010, January 30). Education Secretary Duncan calls Hurricane Katrina good for New Orleans schools. *Washington Post*, p. A06. Retrieved from http://www.washingtonpost.com/wp-dyn/content/article/2010/01/29/AR2010012903259_pf.html

Baglieri, S., & Knopf, J. (2004). Normalizing difference in inclusive teaching. *Journal of Learning Disabilities*, 37(6), 525–529.

Baynton, D. (2001). Disability and the justification of inequality in America. In P. Longmore & L. Umansky (Eds.), *The new disability history: American perspectives*. (pp. 33–57). New York: New York University Press.

Biklen, D., & Burke, J. (2006). Presuming competence. *Equity & Excellence in Education, 39*(2), 166–175.

Blanco, K. (2005, November 9). Governor Kathleen Blanco: Recovery school district bill, Nov. 9, 2005. Retrieved from http://www.blancogovernor.com/index.cfm?md=newsroom&tmp=detail&catID=4&articleID=1193&navID=13

Carr, S. (2013). Hope against hope. Three schools, one city, and the struggle to educate America's children. New York: Bloomsbury Press.

Cassandra Berry et al. v. Paul Pastorek et al. E.D. La. 2:10-cv-10-1049. Motion to dismiss case oral argument transcript. April 26, 2011.

Collins, K. M. (2013). *Ability profiling and school failure: One child's struggle to be seen as competent* (2nd ed.). New York: Routledge.

Collins, K. M. (in progress). Learning from the stories of "leftover children" and their families: Corporate school reform at intersections of race, class, and dis/ability in New Orleans. Faculty research grant in progress, Penn State University.

Connor, D. J., & Gabel, S. (2013). "Cripping" the curriculum through academic activism: Working toward increasing global exchanges to reframe (dis)ability and education. *Equity and Excellence in Education, 46*(1), 100–118.

Connor, D. J., Gabel, S., Gallagher, D., & Morton, M. (2008). Disability studies and inclusive education: Implications for theory, research, and practice. *International Journal of Inclusive Education, 12*(5–6).

Cowen Institute (2013). *The state of public education in New Orleans: 2013 Report.* Cowen Institute for Public Education Initiatives. New Orleans, LA: Tulane University.

Danforth, S., & Gabel, S. (Eds.) (2006). *Vital questions facing disability studies in education.* New York: Peter Lang.

Davis, O. (2013, January 11). Teach for America apostates: A primer of alumni resistance. *Truthout.* Retrieved from http://truth-out.org/articles/item/17750-teach-for-america-apostates-a-primer-of-alumni-resistance

Delgado, R. (1989). Storytelling for oppositionists and others: A plea for narrative. *Michigan Law Review, 87*, 2411–2441.

Dingerson, L. (2006). Dismantling a community timeline. *High School Journal, 90*(2), 8–15.

Dingerson, L. (2008). Unlovely: How the market is failing the children of New Orleans. In L. Dingerson, B. Miner, B. Peterson, & S. Walters (Eds.), *Keeping the promise? The debate over charter schools* (pp. 17–33). Milwaukee, WI: Rethinking Schools.

Ferguson, P., & Nusbaum, E. (2012). Disability studies: What is it and what difference does it make? *Research and Practice for Persons with Severe Disabilities, 37*(2), 70–80.

Ferri, B. (2008). Doing a (dis)service: Reimagining special education from a disability studies perspective. In W. Ayers, T. Quinn, & D. Stoval (Eds.), *Handbook of social justice in education* (pp. 421–430). Mahwah, NJ: LEA.

Ferri, B. (2011). Disability life writing and the politics of knowing. *Teachers College Record, 113*(10), pp. 2267–2282.

Ferri, B., & Connor, D. J. (2005). Tools of exclusion: Race, disability, and (re)segregated education. *Teachers College Record, 107*, 453–474.

Ferri, B., & Connor, D. J. (2006). *Reading resistance: Discourses of exclusion in desegregation and inclusion debates.* New York: Peter Lang.

Frankenberg, E., & Siegel-Hawley, G. (2009). Equity overlooked: Charter schools and civil rights policy. Los Angeles, CA: The Civil Rights Project/Proyecto Derechos Civiles at UCLA. Retrieved from www.civilrightsproject.ucla.edu

Frankenberg, E., Siegel-Hawley, G., & Wang, J. (2010). *Choice without equity: Charter School segregation and the need for civil rights standards.* Los Angeles, CA: The Civil Rights Project/Proyecto Derechos Civiles at UCLA. Retrieved from www.civilrightsproject.ucla.edu

Friedman, M. (2005, December 5). The promise of vouchers. *Wall Street Journal.* Retrieved from http://www.naomiklein.org/shock-doctrine/resources/part7/chapter20/friedman-promise-vouchers

Gabel, S. L. (Ed.) (2005). *Disability studies in education: Readings in theory and method.* New York: Peter Lang.

Gabor, A. (2013, September 20). Post-Katrina, the great charter-school tryout. *Newsweek.* Retrieved from http://www.newsweek.com/2013/09/20/post-katrina-great-new-orleans-charter-tryout-237968.html

Garda, R. (2011). The politics of education reform: Lessons from New Orleans. *Journal of Law & Education, 40*(1), 1–42.

Hill, P. H. (2005, September 21). Re-creating public education in New Orleans. *Education Week.* Retrieved from http://www.edweek.org/ew/articles/2005/09/21/04hill.h25.html

Individuals With Disabilities Education Act, 20 U.S.C. § 1400 (2004).

Institute on Race and Poverty. (2010). *The state of public schools in post-Katrina New Orleans.* Minneapolis: University of Minnesota Law School.

Klein, N. (2007). *The shock doctrine: The rise of disaster capitalism.* New York: Picador.

Kliewer, C., & Biklen, D. (2007). Enacting literacy: Local understanding, significant disability, and a new frame for educational opportunity. *Teachers College Record, 109,* 2579–2600.

McDermott, R. P. (1993). The acquisition of a child by a learning disability. In S. Chaiklin & J. Lave (Eds.), *Understanding practice* (pp. 269–305). New York: Cambridge University Press.

New York Times. (2011, October 15). Lessons from New Orleans [editorial]. *New York Times.* Retrieved from http://www.nytimes.com/2011/10/16/opinion/sunday/lessons-from-new-orleans.html

O'Neill, L. (2013, November 18). This is autism (by Lief O'Neill, age 10) [Web log comment]. This is autism flash blog. Retrieved from http://thisisautismflashblog.blogspot.com/2013/11/this-is-autism-by-lief-oneill-age-10.html

P. B. et al. v. Paul Pastorek et al. (2010). E.D. La. 2:10-cv-04049.

Polkinghorne, D. (1995). Narrative configuration in qualitative analysis. *Qualitative Studies in Education, 8*(1), 5–23.

Quigley, B. (2007, June 9). Part I: New Orleans's children fighting for the right to learn. *Truthout*. Retrieved from http://truth-out.org/archive/component/k2/item/72377:bill-quigley--part-i-new-orleanss-children-fighting-for-the-right-to-learn

Ravitch, D. (2013). *Reign of error: The hoax of the privatization movement and the danger to America's public schools*. New York: Alfred A. Knopf.

Saltman, K. (2007). Introduction. In K. Saltman (Ed.), *Schooling and the politics of disaster* (pp. 1–21). New York: Routledge.

Saulny, S. (2006, August 21). Rough start for effort to remake faltering New Orleans Schools. *New York Times*. Retrieved from http://www.nytimes.com/2006/08/21/us/21recovery.html?pagewanted=all

Schweick, S. (2009). *The ugly laws: Disability in public*. New York: New York University Press.

Southern Poverty Law Center (SPLC). (2010, December). *Access denied: New Orleans students and parents identify barriers to public education*. New Orleans, LA: SPLC. Retrieved from http://www.splcenter.org/sites/default/files/downloads/publication/SPLC_report_Access_Denied.pdf

Valle, J. W., & Connor, D. J. (2011). *Rethinking disability: A disability studies approach to inclusive practices*. New York: McGraw-Hill.

Conclusion

All That Jazz: Using Disability Studies in Education to (Re)Envision the Applied Field of (Special) Education

JAN W. VALLE, CHRIS HALE, AND DAVID J. CONNOR

We began this volume with a note on the cover art and how we believe work within DSE is very much like jazz. In this concluding chapter, we provide a synthesis of the "work of the ensemble" as represented in the preceding chapters.

As editors, we solicited manuscripts from a range of DSE scholars who could speak to their ongoing work in the areas of theory, research, practice, and policy. As discussed elsewhere, disability studies in education (DSE) grew out of disability studies (DS). In other words, DSE scholars seek to *apply* the tenets of DS within the context of education. DSE scholars rely upon ideas from the humanities as do DS scholars; however, education is considered an "applied field" (like, for example, social work and nursing) because of its preparation and enculturation of professionals to enter the field and its ongoing "professional development" for those working in the field. It is this professional community that DSE scholars hope to influence in areas such as teacher education, pedagogy, institutional structures, curricula, parent-school relations, and the professional literature.

The Work of the Ensemble

Much like sections of a jazz band, members who subscribe to the ideals of DSE "play" (and write) within the sections of theory, research, practice, and policy. Although most musicians play multiple instruments, it is most common for a musician to specialize in a single instrument. Likewise, most DSE scholars write across the areas of theory, research, practice, and policy, but tend to focus upon a particular area of interest. The authors we invited to contribute are those who "play" most often in the sections we outlined for this volume. They are the musicians within our ensemble. There are three members in each of the four sections.

The Influence of DSE Upon Theory

The volume opens with "Exploring Some Moral Dimensions of the Social Model of Disability," by Deborah Gallagher, a well-known and seasoned DSE scholar who has long tackled complex philosophical issues in the literature. Gallagher challenges the reader to consider the moral dimensions of our current response to educating students with disabilities in American public schools. In making a case for thinking about disability as a moral category, she considers utilitarianism, libertarianism, and communitarianism as possible grounding philosophies toward this end. Gallagher well-argues a case for communitarianism as the philosophical framework for DSE work. Communitarianism challenges the "pull yourself up by the bootstraps" American mentality that constructs disability as a personal trial to overcome with the ultimate goal to achieve independence. In contrast, communitarianism offers an understanding of disability as a social responsibility and values interdependency over independence. Gallagher moves from theory to practice in her connection of these ideas to the practice of inclusion and the implications of communitarianism for students with disabilities.

Beth Ferri joins Gallagher in philosophical "play" with her integration of feminist studies and DS/DSE in "'As a Cripple I swagger': The Situated Body and Disability Studies in Education." Ferri explores the intersectionalities between Simone de Beauvoir (who explores her experience of moving through the world as female) and Nancy Mairs (who explores her experience of moving through the world both as female and disabled), and their respective theorizing about embodiment. Ferri's work complicates notions of what it means to be female, what it means to have a disability, and what it means to be both female and disabled. She challenges us as readers to rethink how we perceive, understand, and think about the body. Her work holds particular significance in its challenge to the medical model framing of disability (that undergirds American special education) as a pathological condition in favor of an understanding of disability as a complex identity that arises out of both *situation* and *point of view*. Imagine how differently special education would look if we began with standpoint rather than pathology.

Phil Smith rounds out this section with a fierce "riff" on theory. His work challenges the reader in terms of both format and content. His words skitter across the page like jazz—loud, tumbling, provocative, soft, seductive, radical—free from conventions of academic literature. The effect leads the reader to ask: What is it? What does he mean? Why is he saying these things? Smith's "stream of consciousness" style suggests the musical wanderings of a jazz musician. We are privy to a fertile mind, both playful and serious, connecting anything and everything in a weird, wonderful, and sometimes woeful web of meaning. His expressions of anger, disdain, derision, frustration, and rebellion against the seemingly insurmountable structures of oppression cause us to stop in our tracks and see ways in which so many of these structures are connected. Despite these sobering observations, there is hope within that dark humor.

The Influence of DSE Upon Research

Jan Valle opens this section with an exploration of arts-based research and DSE in "Enacting Research: Disability Studies in Education and Performative Inquiry." In this chapter, Valle makes a case for integrating arts-based research (ABR), specifically theatre arts, and disability studies in education as means to provide access to DSE research and practice for an audience beyond the academy. She shares two examples from her work to illustrate how ABR methods can support the work of DSE scholars: (1) *The M.O.M. Project*, an ethnodrama based on narratives told by mothers of children with disabilities, and (2) a student research project with elementary school students labeled as autistic—conceived and carried out by three graduate students in the City College of New York's educational theatre program. Both examples reflect "real-life" applications of DSE by researchers in the field. In the case of these examples, DSE literally takes "center stage."

Subini Annamma enters next with her chapter, "'It was just like a piece of gum': Intersectionality and Criminalization of Young Women of Color With Disabilities in the School-to-Prison Pipeline. In her research with five queer young women of color with disabilities, Annamma relies upon DSE (as well as critical race theory, DisCrit, and queer theory) in her analysis of the process by which these young women end up in juvenile incarceration. She explores the role of labeling, surveillance, and punishment in the eventual "criminalization" of these young women. The sticking of stigma ("like gum on a shoe") is a powerful analogy provided by one of the research participants to describe the effects of labeling. Annamma's work, echoing notes of Ferri's chapter, reveals ways in which the positionalities (or standpoints) of these young women inform and impact their life choices. Their voices speak to the urgency of (re)theorizing and problematizing the persisting issue of overrepresentation in American special education.

Writing from the standpoint of a DSE scholar with a disability, Joseph Valente offers an emic perspective as a researcher researching disability in his chapter, "An In-Betweener Ethnographer: From Anxiety to Fieldwork Methods in a Cross-Cultural Study of Bilingual Deaf Kindergartners." Valente's work illustrates the growing pains of becoming a researcher and the choices made in all aspects of inquiry—thereby revealing the constructed nature of research. Complicating the already complex arena of research, Valente shares his experience as a deaf researcher studying international kindergartens for Deaf students. His dual analysis engages with disability as identity, revealing the fluid and porous nature of disability—repeating the rhythms established by Ferri and Annamma. In the end, the reader recognizes that Valente speaks to the autoethnographical aspect of *all* research and the potential of DSE as a framework for the questions *all* researchers have about themselves.

The Influence of DSE Upon Practice

In the chapter, "Practicing What We Teach: The Benefits of Using Disability Studies in an Inclusion Course," David Connor documents the application of DSE within a college course on inclusion at Hunter College (New York City)—a strong example of influencing the professionalization of teachers. Connor describes how he engages college students in identifying what they believe about disability (and why) and how those beliefs impact how they will teach in a classroom. The reader learns from Connor how to make transparent the medical and social models of disability as well as how to help students rethink/relearn notions of disability. Much like Valle describes in Chapter 4, Connor integrates DSE into class activities that call attention to the reality of people with disabilities from their standpoints. The chapter is replete with examples of DSE-compatible resources and materials to facilitate reflective analysis about American special education practices.

Geert Van Hove and Elisabeth De Schauwer continue Connor's theme of applying DSE at the university level in "Why We Do What We (Think We) Do: Creating a Campus Coalition From the Perspective of Disability Studies in Education." This chapter describes the work of a group of DSE researchers at Ghent University in Belgium who, for more than a decade, have been building a network through which their collective work moves beyond a theoretical framework to touch the lives of people with disabilities and their families. Toward this end, the university group established partnerships with the self-advocacy movement Onze Nieuwe Toekomst (Our New Future),[1] and the parents' association Ouders voor Inclusie (Parents for Inclusion) and with Steunpunt Inclusief Hoger Onderwijs (Expertise Centre for Students with Disabilities in Higher Education Institutions). Much of the impetus for this work comes out of their standpoint of *ethics*—a refrain begun in this volume by Gallagher. Their "coalition" of partnerships is devoted to the integration of university and community. The university invites families and persons with disabilities to "co-teach" in their classes as well as engage in research as a "community of practice." The knowledge of families and persons with disabilities is regarded as equally valid to that of university professors. Moreover, the coalition is committed to political engagement and dialogue among cultures in regard to disability.

Nirmala Erevelles rounds out this section with her chapter, "Madness and (Higher Education) Administration: Ethical Implications of Pedagogy Using Disability Studies Scholarship." As a scholar who often writes about uncomfortable or taboo subjects (e.g., race, sexuality, queerness), Erevelles fearlessly tackles the subject of "madness" at the university level. In response to shootings on American campuses in recent years, colleges and universities have responded by creating administrative policies intended to identify and monitor students with potential or documented mental illness. Erevelles troubles these kinds of narrow institutional policies that equate mental illness with violence. Starting from an ethical standpoint (continuing the riff begun by Gallagher, Van Hove, and De Schauwer), Erevelles describes how she uses *Mad at School* (2011) by Margaret Price to help her university students critically "read" university policies on mental illness. Providing a variation on the theme started by Connor, Erevelles likewise provides examples of ways she integrates DS/DSE into course materials and how students engage with the materials she selects. The result is a radical reframing of disability that provides students with tools to challenge scare-mongering in regard to mental illness.

The Influence of DSE Upon Policy

Julie Allan sets the stage for the policy section of this volume with her chapter, "Critiquing Policy: Limitations and Possibilities." Allan considers the rather limited success of formal critiques of educational policies in Sweden, the United Kingdom, and the United States. As a DSE scholar with much experience engaging at the national policy level, Allan emphasizes the need for criticality as a duty of sorts. Relying upon DS/DSE as a tool for contrapuntal critique, Allan calls attention to social inequities in various societies and the role of policymakers. She cautions the reader about the consequences of failing to critique educational policies and the resulting impact upon students with and without disabilities.

Missy Morton enters next with her chapter, "Using Disability Studies in Education to Recognize, Resist, and Reshape Policy and Practices in Aotearoa New Zealand," in which she describes the tensions between a national push for inclusive education and a strong national neoliberal agenda. Drawing upon the somewhat parallel histories of disability laws and rights in other countries (e.g., the United Kingdom, the United States), Morton makes suggestions for how teacher educators can help both pre-service and in-service teachers recognize, resist, and negotiate deficit discourses of human difference. New Zealand's student-centered individualized education program is presented as an example of collective resistance to standardization translated into national policy.

Concluding this set is Kathleen Collins' chapter, "A Disability Studies in Education Analysis of Corporate-Based Educational Reform: Lessons From New Orleans," in which she describes the opportunistic privatized school reform that occurred in New Orleans as a result of Hurricane Katrina. Using a DSE lens, Collins renders visible the reform's "discourses of exclusion" for students with disabilities through a document analysis of legal artifacts. Her insightful analysis of individual and family testimonies within *P. B. et al. v. Pastorek*, a pending class-action lawsuit, provides both a verification of the power of personal voice and an incisive critique of exclusive policies and practices under this reform.

Coda

Coda (Italian for "tail") is a musical term used to designate a passage that brings a piece to an end. So it is that we end with a coda to this volume. As previously stated, DSE is a newly established academic discipline with scholars at work for just over a decade. This collection documents the ongoing work of DSE scholars as they apply the tenets of the discipline to real-life context. We hope that this sampling of work in DSE inspires our readers to join the ensemble of those interested in disability and education around the globe.

We end with a quote by Chinnery (2003) whose comparison of the work of professionals to jazz players seems an appropriate inspiration for the collective work of DSE scholars:

> Engage in rigorous study and practice in order to build up ... memory of repertoires, then, at the moment of performance ... suspend deliberation and abandon the known in order to embrace risk and vulnerability. It is about the capacity to vulnerability and exposure to the Other, to the pains and pleasures of human life. (p. 13)

Note

1. Self-advocacy movements are movements of people with special needs where they are encouraged to speak up for themselves, with the emphasis on actions that help to find how the human rights concept actually affects their lives.

Reference

Chinnery, A. (2003). Aesthetic of surrender: Levinas and the disruption of agency in moral education. *Studies in Philosophy and Education, 22*(1), 5–17.

Contributors

Julie Allan is Professor of Equity and Inclusion at the University of Birmingham, U.K., and Visiting Professor at the University of Borås in Sweden. Her work encompasses inclusive education, disability studies, and children's rights, and she has a particular interest in educational theory and the insights offered through poststructural and social capital analyses. Julie has been advisor to the Scottish Parliament, the Welsh Assembly and the Dutch and Queensland governments and has worked extensively with the Council of Europe. She has published several books, including *Rethinking Inclusive Education: The Philosophers of Difference in Practice* (2007, Springer); *Social Capital, Children and Young People: Implications for Policy, Practice and Research*, with Ralph Catts (2012, Policy Press); and *Psychopathology at School: Theorizing Mental Disorders in Education*, with Valerie Harwood (2014, Routledge).

Subini Ancy Annamma, PhD, is a postdoctoral fellow with the Interdisciplinary Research Incubator for the Study of (In)Equality (IRISE) at the University of Denver. Before entering graduate school, she was a special education teacher working with culturally and linguistically diverse students with emotional, behavioral, and learning disabilities in public schools and juvenile justice. All of Dr. Annamma's work—research, pedagogy, and activism—focuses on increasing access to equitable education for historically marginalized students and communities, particularly children identified with disabilities. Her equity commitments emphasize an interdisciplinary approach drawing from the fields of urban education, sociology, criminology, and geography. Specifically, Dr. Annamma examines the social construction of race and ability; how the two are interdependent, how they intersect with other identity markers, and how their mutually constitutive nature impacts education experiences. She centers this research in urban education settings and focuses on how student voice can identify exemplary educational practices.

Kathleen Collins, PhD, is an assistant professor of language, culture and society and co-director of the Center for Disability Studies in the College of Education at Pennsylvania State University, University Park. Kathleen's program of research aims to identify and interrupt the discourses, policies, and literacies that contribute to the identification and location of dis/ability. Kathleen is the author of *Ability Profiling and School Failure: One Child's Struggle to Be Seen as Competent* (2nd edition, 2013, Routledge). Her research has also appeared in *Equity and Excellence in Education*; *English Journal*; *International Journal of Inclusive Education*; *Language Arts*; *Language, Speech, and Hearing Services in Schools*; *Learning Disabilities Quarterly*; *Research in the Teaching of English*; *Teachers College Record*; *Urban Education*; and *Young Children*. Kathleen was awarded the prestigious 2012 Ellen Brantlinger Junior Scholar Award for outstanding work within disability studies in education.

David J. Connor is a professor and chairperson of the Special Education Department, Hunter College, part of the City University of New York (CUNY). He is also a faculty member at large in the Urban Education doctoral program at CUNY's Graduate Center. David is the author of several books: *Reading Resistance: Discourses of Exclusion in Desegregation and Inclusion Debates*, co-authored with Beth Ferri (2006, Peter Lang); *Urban Narratives: Portraits-in-Progress—Life at the Intersections of Learning Disability, Race, and Social Class* (2008, Peter Lang); *Rethinking Disability: A Disability Studies Guide to Inclusive Practices*, co-authored with Jan Valle (2011, McGraw-Hill); and *Teaching and Disability*, co-authored with Susan Gabel (2014, Erlbaum). He is also co-editor, along with Beth Ferri and Subini Annamma, of *DisCrit: Critical Conversations Across Race, Class, and Dis/ability* (forthcoming, Teachers College Press). His research interests include learning disabilities, inclusive education, and intersectional understandings of disability. For more information, see http://hunter-cuny.academia.edu/DavidJConnor.

Scot Danforth, PhD, is a Professor in the College of Education at San Diego State University. He is a disability studies in education and inclusive education scholar. He was (with Susan L. Gabel) co-founder of the Disability Studies in Education Special Interest Group of the American Educational Research Association. He served (with Brenda Brueggemann) as co-editor of *Disability Studies Quarterly*. His books include *Becoming a Great Inclusive Educator* and *The Incomplete Child: An Intellectual History of Learning Disabilities*.

Elisabeth De Schauwer is an assistant professor at Ghent University. She earned a PhD in educational sciences from the same university. In her postdoctoral research work, Elisabeth stays close to families with children with disabilities, members of the self-advocacy movement, and professionals who try to make a significant difference in the lives of children, youngsters, and adults with disabilities. In addition to this research, with Dr. Bronwyn Davies of Australia, Elisabeth works to deepen theoretical concepts about differences.

Nirmala Erevelles is Professor of Social and Cultural Studies in Education at the University of Alabama. Her teaching and research interests lie in the areas of disability studies, critical race theory, transnational feminism, sociology of education, and postcolonial studies. Specifically, her research focuses on the unruly, messy, unpredictable and taboo body—a habitual outcast in educational (and social) contexts. Erevelles has published articles in the *American Educational Research Journal, Educational Theory, Studies in Education and Philosophy, The Journal of Curriculum Studies, Teachers College Record; Disability & Society, Disability Studies Quarterly,* and *The Journal of Literary and Cultural Disability Studies,* among others. Her book *Disability and Difference in Global Contexts: Towards a Transformative Body Politic* was published by Palgrave in 2012.

Beth A. Ferri, PhD, is a professor of inclusive education and disability studies at Syracuse University, where she also coordinates the doctoral program in Special Education and is an associate faculty member in Women's and Gender Studies. Professor Ferri has published widely on the intersection of race, gender, and disability, including articles in *Teachers College Record; Race Ethnicity and Education; International Journal of Inclusive Education; Remedial and Special Education; Gender and Education; Disability Studies Quarterly, Disability and Society,* and *The Journal of African American History.* Her first book, written with David J. Connor, titled *Reading Resistance: Discourses of Exclusion in Desegregation and Inclusion Debates,* documents how problematic rhetorics of race and dis/ability were used to maintain and justify segregated education after the historic *Brown v. Board of Education* decision. Her most recent book, *Righting Educational Wrongs: Disability Studies Law and Education,* was published by Syracuse University Press (2013).

Deborah Gallagher is Professor of Education at the University of Northern Iowa. Her scholarly work centers on the philosophy of science and moral philosophy as it pertains to research on disability, pedagogy, and policy in education and special education. In addition to numerous articles and book chapters, she is the lead author of a book entitled *Challenging Orthodoxy in Special Education: Dissenting Voices* (2004, Love Publishing Company).

Chris Hale is an assistant professor of special education at the College of Staten Island, City University of New York. He is a critical special educator who is theoretically, politically, and dispositionally aligned with a disability studies in education perspective. His research interests include the intersection of ethics, special education law, and institutional practices; the dispositions, beliefs, and attitudes of pre-service and novice special education teachers; the juncture of social class and disability; and the lived experience of children and families associated with urban special education systems.

Missy Morton is Associate Professor and Head of the School of Educational Studies and Leadership at the University of Canterbury, Christchurch, New Zealand. Her research and teaching include qualitative research, inclusive education, and assessment for learning. Working in disability studies in education, she is particularly interested in how ideas and strategies from critical ethnography can be taken up in curriculum, pedagogy, and assessment for inclusive education. With David Mills, she is co-author of *Ethnography in Education* (2013, BERA/Sage). She is editor of *Supporting Inclusive Education: Learning From Narrative Assessment* (forthcoming), and co-editor of *Tales From School: Learning Disability and State Education After Administrative Reform* (forthcoming), both published in the Sense series Studies in Inclusive Education. She has served as co-editor of two special issues of the *International Journal of Inclusive Education*. Missy was a member of the working group that wrote the *New Zealand Disability Strategy* and is a founding member of the Inclusive Education Action Group.

Phil Smith is, in a nutshell, post-everything—he is so after that. He teaches at Eastern Michigan University, where he slips disability studies stuff and the occasional cranky rant into courses he teaches, and hopes the bureaucraps and curricula police won't notice. Phil received the Emerging Scholar Award in Disability Studies in Education in 2009, has had papers published in a buncha different journals, as well as a lotta book chapters. He's published two books in the Peter Lang Disability Studies in Education series: *Whatever Happened to Inclusion? The Place of Students with Intellectual Disabilities in Education* (2010), and *Both Sides of the Table: Autoethnographies of Educators Learning and Teaching With/In [Dis]ability* (2014). He's also a published poet, playwright, novelist, and visual artist, and izza critical scholar and a whatever-comes-after-qualitative researcher. For more than 25 years, in a variety of contexts and roles, he has worked as a disability rights activist, and served on the boards of directors of a number of regional, state, and local organizations, including the Society for Disability Studies. He's disabled, queer, a walkie, and presents as cis-male. He rides his bicycle a lot, and tries to remember to wear his socks. A transplanted Yankee, he makes maple syrup and spends most of his time beside Lake Superior, where loons, wolves, moose, and bald eagles peek in the windows of his cabin.

Joseph Michael Valente is an assistant professor of early childhood education at Pennsylvania State University. He is also the co-director of the Center for Disability Studies and core faculty in the Comparative and International Education program. Dr. Valente is the co-principal investigator of the video ethnographic study "Kindergartens for the Deaf in Three Countries: Japan, France, and the United States," funded by the Spencer Foundation; and author of the research-novel *d/Deaf and d/Dumb: A Portrait of a Deaf Kid as a Young Superhero* (2011, Peter Lang). To learn more about Dr. Valente's work, you can visit his website: www.joevalente.net.

Jan W. Valle is an associate professor in the Department of Teaching, Learning, and Culture at the City College of New York and director of the Childhood Education program. She has been an educator for more than 30 years. Her research interests include inclusive education, parents and families of children with disabilities, disability studies in education, and disability and theatre arts. She is the author of *What Mothers Say About Special Education: From the 1960s to the Present* (2009, Palgrave Macmillan), and co-author with David Connor of *Rethinking Disability: A Disability Studies Approach to Inclusive Practices* (2011, McGraw-Hill).

Geert Van Hove is a professor at Ghent University and the Free University of Amsterdam. His main research and teaching work is situated within disability studies, inclusive education, and qualitative research methods.

Disability Studies in Education

GENERAL EDITORS: SUSAN L. GABEL & SCOT DANFORTH

The book series Disability Studies in Education is dedicated to the publication of monographs and edited volumes that integrate the perspectives, methods, and theories of disability studies with the study of issues and problems of education. The series features books that further define, elaborate upon, and extend knowledge in the field of disability studies in education. Special emphasis is given to work that poses solutions to important problems facing contemporary educational theory, policy, and practice.

To order other books in this series, please contact our Customer Service Department:

(800) 770-LANG (within the U.S.)
(212) 647-7706 (outside the U.S.)
(212) 647-7707 FAX

Or browse by series:

WWW.PETERLANG.COM